MUDVILLE'S
REVENGE

MUDVILLE'S REVENGE

The Rise and Fall of American Sport

TED VINCENT

Seaview Books
NEW YORK

Manufactured in the United States of America.

FIRST EDITION

Library of Congress Cataloging in Publication Data

Vincent, Ted.
     Mudville's revenge.

     Bibliography: p.
     Includes index.
     1. Sports—United States—History. I. Title.
GV583.V56   796'.0973   80-52410
ISBN 0-87223-661-7   AACR2

Design by Tere LoPrete

Contents

MUDVILLE'S

REVENGE

Introduction:
Mudville's Revenge

This sports history is written to give courage to those of us who identify with Mudville. It is for the sports fans who suspect that the media hype for "the biggest" and "the most spectacular" may not really be for the best.

This book is for those who find as much pleasure in watching a hard-fought basketball game on the local playground as watching the NBA on CBS. If you have recently taken up jogging or one of the other do-it-yourself sports, and you still feel there is room for sitting back with a beer and rooting for somebody else to do it, this book is for you. But if you relish your participatory sport because it is untainted by the debasement of "spectatorism," your consciousness is probably raised too high for this book.

If you take your kids to Disneyland and find you keep telling them how much more fun it was pitching pennies and knocking down bottles with softballs at the old county fair, this book may give you strength when your kids tell you, "That sounds stupid."

This could be called the Avis people's sports history, the record of the second best who had to try harder. It is for Philadelphians—how much more Avis can you get than to live halfway between New York and Washington? Outsiders perceive Philadelphia sports fans as intolerant. "Philadelphia is such a tough place the people would boo a cure for cancer," goes the old joke. But I believe what strangers perceive as nastiness is just the Philadelphians' way of caring deeply about their teams. Take my mother-in-law up in northeast Philly. She's a sweet little lady in her seventies, who seems to get her boundless energy from the years of frustration over Phillies games. "Mike Schmidt is going to strike out. He always strikes out when it counts," she says as she listens to the game while nervously pushing the vacuum cleaner. When Schmidt hits a home run to tie the game she exclaims, "Big deal! They always lose when it goes into extra innings. You'll see."

Brooklyn Dodger fans had a fierce loyalty to their team, and something more. I spent much of my youth in old Ebbets Field, and in retrospect my fondest memories are not of game-winning hits but of the fun Dodger fans had during the game. There was the grandmother in the bleachers with her cowbell; there was the always-out-of-tune "Brooklyn Sym-phoney," consisting of any fan who wanted to bring a musical instrument and sit in the general admission section behind first base; and there was the endless buzz of animated discussion between total strangers. Dodger fans had opinions on everything.

All of Brooklyn fell into a deep funk when the beloved "bums" were robbed of the 1951 pennant by that Bobby Thomson home run. Thomson's "shot heard round the world" gave me periodic nightmares for years. The day after the horrible event I wandered the streets with others who were mumbling about Brooklyn being Mudville.

It was back in 1888 when mighty Casey strode to the plate in the bottom of the ninth with a chance to win it for the original Mudville nine—or at least that was the year Ernest Lawrence Thayer wrote the poem which concluded

> Oh! somewhere in this favored land the sun is shining bright,
> The band is playing somewhere, and somewhere hearts are light.

> And somewhere men are laughing, and somewhere
> children shout;
> But there is no joy in Mudville—mighty Casey has
> "Struck Out."

"Casey at the Bat" has been recited a thousand times on vaudeville stages, and is periodically resurrected in baseball histories and in studies of American folklore. It is certainly better remembered than Thayer's sequel, "Casey's Revenge," wherein Casey once more strides to the plate and this time hits a grand slam. Similarly, the Brooklyn Dodgers are better remembered for their near-misses than for the one time they came through in the clutch and beat the Yankees in a World Series. It is the Dodgers' immortal cry, "Wait till next year," which makes the bums an endearing part of the American past.

The original Mudville and Brooklyn had a lot in common. Ernest Lawrence Thayer probably had in mind his hometown of Worcester, Massachusetts, when he wrote of Mudville. When Thayer was a teenager Worcester had a team in the National League, a team that was booted out, along with the Troy Haymakers, to make room for the New York Giants and Philadelphia Phillies. New York and Philadelphia had better financial potential; the Dodgers went to Los Angeles for similar pecuniary reasons.

Worcester of Thayer's youth was a vibrant city, proudly claiming to be the manufacturing capital of New England. Brooklyn, too, had a special quality about it when I lived there, a pride that extended beyond the Dodgers. There was reverence for our quaint accent; and in the moviehouse on Flatbush Avenue a mention of Brooklyn by some actor on the screen was occasion for a noisy celebration in the theater. In Thayer's time the ball team in the growing city of Worcester was sort of a civic venture. It was organized by members of Worcester's volunteer fire department. Club president was Mayor Charles B. Pratt, a modernizer for his city—he built Worcester's first theater and introduced electric streetcars.

When Casey struck out, gloom had prevailed "from the mayor down the line," but there were consolations. Casey's wasn't the only team in town. The fans played the game, too. The *New York Times* estimated that there were more than 2,000 baseball teams in New England around this time. And although the Brooklyn of my youth didn't have much room for baseball fields, on any given summer day there were probably 2,000 stickball games being played in the streets of the city.

The Mudvillian towns are rarely in the sporting limelight today. Teams represent major metropolitan marketing areas rather than the more anthropomorphic communities. Sandlot ball fields stand empty much of the time; the townsfolk can't get up the energy to go out and create their own version of Casey at the bat. People take their games over TV, and the media's superstar mystique seems to have conditioned fans to believe that the athletic activity of ordinary mortals is embarrassing.

Now it is time for Mudville's Revenge. Let us assume it unfolds as follows: It is tied in with a renaissance of the American town and neighborhood, bringing back the vitality expressed in sporting form at Ebbets Field, or much earlier when Worcester was in the National League, and little Lowell had a better ball team than Boston. It is rejection of the notion that big is always better. It is anti-high-rise initiatives on the ballot, and a realization that public bonds for superstadiums could be better used for tennis courts, softball diamonds, and jogging trails. It is people doing things themselves rather than having things done for them—becoming sports contestants rather than watching the games on television. It is taking advantage of the new opportunities to be both spectator and participant at the same time, as in running the Bay to Breakers or New York marathon.

Mudville's Revenge is learning of the vitality in the American communities of the past, when places like Worcester and Lowell had not only quality sport but theater productions straight off first runs on Broadway. This was a time when virtually every eligible voter went to the polls on Election Day, and there were parades through the streets for one cause or another week after week. Mudville's Revenge is learning how close-knit groups of society's underdogs have built American sports. There were the laboring people who banded together in 1858 and in open opposition to establishment "old fogeys" founded the first association of baseball clubs. The "old fogeys" wanted Americans to play cricket. There were the ethnic clubs and trade unions which put track and field on the sporting map during the 1880s. There were the tenement-district YMCAs and settlement houses which built basketball in the early years of this century, before the small Catholic colleges elevated the game in stature during the 1930s. Following in this tradition, advances in sport today are made by women, and by the carriers of unorthodox life-styles who gather in the coffeehouses next to the tennis store across from the community vegetable garden. They establish a base in the "alternative school," where the popular sports are gymnastics, judo, and coed volleyball. They pour into the streets by the thousands for distance runs.

This book is a historical exploration of the emotion in sport, the qualities of attachment and concern that cannot be adequately measured by mere attendance figures. It is an exposition of how Mudville has always had the nation's quality sports shows, although not necessarily in the mechanical sense of won–lost records. It is the cosmic superiority of the Mudvillian Brooklyn Dodgers over their high-priced Yankee rivals from the Bronx. The Yankees were highly respected in the sports world, but the Dodgers were deeply loved.

So your heroes have lost again. Once more the championship is denied. It is my hope that the following account of how sports developed will provide you with Mudville's Revenge.

The processes at work in generating sports popularity are explored here in three cases, each illuminating a distinct part of the sporting scene. The first case is the sporting crazes of the late nineteenth century, in particular the development of

track and field. It is the rarely told story of the period when
running and jumping was largely a professional sport, and an
extremely popular one at that. Second, the development of the
national game of baseball is presented with special attention
to the close relationship between baseball promotion and the
involvement of the promoters in the daily social, economic, and
political life of their town. Third, the story of the rise of basketball brings to light the important role of ethnic communities in early-twentieth-century sport; and the basketball story
also affords opportunity to explore such topics as how the
nation got public playgrounds, the development of point-spread
gambling, and the recent emergence of women in sport.

A word is in order on why football is not covered here.
First of all, football arose as an Ivy League college game at a
time when colleges were exclusive institutions for the youths
from families that no longer needed to hustle to get by. This
study centers upon sports which developed through substantial
contributions by *both* players and promoters from the struggling classes on their way up the social ladder. The initial
growth of track and field, for instance, was marked by a period when many of the best meets were sponsored by trade
unions and other laborers' clubs. Professional baseball had a
stage when clubs were genuinely membership clubs, rather
than incorporated businesses. Basketball's development owed
much to the intense effort of ethnic minorities in the teeming
tenement districts.

While college football obviously doesn't fit here, professional football might. It certainly began as a sport for the
brawny brutes from the foundry and the rolling mill. However, the expense of the game minimized the promotional role
of the small-time entrepreneur. From its inception, pro football needed financial "angels." The first professional league
needed financing from Andrew Carnegie. The professional
teams that sprouted up around the time of World War I were
usually attached to some industrialist's labor relations department. The memorable Columbus Panhandles, for example,
represented the panhandle works of the Pennsylvania Rail-

road Company, and the team was run by Joe Carr of the railroad's worker relations department. Carr later became the commissioner of the National Football League.

The NFL, launched in 1919, needed corporate benevolence to get through its first struggling seasons. The League did have its share of adventurous promoters of the hometown booster club variety. There was a Hupmobile dealer in Canton; and a cigar store manager and dry cleaner owned the Akron club. But the new league was hard-pressed to keep a quorum of clubs in business. Toward this end factory-sponsored teams had a critical role; and much of this industrial financing was obtained under unattractive circumstances, i.e., attempts to buy off labor unrest.

The Green Bay Packers football team was funded in the summer of 1919 by the Green Bay Indian-Acme Packing Company. In the nine months prior to the creation of the team, National Labor Conciliation Board troubleshooters were called in four times to mediate disputes at this packing company; and in roughly the same period some 11,000 workers were out on strike in assorted industries in and around Green Bay. The idea for the team came from a young front office employee, Curly Lambeau, who had the previous year played football under Knute Rockne at Notre Dame. Lambeau walked into his boss's office one August day and talked him into $500 to start the Packers. Lambeau told his boss the pro team "would be good for Green Bay and good for the company." The Packers took the field that fall; for at least the next three years strikes at the company were unknown, and strikes ceased almost entirely in the Green Bay area.

The Chicago Bears entered the NFL in 1920 under the name of the Decatur Staleys. The team had originated in 1919 with funds from the Staley Starch Company, whose workers were on strike that summer. At the suggestion of young George Halas, Mr. Staley was coaxed into sponsoring the team and hiring Halas as full-time coach. The Hammond Pros were funded by a Hammond steel mill owner and entered the league in 1919, on the heels of strikes involving 8,400 Hammond steel workers. The Dayton Triangles, supported by an electrical company, joined the league at a time of strikes involving thousands of Dayton workers in the electrical and machinery industries. The Eastman Kodak Company funded the NFL's charter club from Rochester. Labor unrest at the Kodak plant had required government mediators four times in the previous fourteen months. Joe Carr of the Columbus Panhandles had experienced one of the biggest strikes of the early twentieth century back in 1914 when 90,000 Pennsylvania Railroad workers went out. One early NFL club, and a number of independent teams of the period, were sponsored by that archenemy of the trade union movement, the American Legion.

Begun as a game for the elite in college, utilized by management to undercut labor militancy, and today a bastion of macho paramilitary values, football is a tailor-made sport for political conservatives. It may be a great visual attraction for spectators, but so were chariot racing and gladiatorial combat. Just as the paternalistic patricians gave the Roman plebeians their games, so is football a sport for the privileged to give to the modern masses. Mudvillian sport is more of a do-it-yourself enterprise of groups attempting to raise themselves up by their own effort. Football doesn't belong in this study.

TRACK AND FIELD

CHAPTER

I

The Democratic Era
of Sport

During his presidential campaign of 1880 James A. Garfield said in a speech at Lake Chautauqua, New York: "We may divide the whole struggle of the human race into two chapters: first, the fight to get leisure; and then the second fight of civilization—what shall we do with our leisure when we get it?" In 1880 organized sport involving leagues, associations, enclosed stadiums, and substantial coverage in the newspapers was a relatively new phenomenon, only some twenty years old. Most of our modern sports experienced their initial popularity and took organized form at some time between the Civil War and the end of the nineteenth century. The newfound popularity of sport shocked conservative ministers of the Gospel, and was misunderstood as well by powerful business interests, who were slow to see the potential of mass sport for extending their influence.

Compared with today, the distinguishing feature of sport a hundred years ago was that the professional games and contests had not yet been monopolized by corporate wealth, and a fledgling amateur system was not yet under the control of college deans, retired military brass, and corporation executives. The period from the 1860s into the early 1890s was the democratic and pluralist era of American sport, in which a grocer or saloon keeper had as much chance as a millionaire of producing an event that grabbed headlines in the national sporting magazines.

The teams in the early years of professional baseball were group enterprises, and always run by the townspeople. An absentee owner was unthinkable. Baseball clubs were really clubs, with hundreds of members. And when a club became a company, shares of stock were sold to the public, giving a wide range of people a chance to own a piece of "our team." The organizational form for early professional teams is typified in the Philadelphia Athletics of the 1870s, the ancestors of the current Oakland A's and prominent in baseball from the beginning, excepting a few years in the 1890s as a minor operation. For all but one season of the 1870s the Philadelphia Athletics didn't have an individual owner. And the team performed not for a company but for a large membership club. Control changed from year to year through revolving positions on a board of directors and on committees. The officers were ordinary people from Philadelphia. In 1872 the officers of the club were: two liquor dealers, two attorneys, two clerks, a secretary, a livery-stable keeper, a pawnbroker, a sportswriter, two players, and the team manager. Throughout the 1870s the identifiable club officials of the Athletics included only one person of substantial wealth, a Stephen Flannigan, who owned a steamship company.

The input to the popular spectator attractions on the part of the wealthy and powerful was limited for several reasons. They were inhibited by objections from religious and intellectual leaders of the old puritanical gentry, who still pulled weight in public affairs. Sports were a risky financial investment and didn't match the profit potential available in the booming areas of manufacturing, railroads, and banking. Very few baseball teams lasted as did the Philadelphia Athletics; three out of every four professional teams of the nineteenth century went out of business within two years. Those among the wealthy who did go in for sports, the "gentlemen sportsmen," were often nouveaux riches who coveted acceptance by the families of traditional wealth, and felt more acceptable when their amusements were distinct from the popular sports of the masses. The gentlemen sportsmen favored prestigious participatory sports, such as polo, yachting, and tennis, rather than the spectator attractions.

During the democratic era in sports the athletes themselves were often able to do the organizing and promoting. Ordinary fans started teams whose exploits were reported in a sporting press which was developed by similar individuals. *Sporting News* was founded by two telegraphers; *Sporting Life*, by a printer; and the *Police Gazette* was made into a national organ for boxing fans by Richard K. Fox, an immigrant from Ireland who had arrived in this country almost penniless. Top-quality sporting events were not restricted to a few major cities, but enlivened many towns now stereotyped as cultural and sporting wastelands. The distinction between amateur and professional was not clearly drawn, and novices competed against experts. Open competition invited broad participation, as though everyone had a chance to play sandlot ball against a Pete Rose or Reggie Jackson. In track and field, handicap events were common, providing encouragement for the less proficient athletes.

Before the Civil War, organized sporting contests were a rare treat. Durant and Bettmann, in their *Pictorial History of American Sports*, describe the slim pickings for the antebellum sports fan. "Now and then he could take in a ball game or a horse race and, once in a blue moon, a prize fight, if he was willing to risk getting slugged by some hoodlum or having his pocket picked. . . . His comfort wasn't considered at the few sporting events he could attend. There were no stadiums or indoor arenas. He stood on his feet while watching ball games, prize fights and foot races."

Americans had been engaged in sports since colonial times, as evidenced in the numerous edicts and diatribes written by Puritans condemning everything from horse racing to deer hunting. However, what passed as athletics in colonial America was along the lines of informal competitions between neighbors to see who was the fastest woodchopper. Missing were the afficionados whose reporting and record keeping turns mere exercise and games into sport. For example, in his history of British sport in the 1700s Montague Shearman cites a report from Virginia concerning a long-jump leap of over 22 feet by the young George Washington. Had there been amateur records, this probably would have been the world's best mark for that century; and had the colonies had a sizable sporting crowd to make a fuss over Washington's leap, we might today speak of the father of our country as our first track and field star.

For fifty years the new nation went without the trappings of a sporting society. Sport seemed a waste of time and out of place in a land of hardworking farmers who had but recently renounced a self-indulgent king and hereditary nobility. The first general sports book published in the United States appears to have been the 1820s volume titled *Children's Amusements: When School Is Over for the Day, the Sprightly Boys Run Off to Play*. Among the accepted play for children the author listed archery, cricket, skating, fives, and various ball games.

An adult sporting world began to take form in the 1830s when grandstands were constructed at racetracks and the first sporting journals appeared. The growth of sport was quite gradual, however, until the spectacular boom began around the time of the Civil War. Accelerated interest in sport is reflected in the growth of the National Association of Base Ball Players. Founded in 1858 with 25 clubs, the Association had 50 member clubs on the eve of the Civil War. In 1865 there were 97 members, a year later 202, and in 1868 close to 350. By 1869 the *New York Times* estimated that there were over 1,000 clubs, including those operating outside and inside the association; and there were doubtless many additional informal teams playing the game.

The rapid growth of sports in the United States has left scholars perplexed. They mention the effect of urbanization in facilitating the gathering of a crowd; there is discussion of the increase in leisure time produced by the Industrial Revolution; it is shown how improved rail travel sparked intercity competition; the sporting press is seen as capitalizing on the speedy information provided by telegraph companies; and the creation of an advertising industry is shown to have had its impact on the popularity of sport. But the reasons given are too mechanical, and treat sport as one more marketable product in a consumer society. The intensely fraternal motivations of the emerging sporting crowd are overlooked. In the final analysis, one historian admits no answer as to "just why" the boom occurred when it did, while another finds the extent of the sports phenomenon "not easy to explain."

Heroes and teams showered with glory seemed to come out of nowhere. In track and field, new world records were set with ease by the ubiquitous inventors of new events, such as the professional jumping event known as "the run, eight hops and a jump," and the one called "the stand, one hop, two strides, one hop, two strides and a jump"—world record 73′ 2″. For accomplishments to mean anything there have to be people who will make something out of it. More than athletes were needed to make the abovementioned jumps noteworthy; there was the active cooperation of track fans, whose presence made the event worth recording. The rise of sport is more easily comprehended when fans are credited with more than a passive role. In the formative years of track and field, for example, sponsorship most often came from an ethnic organization, whose members were expected to round up their relatives and friends, so that a big crowd would be on hand when, hopefully, someone would hop, jump, run, throw something, or ride a bicycle to a new world record. The payoff for the club would be a sizable paragraph in the sports page of the next day's newspaper. Reading the story, the club members could feel that they were more than just passive fans taking vicarious thrills. They had rounded up the spectators, who paid the admissions that covered the prize money and attracted the top-rate performer, who in turn set the record that publicized the club and brought in new members.

In every historical period there are the few of economic and social power who seek to dictate cultural taste. Occasionally they fail. In the origins of American sports the control of the elite was temporarily absent; in part because sports was seen as something not to be controlled but to be repressed. A sporting world was being created in a still-puritanical country whose gentry, clergy, and other "respectable" elements had from colonial times condemned sports and frolics as unfit for a hardworking Christian people.

"Society would drop a man who would run around the Common in five minutes," declared the Boston "Brahmin" Oliver Wendell Holmes in 1858. The popular amusements and sports became the preserve of a crowd labeled "the mob" by that venerable journal the *New York Times*. The erudite *Fortnightly Review* wasn't sure who the crowd was, but was certain it was not composed of "men of breeding." The raucous and untamed baseball fans of the period were proudly classified as "the working classes" by Samuel Gompers of the American Federation of Labor; and *Sporting News* termed them "the masses." Henry Chadwick, the dean of American sportswriters, reminisced about the way the prominent dailies rarely mentioned baseball well into the 1860s, and when they did, they "affected sneer and ridicule." Avoided even more thoroughly were sports such as boxing, which one New York gentleman of the day termed "one of the most fashionable abominations of our loafer ridden city." The publishers of the new tabloid "yellow" journals, however, were quick to provide what the gentleman called "the horrid details, with all their disgusting technicalities and vulgar slang."

The urbanization and industrialization of America, begun in the 1850s and greatly accelerated in later decades, created a large mass of people who were not served by traditional spokesmen of culture. The minister, the banker, the dean of the local academy, and the family of landed wealth had their own version of leisure; at the concert of the string quartet, at the church bazaar, boating on the lake, or attending a lecture about the Australian aborigines or other faraway peoples. The traditional church did not reach out to the new urban dweller; inner-city churches were left with many an empty pew after the old gentry had moved out to the suburbs; only then did the religious leaders discover the virtue of the involved church of the social gospel. The aloof intellectual establishment was nurturing Social Darwinist notions which held the typical worker and his family to be an inferior breed of human being, unqualified to share in the refined cultural and leisure pursuits of the "fittest" classes.

Popular sports were generated from below as one answer to the crying need for organized social activity in the new urban setting. They developed during a time when cities experienced a growth rate of from 100 to 200 percent in a decade. Uprooted populations had a desperate need for new social ties. When people formed an occupational club, ethnic organization, fraternal order, political club, or trade union, they tended to add sports activities as a way of attracting members and solidifying friendships. In the beginning, the majority of baseball clubs were just that—"clubs" of many members, like the Athletics of Philadelphia. Track meets featuring the best athletes were sponsored by such groups as Hibernians, Caledonians, Odd Fellows, and trade unions. The meets were embellished with sack races for the youngsters and special events for the elderly. And when a meet was over, the band started up the music for the evening dance party. High-stakes billiard tournaments stretching out over an entire week provided a sense of purpose for many a pool-hall loafer who was going to be there anyway.

The rise of sport perplexed the critics, who were at a loss to explain what it was that drew the crowds. A hostile reporter at a Madison Square Garden six-day professional walking marathon in 1882 wished he could understand "the peculiar phase of idiocy in the American character" which kept thousands of men and women watching this spectacle well past midnight. Horace Greeley had a tongue-in-cheek explanation "of our public vices." He said they subsisted on rum, and that without

liquor, horse racing, gambling halls, and lotteries as well as
theaters would wither away. "I don't know of a theatre," said
Dwight L. Moody, evangelist king of the 1870s, "that hasn't a
bar connected with it, or near it. What is that bar there for?
Fallen women go to the theatres, and for no good purpose."
During the decades of the rise of sport the per capita liquor
consumption almost trebled. There was need of some tran-
quilizer, some avenue of escape from the tensions of city life,
the "splendid chaos" which Rudyard Kipling called Chicago
—and having seen it he exclaimed, "I urgently desire never to
see it again."

The popularity of spectator sports soared in the aftermath
of the Civil War. To put out of their minds the bloody conflict
which took a million lives, Americans were throwing away
their puritanical inhibitions about amusements—flocking to
gaming rooms to have a go with the faro cards, and laughing
themselves hoarse at minstrel shows and at the new variety
acts called "vaudeville." Theater, sports, and gambling si-
phoned off the energy of the discharged veterans, then congregating in the cities, creating a bachelor culture of saloons,
pool halls, and boardinghouses. "Another Pool Hall on
Broadway," headlined the New York *Clipper* on the story of
the clutter of billiard parlors, saloons, theaters, dime mu-
seums, and the like stretching up from the Bowery toward
midtown. The cities were swollen by an ever-increasing stream
of immigrants from Europe seeking employment in the new
factories and mills. The war veterans who had chosen not to
return to their farms and villages were now joined in the city
by friends and relatives. From Maine out through Illinois,
farms were abandoned by the thousands, and villages stood
deserted. A traveler in rural Vermont described the eerie feeling of villages with "abandoned wagonshops, shoeshops, saw-
mills and other mechanical businesses."

The country had always had its rich and its poor, but outside of the plantation South there had been little precedent in
antebellum years for the blatantly obvious class distinctions
arising in the burgeoning cities. Whereas in the villages the

inns and taverns had served everyone, there were now in the cities separate hotels and separate drinking establishments for the separate classes. Where there had been a village livery stable, there was now in the city the private riding academy for the elite, while the nearest the masses got to riding a horse was watching its backside as they rode the trolley. In rustic America a dinner and dance put on by the best people in town lacked the splendor of a big-city, high-society cotillion held in a huge dance palace with a sixty-piece orchestra. Showing your latest hound dog to a neighbor was certainly not in a class with the Westminster Kennel Show in Madison Square Garden.

The America which Alexis de Tocqueville had described in the 1830s as industrious but plain was turning gaudy as it entered the Gilded Age, which the critic Thorstein Veblen found marked by "conspicuous consumption" and "conspicuous leisure." We can still see its glitter today in the Victorian homes and older office buildings, with their marble staircases and statues in the lobby. Those who had little to flaunt could, at least, find notoriety through identification with the rough and ribald world of public amusements. The more plebeian New Yorkers had their turn at the Garden too. Six-day marathons brought them there in great numbers during the late 1870s and early 1880s. Paying 25 to 50 cents to watch a marathon, a baseball game, or a billiard tournament was the poor folks' way of putting themselves on public display, as the gentlemen and ladies did by attending a Grand Ball, or paying $1.50 to $3.00 to see the great Edwin Booth on the Broadway stage.

One of the more important reasons for the baseball craze was that the teams provided the newly arrived and lonely urban masses a topic around which conversation at the pub could lead to friendships. No history of the early game is complete without mention of the semiliterate fan who could quote all the batting averages and betting odds, and harangue for hours about "our team." The way ball clubs were organized added substance to the "our team" claim. If the fan was not one of the team's club members or stockholders, he was likely to have some of them for friends. The promoters of baseball, well into the 1880s, were typically only a notch above the gate crashers in the sporting crowd.

In building public stadiums, organizing leagues, and funding cash prizes, the input of the respectable rich was minimal; they were absorbed with their kennel shows, horse shows, and yacht parades, and their penchant for exotic sports like court tennis and the aristocratic game of cricket. Financial backing by the proletariat was likewise minimal. But urbanization spawned merchants and a white-collar class that provided goods and services to the poor and as a result of promoting sports found a common social ground with them. Organizing and attending sporting events, and ostentatiously betting on the outcome, was one way for the new middle class to display its importance; many of its members were too recently off the farm to show their acquired status by proper manners. The middle classes were the fortunate of the city newcomers who knew how to read and "figur." A good number of them were transients, who for lack of a position went by the title "commission merchant," signifying a willingness to venture into any promotion which might turn a fast buck. Others took to the rapidly expanding civil service. Back before the Civil War, for example, when Cleveland, Detroit, and Milwaukee each had less than 50,000 people, these and similar cities had need of only one or two tax collectors. But within ten years these cities had nearly tripled in size, which meant, given the workings of bureaucracy, an increase of not three or four collectors, but a dozen or more.

The link between the laborer and the petit bourgeois was made stronger by the absence of middle-class suburban tract homes. The shopkeeper didn't commute to work; he lived above the store. There were only two sides to town rather than three. San Francisco had Nob Hill for the fortunate, and the Mission District for the unfortunate; it wasn't until the 1880s that the San Francisco middle class got their own neighborhood, the subdivision of fine Victorian homes known as the

Fillmore District. Historian Paul Worthman found that in the boom town that was Birmingham, Alabama, of the 1870s the neighborhoods of laborers and shopkeepers also had a surprising degree of racial integration, including interracial saloons that were not eliminated until the 1890s.

Merchants in mine and mill towns of the 1870s and 1880s often sided with workers in labor strikes, particularly when the struck business was owned by some absentee capitalist, who had a company store that undersold local merchants or who owned the railroad that brought goods into town at inflated wholesale prices. In other cases, ethnic loyalties prompted small businessmen to side with striking workers of their nationality. In the textile and shoe towns of New England the typical worker on strike was an Irish-American, who socialized in the saloons in the Irish part of town, where the city baseball team was organized. The Irish put New England on the sporting map in boxing and track and field as well.

In the huge metropolitan centers there was being created not only a high society but also a sidewalk society. On the latter Jane Jacobs commented a few years ago, "Reformers have long observed city people loitering on busy corners, hanging around in candy stores and bars and drinking soda pop on stoops, and have passed a judgment, the gist of which is: 'This is deplorable!' If these people had decent homes and a more private or bosky outdoor place, they wouldn't be on the street." Within this community a century ago there were those who organized sports, such as the track meets of ethnic organizations and the baseball teams of neighborhood political wards. Also within the neighborhood were entrepreneurs who saw the crowd as a potential market to be channeled through the turnstiles at public amusements. These entrepreneurs had the personal contacts necessary for bringing people together, and they could grudgingly accept the manners of street people, although wishing for refinement. The reputation of baseball fans, however, remained a poor one on into the 1890s, during which decade there were cases of ball teams being taken to court on the grounds that the people going to and from the ball park depreciated neighborhood property values. Sportswriters tried to elevate the game's reputation by mentioning the presence of the mayor or other dignitaries in the grandstand. Then again, J. P. McGuire, national head of the carpenters' union, was quite proud to proclaim in 1890 that "four-fifths of the spectators at any game on any day are men who do manual labor for a living." Whoever they were, the spectators were not bound by a narrow-minded code of behavior.

The public amusements were open to all in ways which allowed the acting out of a life-style quite alien to the Victorian standards of the upper classes. This moral conflict between the classes is evident in the relationship of women to sport. Working-class women toiled twelve-hour days in sweatshops, while "proper ladies" were not expected to work up a sweat anywhere. From the fact that women saloon owners were numerous, as shown in *Bonfort's Liquor Circular*, it is clear that Victorian standards failed to take, not only for many of the working class but among certain business people too, particularly business people working and living in the poorer neighborhoods. There were women involved in the outlawed sport of boxing, and there were also professional women wrestlers. Professional track and field had quite a few women runners, including one Ada Wallace who was said to have matched the record of one of the country's best male marathoners. Victorian ladies in their corsets and bustles were schooled to avoid sport. An 1879 *Treatise on Etiquette and Dress of the Best American Society* informed the ladies that even in social boating they should defer to the men for rowing, since "it is impossible for anybody to row with comfort or grace if she laces tightly."

In that moralistic age, when the crowds at sporting events were characterized as a foul-mouthed horde, for a woman merely to sit in the grandstand was to invite a reputation for low-class and unladylike behavior. In the interest of providing women a chance to attend baseball games and keep their reputations, promoters set aside special sections for women and children, in which no unaccompanied male was allowed. There were also periodic attempts of women to form their own professional ball teams. Sportswriters were scornful of these efforts, but one barnstorming women's team managed to last through at least two seasons.

The class composition of the sporting crowd is suggested in its ties to pool halls. At the height of the billiards craze, in the years just after the Civil War, every sizable city had its splendidly decorated barn-sized billiard parlors. In addition, there were an uncountable number of "billiard saloons." The strenuous efforts of blue-nosed moralists to tax and legislate billiard establishments out of existence seems the best evidence that, then as now, pool halls were hangouts for shady characters. Back then, however, billiards was a major spectator sport, which attracted those eager to be seen at the "in" places, particularly those who couldn't get into the really posh places, like the private rooms of the St. George Cricket Club. Billiards was in the winter months what baseball was in the summer. In the sporting journals of the 1860s billiards received easily as many column inches of coverage as did baseball. The two sports seemed to draw the same ill-mannered crowds; and whereas baseball had its code of proper behavior, billiards had the pamphlet of pool-table manufacturer George E. Phelan, *How to Conduct Yourself in a Billiard-Room*. An image of respectability was conveyed in lithographs of the day showing the assembly at pool halls wearing dark suits and bowler hats. Then again, as noted in the New York *Clipper* of December 6, 1873, "The downtown rooms were never before so crowded as on Thanksgiving Day, but it was by men . . . waiting for some one to come in who would loan them five cents to pay car-fare up home."

Billiards champions and room keepers played prominent roles in organizing and backing a number of the first professional baseball teams. In Brooklyn the biggest pool hall in town was A. R. Samuells' converted warehouse, which had fifty tables and a special section with five hundred seats from which spectators could view the course of tournaments, played

for prize money running into the thousands of dollars. Samuells was a Democratic ward leader, prominent member of the
Brooklyn Atlantics Baseball Club, and the backer of a
number of professional sprint racers. Out in Chicago, the self-
styled finest billiard hall in the land had raised seats accom-
modating over 2,000 tournament spectators. This establishment was financed by the accumulated prize money of billiards
expert Tom Foley. A noted man-about-town, Foley also
managed and played for Chicago's first professional baseball team, and a few years later was elected to the city council
on a workingmen's party ticket.

Democracy in sport was threatened by the creation of exclusive leagues and associations. It became apparent quite
early, to certain promoters, that there was more prestige,
and/or profit, in such combinations than in attempting to collect all the best athletes on one team, which for lack of competition would have rather meaningless victories. However,
monopolistic organizations and regulation were not readily
accepted by the majority involved in any sport. Baseball's
major leagues didn't have an effective monopoly on the talent
in the game until 1891. In amateur sport, the powerful regulatory agency the Amateur Athletic Union, the AAU, wasn't
created until 1888. The early sporting crowd had carried over
into the Industrial Revolution the free-market values of the
age of Andrew Jackson, the idea that "competition is the life
of trade." Competition in manufacturing, railroads, and finance was being restricted, driving the excluded to seek competitive situations elsewhere, sporting activity being one opening.
   The struggle to keep sports competitive was not conducted
by socialists and radicals, however, but rather by the stalwarts
of free enterprise fighting against corporate monopoly. As
Americans entered the Industrial Revolution, their ears were
still ringing with Jackson's damnation of "the monied capitalists" and the "powerful monopolies and aristocratical es-

tablishments." His stand was echoed by Samuel J. Tilden, Democratic candidate for president in 1876, declaring, "The capitalist class has banded together all over the world and organized the modern dynasty of associated wealth." To Grover Cleveland, the effect of this was like "an iron heel" stamping out liberty.

Despite the Jacksonians, by the 1870s the wealth and social power of the country had become centralized. It could be noted in the concentration of commercial and financial power in a few large cities. However, centralization of sports and theater talent in a few metropolitan areas was slow to develop. The expense of attracting well-known actors and promoting sporting events was, for a time, small enough to match the resources of hometown boosters. In 1878, for example, Boston had obviously become an economic center dwarfing in significance the textile town of Lowell, but the baseball fans of Lowell didn't have to feel insignificant. Their team, organized by a collection of petty clerks and merchants, had met the Boston club on the playing field and had handed the Bostons a succession of defeats.

There was a larger context to the struggle of smaller cities to maintain cultural parity with the metropolis. From Mobile to Topeka to Kalamazoo, town folk went into debt to modernize, with street lighting, electric streetcars and telephone service, as well as through the building of opera houses and baseball parks. Mobile had hot competition with New Orleans in baseball, but there was an even hotter contest to see which city would become *the* port of the deep South. So much money was spent on public improvements in Mobile that the local government went into bankruptcy. The smaller cities no more wanted to accept the new geographic power alignments than the shopkeepers and mechanics were willing to accept the new class divisions. The common people continued to believe that they, too, were important in public affairs, as they had believed themselves to be in Andrew Jackson's time. In press releases the organizers of baseball clubs identified themselves as "leading citizens," and more often than not these individ-

uals were the local haberdasher, blacksmith, and court clerk,
with a lawyer or two mixed in with other members of the petite
bourgeoisie and skilled trades. Politics offers another sign of
the self-important feeling of the common people: 80 to 90
percent of the eligible voters went to the polls in local elections; and up to the turn of the century city councils had a
remarkably broad social composition—a large representation
of shopkeepers, clerks, and craftsmen to complement the lawyers and the wealthy who so thoroughly dominate most of city
government today.

The very substantial role of urban political machines in
sports promotion can be seen in the involvement, in one manner or another, of virtually every well-known political boss of
the period. Out of over 1,200 nineteenth-century ball-club
officials and backers, at least half were active politically. One
hundred of them served in the state legislature and almost
twice that number were aldermen or councilmen. The promotion of sports was the specialty of politicians who lived off the
votes of the poor by defending them against easily managed
enemies—not the enemies who were the heads of strike-torn
factories, but temperance crusaders, Sabbatarians, law-and-
order societies, and puritanical opponents of spectator sports.
The sporting role was all the more easily adopted by the many
politicans/promoters who had themselves risen from poverty
and knew well how to make sports part of a demagogic package of rhetoric and grandstand plays.

The outspoken enemies of spectator sport took their battle
to the courts, the legislatures, and Congress. There were
enough attempts to outlaw or restrict boxing, wrestling, billiards, pro baseball, and other amusements to provide the
leading sporting journals an average of almost a story a week
for the 1880s. To the moralists, boxing, cock fighting, and the
like were simply bestial activities. But when it came to baseball it wasn't so much the game that drew criticism as it was
the crowd behavior: the drunks, the gamblers, the pickpockets, the mashers who bothered the women, the fans who yelled
obscenities and threatened the umpire. It seemed that certain

people didn't like certain other people gathering in big crowds, a situation that gave those attending late-nineteenth-century spectator sports something in common with the defiant long-haired youth at rock concerts of the late 1960s. In the years of the Industrial Revolution the working classes were not expected to have fun; they were expected to work. One of the biggest crowds of the period was the estimated 50,000 who lined the streets of Chicago in 1867 to watch the professional walker E. P. Weston complete a cross-country trek from New England. A critic found it repulsive that so many of those cheering Weston to the finish line had walked off their jobs.

The resentment toward gatherings of commoners for sports had sprung from earlier gatherings of a political nature. The rallies and torchlight parades of Jacksonian Democrats had been condemned. When Jackson entered Washington to assume the presidency, a conservative justice of the Supreme Court had declared, "The reign of King 'Mob' seemed triumphant." Responding to the critics, the poet Walt Whitman, a Jacksonian to the core, had written in 1847, "All the noisy tempestuous scenes of politics witnessed in this country—all the excitement and strife, even—are *good* to behold. They evince that the *people act*." By the time of baseball's famous Cincinnati Red Stockings of 1869 the substance seemed to have gone out of Jacksonian political action. But the people were by no means short on rallies and parades. One has to wonder where sports left off and politics entered at the Red Stockings' homecoming parade and celebration, addressed from a hotel balcony by club president A. B. Champion—lawyer, ward leader, and delegate to the Democratic National Convention.

CHAPTER

2

The Era of

the Pedestrians

In the history of track and field sports in the United States, sprinting and distance running and walking contests were the first activities to take an organized form, under the name of "pedestrianism." In the 1840s there were few memorable contests, and the ones that did occur typically involved one or more visiting runners from the British Isles, where the sport had had a much earlier development. American runners, and jumpers and throwers too, came into their own after the Civil War, a period of expansion and discovery in the sports world. Between 1865 and the creation of the Amateur Athletic Union in 1888 there was a gradual snowballing of interest and an uncovering of new attractions in "athletics," a loose term of the day covering running, walking, jumping, weight tossing, and weight lifting. There was an abundance of participants and spectators, and competing for prize money was a common feature. There followed from 1888 to roughly 1970 the era of the Amateur Athletic Union. Early in this period professionalism was virtually eliminated, and in the process many outlets for participation at a nonprofessional level were also eliminated. The 1970s deserve to be considered a new stage in track history. While the AAU and other traditional amateur organizations still wield authority, there has emerged from below an informal running movement which brings back features rarely seen since the 1880s, such as age-group running, significant opportunities for women, and attempts to maximize the quantity of participants, even if it inconveniences the few runners of exceptional quality.

Viewing the sports-page sections devoted to "athletics" and "pedestrianism" in the 1865–1888 period, one is struck by the vitality of sports involving running and jumping. It was the liveliness of a sport with excitable fans, and chances for the athletes from the tough neighborhoods to achieve fame and glory while performing in front of their peers. It was a time when organized running and jumping provided symbolic Mudville with much the same charge and excitement generated by Casey and the ball team.

For a time in the 1880s it appeared that the various forms of track, when combined, might soon match baseball in spectator and participatory following. One piece of evidence was the ease with which sponsors filled rented baseball stadiums for track meets, and occasionally for special match races between top sprinters or distance runners. Other evidence of the popularity of the sport could be found at the amusement parks, like Coney Island, which typically had running tracks and conducted weekend pedestrian meets through the summer months. The annual picnics of trade unions and ethnic organizations provided the setting for many top-rate track and field meets; cross-country walking had a sizable following; enthusiastic crowds jammed indoor arenas to cheer on the contestants in six-day walking marathons; and there was a fledgling world of "amateur" track in the colleges and in organizations like the New York Athletic Club.

At the height of the "pedestrian craze" the sport had most of the ingredients from which so many lively books about late-nineteenth-century baseball have been concocted: colorful characters on the field, creative promoters, and grandstand fanatics. The track story has been largely untold, however, perhaps because the plot line doesn't fit the usual sports story. In the often-told accounts of baseball and football, for exam-

ple, there are in the beginning the snobbish amateurs, baseball's Knickerbockers, and football's Ivy League colleges. And
then there is the triumph of democracy, which is ushered in,
according to the story, by the arrival of the professionals from
the coal mines and steel mills, who open the sport to a mass
audience. Conversely, pedestrianism was initially professionalized and had a remarkably large following of participants and
spectators; later, in the change to amateurism, the sport was
taken over by a wealthy minority. While present-day big-
league baseball or football teams are owned by the wealthy,
the show is ostensibly produced for everybody, whereas AAU
and college track has always been a rather haughty production. Today, the amateur system is undergoing reforms. Competitive opportunities are being expanded. And the story of
track in the free and loose era of the pedestrians takes on
added meaning.

The story of the athletic movement of the post–Civil War
era begins much earlier, and can best be understood by first
looking at the birth of modern athletics in England, where
professional running and walking contests were to be noted as
early as Queen Elizabeth's time, according to the British
sports historian Montague Shearman. Well-organized "professional pedestrianism" with record keeping dated from the
1660s. It was a professional rather than amateur sport largely
because of the Puritans, who, although defeated politically,
continued to influence the moral standards of the rising British
middle classes. Participation in sweaty sports by adults was
considered ungentlemanly. The more adventurous and friv-
olous of the gentlemen found an outlet for interest in running
and jumping contests by becoming sponsors and spectators of
runners from the lower classes.

The sponsorship of runners by those who couldn't quite
afford the purchase price of a good racehorse launched professional track. In its beginning, as Shearman explains, capable
runners were to be found in abundance among the footmen,

whose profession involved delivering messages and other tasks such as running ahead of the master's carriage and warning of rocks and potholes. There were other athletic activities developed out of occupations; hammer throwing, for example, utilized what was originally the large sledgehammer of the laborer, and rowing was initially popularized in competitions among ferrymen on the Thames.

The reluctance of gentlemen to become participants in track and field was intensified by the connection of the sport with county and town fairs, those annual events where farmers of the countryside gathered to purchase their supplies for the season and join in a general frolic ending in dance and alcoholic revelry. By the 1600s the merchants who organized the fairs almost always included an athletic program, and such programs were the early versions of the track meet. Running and jumping contests were also common features of wakes in the rural areas. By the 1800s fairs and wakes were less frequent, and the production of annual meets began to be the work of clubs and individuals. The program for a meet sponsored by a Major Mason of the town of Necton in 1817 included footraces, jumping matches, wheelbarrow races blindfold, jumping in sacks, and some difficult-to-comprehend events such as "grinning" matches and "spinning" matches. In these meets women as well as men competed.

The British offered to the Americans an approach to running and jumping that included hired competitors, with "wagering and betting of all kinds"; and informal competitions at fairs for such prizes as articles of clothing, or in the case of one race for old women, a pound of tea.

By the 1830s America had begun to experience the processes of urbanization and industrialization which two centuries earlier had created in England a leisure class that sponsored sports. During the 1830s horse tracks with grandstands for spectators were constructed in and around the major eastern cities of the United States. Magazines devoted to horse racing appeared, and one, W. A. Porter's *Spirit of the Times*, took to publishing occasional reports on ball games and footraces. American sports were stimulated by visiting Englishmen. Some came to win money with their imported racehorses and gaming cocks. Others came on what amounted to wild-animal safaris. These visits were encouraged by reports such as the one in *New Sporting Magazine* of January 1840 describing the excitement of buffalo hunting in the Rocky Mountain area.

Organized running in the United States began as an off-day feature at the new horse tracks. The owners of the premises would put up a modest $200 to $300 purse and the gamblers would sponsor whomever they could find to compete, the runners being generally from the poorer segments of society, as evidenced by the rather frequent appearances of black and native American contestants. The contestants were generally youthful, and many carried the title "Boy" as in the "Plow Boy" John Wesley Cozad, and the "Broom Boy" John Thomas.

Until the 1860s runners in America were in the shadow of their British counterparts. If a promoter wanted a sizable crowd, he knew his best prospects lay in negotiating with English sportsmen to bring over some of their runners. It wasn't that American competitors were all that inferior. During the 1840s a sprinter from New Haven, George Seward, established world records in the 100- 120- and 200-yard dash that stood for over three decades. The problem was that until the 1860s there wasn't enough social focus on the sport for many people to care, except when the match could be advertised as "England vs. America." The international contests drew enormous crowds.

Two "England vs. America" 10-mile runs in 1844 deserve a special place in track history. For the first time in such competition American entries were recruited from many states. There were also Canadian and Irish runners. Four Englishmen, including the renowned John Barlow, faced thirty-two challengers in the first contest. The purse was an unheard-of sum of $1,000. On the day of the race a crowd of from 25,000 to 30,000 spectators was on hand at the Beacon Raceway near Hoboken, New Jersey. The infield was packed with people, and they spilled over onto the running track. The English were favored among the gamblers, but the winner turned out to be a New Yorker, John Gildersleeve. He was a chair gilder by trade, and he had little previous running experience. Now he was a celebrity.

The Englishmen asked for a rematch, which was set for early November. The English had a habit of coming to America and letting the locals win one race in order to generate betting interest in a rematch, in which the visitors would go all out, and in winning recoup the earlier loss and gain large additional profits. The purse for the second race was raised to $1,400; there was now substantial betting on the new American star. The British star John Barlow had finished third behind a fellow countryman in the first outing. To save the honor of England and reward his financial backers, Barlow knew from John Gildersleeve's respectable winning time in the first race, a special effort would be needed in the rematch.

The crowd was even larger for the showdown contest—at least 40,000. The reporter for *Spirit of the Times* despaired of taking a count and said it was simply the biggest crowd ever seen at an American racing track, "an army three times larger than that with which Napoleon made his Italian campaign." Barlow led from start to finish and established a new 10-mile record of 54:21. Gildersleeve ran well under his time in the first race, but finished fourth behind another Englishman. The American Indian John Steeprock took second. There was grumbling among American gamblers that the British had set them up for the take. A check of Barlow's running record in England turned up a race the previous year that had been declared no-contest because Barlow was suspected of being in on a fix.

Subsequent international running matches in the United States failed to draw the enormous crowds of 1844. The luster of such contests had fled with the thousands of dollars in

wagers taken back to England. The event had launched pro
track into the limelight, and simultaneously exposed the
weakness which eventually destroyed the sport. Pro track was
easy to fix, and it was even more easily accused of a fix. John
Barlow ran for many more years, set many a record, and was
not involved in further scandals of note. Perhaps in the first
race at Hoboken he was a bit out of condition due to the long
ocean voyage just completed. Then again, he might have been
loafing.

The connection of running with racetracks probably did
little to elevate the sport's reputation. The equation of the
human runners with the animals was evidenced in the identi-
cal form employed in the sporting papers for charting results
of human and horse races. Noted in each case were distance,
purse, and condition of the track. The purse for the human
beings rarely matched the sum put up for even the slowest
nags. By the 1850s the prestige racetracks had excluded
human runners entirely.

American pedestrians emerged from the shadow of the race-
horses in the years following the Civil War. Pedestrianism had
a substantial position in the newfound sporting interest that
had the public flocking to baseball games, pool halls, rowing
contests, and prizefights. There were now distinct sections in
the sporting journals devoted to what some editors termed
"pedestrianism" and others "athletics." The publication in
1867 of Beadle's *Dime Handbook of Pedestrianism* seemed to
mark the arrival of the sport as a significant feature in American life; the Beadle Company's dime novels, joke books,
handbooks, and annuals were for that historical period as
much a reflection of tastes and fancies in mass culture as is the
television medium today.

In the postwar era there were many new forms of the sport,
in addition to the occasional runs still found at the racetrack.
Jumping matches involving wagers in the hundreds of dollars
were reported in the press. The clubs of immigrant groups

from the British Isles were beginning to turn their annual picnics into track meets on the model of the Old World county
fair meets, with their numerous contests for men and for
women, and for the young and for the elderly. The track
meets in this period were not, however, nearly as significant a
feature of the sport as were the single-event contests. The featured performance might be a sprint race, a jumping match, or
a long-distance walk or run. These single-event affairs, typically for cash prizes, were the activities sportswriters referred
to specifically as pedestrianism, even when it was a jumping
match.

The 50,000 Chicagoans who turned out to view Edward
Payson Weston finishing his 1867 walk from Portland, Maine,
had been furnished daily reports on his progress. Extensive
press coverage whetted public interest in many other city-to-
city contests. There was also something of a craze for efforts
to walk X number of miles in X days or hours, often in attempts at smashing some record established by the English.

For a sport in which there was usually but one lone contestant, the public interest and spectator turnouts for distance
walks seem rather remarkable. A walker approaching a town
along the way might expect to find ahead a welcoming party
including the mayor and a brass band. The New York *Clipper*'s coverage of an 1869 cross-country walk by the renowned
Weston included a dispatch from the town of Ellenburg,
where "during services in a prayer meeting, some person announced that Weston was passing through on his 5,000 mile
walk. Two-thirds of the congregation rushed . . . to greet him,
leaving the clergyman conducting services greatly shocked at
their irreverence."

Long-distance walking was for stouthearted members of the
working class. In social standing few competitors could match
even the modest position of E. P. Weston. When he began his
half-century walking career he was a young man in his twen-
ties who had floated through jobs as book salesman, jeweler's
apprentice, circus hand, and newspaper reporter. The walkers
were typically in need of financial aid to pay the tab on the

two- to four-hour-a-night stay in a hotel and other expenses. In most instances their sponsors were sporting men who took bets with those who believed the predicted feat was impossible to accomplish. Agreeing to wear a uniform or sign emblazoned with the name of a business or product was another way to fund a walk. Lamb and Earley note in their biographical sketch of Weston that for his first memorable walk he received financial aid from businessmen in return for passing out bundles of advertisements in towns along his path.

The grueling nature of long-distance walking is described in the *Clipper*'s report of February 27, 1869, on the attempt of R. F. Leonard to do 100 miles in 24 hours. Attempts to join a select circle of 100-mile-a-day peds were something of a fad in 1869. Leonard was a young American Indian who had fought with the Union army during the Civil War. The *Clipper* noted he had no previous competitions in distance walking, but now he was trying to make himself $20 by a pedestrian feat, to be accomplished by covering some two hundred times a course through the streets of St. Joseph, Missouri. He began at midnight, the usual starting time for distance-walking tests. It was pouring rain and he had to carry a lantern to see his way. By early morning a sizable crowd had gathered to cheer Leonard on, and some among them offered extra pay if he covered the 100 miles before midnight. Others began wagering with one another on the prospect. By noon he had walked 56 miles. Around two in the afternoon he asked for a whip, with which he slapped his legs as he went. By dark a man was following behind Leonard providing the stimulation of the whip. A man on either side of him kept pace and watched to catch him if he fell. Leonard went through the last miles in fits and starts, and in much agony, completing the 100 miles 21 minutes ahead of time. He was hoisted from the ground and carried aloft by the crowd, but according to the *Clipper* he knew little of the celebration, having apparently passed out in exhaustion.

Competitive sprinting and jumping also flourished in the post–Civil War years. Added elements of drama and intrigue were provided by handicapping. Important sprint races often took weeks of advanced planning, during which time the previous records of the contestants were compared and appropriate head starts provided to the less able competitors. In the jumping events the superior performers had to wear weights. Aside from match races, it appears that the very best sprinters rarely competed without granting at least part of the opposition a head start. Among the jumpers, the infrequency with which the best competed without weights may explain why late-nineteenth-century jumping records "with weights" were often better than the records "without weights." Handicapping in track and field began back when the sport was tied in with horse racing, and Shearman notes that in the early stages of sprinting in England there were occasional instances when top sprinters were weighted, as was the case with the best horses.

Handicapping offered the unusual sports situation in which the very best athletes were often competing against rank novices. This situation generated greater participation by the more amateurish athletes; and yet, somewhat ironically, these "amateurs" got this opportunity because the contests usually offered prizes of either valuable merchandise or cash. These prizes were the necessary enticement drawing in the superior athletes. In the genuinely amateur track and field meets of the twentieth century the practice of handicapping became almost extinct—in part because the best among the genuine amateurs had little incentive to accept a starting position at the rear of the pack, and in part because handicapping was considered a holdover from an earlier era when the reputation of the sport had been tainted with gambling and various financial features that exploited the athletes.

The particulars of how pro track operated after the Civil War should be, in fairness, understood in terms of life in that period. Running and jumping for dollars had a widespread popularity back in the late nineteenth century, and while part of this popularity related to the sporting types who enjoyed slinking out to a barn to watch professional women wrestlers and boxers, and cock fights, there was another side to the sport that was no more debauched than were the traditional contests in speed, strength, and skill conducted at county fairs and club picnics. The context in which most of pro track operated was unmistakably crude, but in its fully developed state, during the 1880s, it provided an outlet for participation on a scale that would be the envy of today's sports-reform advocates.

To understand how pro track functioned, the first point to note is that even the very best athletes were not professionals in the sense that pro baseball players were. Nineteenth-century pro track never had a league, nor did it have an organized circuit of signed performers. It didn't even have a national register of performers.

Pro track was similar to rodeos in that a comparative handful of experts traveled about taking on local talent, just as the bronc riders of the rodeo travel about even today matching their entry fees with those of the local cowboys, most of whom are in it more for fun than in any realistic expectation of winning a prize.

The match races between top sprinters, which were common from 1865 into the early 1880s, were conducted in a setting much like that of prizefights; but then around 1880 the sport moved onto tracks constructed at the many new amusement parks, where shills tried to get the masses involved in running, as other shills enticed wandering spectators to try their luck at the shooting gallery. In the mass participation at amusement parks, and at the track meets run in conjunction with club picnics and dances, pro track was hardly more "professional" than is participation today in a neighborhood bowling or softball league that awards a cash prize at the season's end. For bowling and softball teams, cash prizes serve to increase interest and ensure that the players show up each week; and the offering of prizes at amusement parks and club meets served similar ends.

In large part, athletics for pay developed because of a lack of opportunity for organized athletics without pay. There were no public running tracks or jumping pits; until 1887

there was not a city in the United States with a public playground. While military academies and private high schools
had begun athletic programs somewhat earlier than this, there
were almost no public schools with organized athletics until
the 1890s. The majority of the public schools didn't get them
until after the turn of the century. Even had the high schools
organized sports, not all that many youngsters went from
grammar school to high school. This was the era of child
labor. The conventional wisdom held that when young people
had energy to burn they had best burn it off in the factory,
mine, or mill.

Because of the long hours and short pay that were the lot of
the proletariat of that time, any chance to escape that toil was
welcomed. As *Sporting News* replied to a reader's inquiry as to
why people became baseball players: "It beats hoeing corn or
shoveling coal." The itinerant sprinter, wandering from town
to town in search of a race, was avoiding hoeing, shoveling, or
some similar endeavor. The crowds that rimmed the banks
and bridges of the Charles River in Boston to watch the scull-
ing races cheered in the hope that their favorites might be
the ones to take home the prize money that could mean a
respite from having to work.

Pedestrianism was obviously a fast-buck hustle, but those
who were society's new success models in that Gilded Age
generally did no productive labor themselves. They were the
speculators in corporate stocks, railroads, banknotes, and
land. They were the predatory lawyers who stole the patent
rights to gadgets dreamed up by those with an instinct for
craftsmanship which seemed no longer rewarded. There had
been a time when "work" meant workmanship, craftsmanship.
The shoemaker of old had constructed entire shoes; but in the
newly built shoe factories the shoemaker was reduced to the
bored and low-paid operator of a last-making or stitching machine. There was as much creativity and craftsmanship in becoming a good sprinter as in what was left of many traditional
crafts. At the starting line for a dash, the sprinters could be

seen in a remarkably creative array of upright and crouched poses. Some even faced backwards, believing a whirl-around made for the fastest start.

For the athlete to make money, there had to be a way to attract money to his or her sport. In the beginning, the prime attraction of pedestrianism was as primordial as running itself —gambling, which has been dated back before the first pyramids by historian Alan Wykes, who found hints that even the cavemen of the Lower Pleistocene age were familiar with betting. The gambling instinct, severely censured during the early history of America, could no longer be suppressed in the aftermath of the Civil War. The age of the Industrial Revolution was also the age of the gamblers, wagering on sports, on stock in mythical gold mines, and on the odds of not getting caught engaging in fraudulent business practices or graft. The 1870s became the decade of the state lottery, the profits of which went not to the state, but to the private parties who had bought a contract from the state. It was the Cuban National Lottery which gave the biggest prizes; and its American agent worked out of an office in New York, on Wall Street. Bookmaking was legal in most localities during the 1870s. Bookies hauled portable booths from one sporting event to the next.

Be it baseball, track, rowing, shooting, skating, swimming, billiards, cock fighting, boxing, or wrestling, the people who showed up to watch the event generally loved to gamble. Paterson, New Jersey, was a popular town for running during the early 1870s. The New York *Herald* and the *Clipper* reported crowds of 2,000 to 3,000 turning out at Paterson for a single race. The stakes generally ran from $100 to $200 a side, and in one instance were "one hundred dollars and a bucket of wine." The papers reported that side betting was heavy at Paterson, although the reported total sums were in the $1,500 to $3,000 range, far below the wagering for a good horse race, which seems to suggest that there were not all that many well-to-do pedestrian fans.

In those forms of pedestrianism conducted along the lines of boxing and wrestling matches, the athletes were among those frequently "taken" by the gamblers and the other shysters of that particular sporting crowd. The announcement that the noted sprinter Henry Crandall was going to run against McNally in Buffalo for $500 a side didn't mean that one of the two would emerge $500 richer. In stakes races, the pedestrians were generally underpaid hired athletes, employed by "sporting gentlemen" who put up the wager and gave the pedestrian a cut of the winnings. Perhaps with a better breed of backer a reasonable number of the more capable pedestrians might have become independently wealthy; but the backers tended to be ne'er-do-well types, betting their shirts on the outcome, playing with the athletes as they would play chips at the roulette wheel. A lost race might find the defeated ped stranded in a strange city with neither meal money nor carfare home. When the backers in track had a real income, it was usually from something like a saloon. For example, Madame Anderson, the leading lady pedestrian, was backed by the proprietor of a Brooklyn billiard hall.

In any of the sports connected with gambling there could be found athletes going under the title "the Unknown." A sporting patron could hardly find a better way to show daring than to risk putting up his athlete against an unknown, the questionable party often turning out to be a ringer of marked ability. One has to believe that there was a distinct air of insecurity at the reported match of two professional women wrestlers in which each was an "unknown." When an athlete's backer showed poor judgment in arranging a match, there was little the athlete could do about it without running the risk of being labeled a troublemaker and being blackballed from high-priced competition. Until the 1880s, when the amusement parks and sponsors of club picnics started offering substantial prizes, the professional runners were pressed to rely upon private backers. If the runner was mediocre, backers were few, and if the runner was superior, the opposition would demand a sizable head start as a condition of the contract. Suggestive is the *Clipper* item of April 2, 1870: "James Harris, otherwise known as the 'Cleveland Boy,' a youth . . . 19 years old, can't seem to get a race booked because . . . none of the 100 yard peds care to allow him the start he demanded."

For sprint races the putting up of the stakes was done with a maximum amount of publicity about who would do what to whom. The stakes were usually held by the sports editor of some newspaper or journal, who would print the signed agreement between the parties concerned. The signed agreement between the backers was a signal to the sporting crowd that the race was legitimate. Occasionally the published agreement stipulated the odds for the betting.

The gambling input contributed to the very shady reputation of professional track. Fixed races, or "throw-offs," as they were called, were common enough to keep sprint running relegated to outlying areas during the 1870s. In lieu of races in New York City the crowds went to Paterson, to the old vice den of Hoboken, or to the newly created vice den of Coney Island. In time the sporting public would decide it was safer to bet on the horses than on the match races of pro sprinters. Contributing to this conclusion were reports such as the one out of Shreveport, Louisiana, in 1875. As revealed in the New York *Clipper*, there had been double-dealing on a grand scale.

The backers of two prominent sprinters had connived with their respective runners to swindle the yokels of Shreveport by playing into the popular belief that sprints were fixed. The design of both parties was to show up in town acting quite suspicious. The contestants were Henry "Yank" Crandall, the American record holder in a number of sprint distances, and "Old Bill" Kendricks. Each of them was using an assumed name. A simple fix using their real names would be too obvious. Crandall was much the superior on record. Then too, little side money could be expected if the public knew the real names. It was side bets that afforded the best profit potential; and to maximize this source the backers of the two runners carefully plotted a series of informational leaks designed to lead the wealthiest of Shreveport gamblers to believe they had the inside dope on a fix. Kendricks arrived in town using the name "Rush." The Shreveport gamblers heard this and promptly began asking questions designed to uncover his true identity. Kendricks' backers strongly hinted that he was really the capable British sprinter Frank Hewitt. Crandall arrived using the name "John Wesley." Before much money was put on the apparent sure-thing of Hewitt against the unrecognized Wesley, the word was leaked that Wesley was really the American champion Crandall. It was suggested that Crandall's backers knew about the scheming Hewitt and had arranged the match in order to send the Englishman home dead broke. The wagering on "Wesley" (Crandall) was intense. But as the subsequently enlightened reporter from Shreveport told the *Clipper*: "The race was a throw-off, Crandall losing to Kendricks. . . . Pedestrianism must be at a fearfully low ebb when the fastest runners in the United States will resort to such tricks to make money."

From the mid-1870s on, there was a gradual decline in pro sprint match racing, but not in the number of sprinters. Great numbers of them were available when the amusement parks began holding sprint contests for prizes, and when the sponsors of picnic meets found they could get substantial press coverage if they invited in top pros. The special dramatic aspects of top-rate sprint contests were appreciated then as they are today. Said one observer, commenting on the growth of sprinting in England during the late 1870s: "The scene at the Hyde Park Cricket Ground, when the men are on their marks for the final heat of an All England Whitsuntide . . . or Sheffield fair handicap, is one of such intense excitement that it must be seen to be realized." The thrill of seeing a runner start from scratch and run down the handicapped competition ahead was part of it too, and this element of excitement is matched only rarely today—only in the relay race, where the final pass of the baton finds the eventual winner starting that last leg many yards to the rear.

In the United States the excitement over sprinting came to be focused at the amusement parks. The 1880s were a decade for the construction of such facilities, and visitors were given the opportunity to try for prizes, not only at the baseball toss and sledgehammer but also on the running track. The typical amusement park built in this period was a collection of concessions, and an enclosed track stadium was a common concession, particularly for the parks located along the eastern seaboard. All-comers meets were held on a weekly basis from late spring through the fall months. D. E. Rose's "Roman Amphitheatre" at Coney Island featured long-distance pedestrianism as well as sprints, but the other tracks went mostly for the sprints, the better known of the track stadiums being located in Boston, Providence, New Britain, Hartford, New York, Brooklyn, Newark, Paterson, Philadelphia, Harrisburg, Hoboken, and Reading. Some track stadiums added an inner ring for roller skating and bicycle races, and Acton & Taylor's Pastime Park in Philadelphia also had races for dogs.

These entrepreneurial track stadiums built their popularity on having a great volume of runners rather than subsisting upon the star appeal that might be held by the few of high quality. Given the lack of public facilities and school athletic programs, the promoters found no problem enticing young people to dish out their hard-earned nickels and dimes to pay the fee to get into organized competitive running. The large volume of runners helped the promoters drag in paying spectators, typically for 25 cents' admission. Friends and neighbors of a kid who had the previous week outrun the cop on the beat in a street chase could now come to the track stadium to see what the youngster could do with his speed in a more constructive setting. Neighborhood businesses and politicians got into the act by adding prize money.

Contestants at the all-comers meets had to pay their way into the stadium and then pay race entrance fees ranging from a dime to a dollar. But there was no shortage of contestants. Races started at 3:00 P.M. and continued until dark, but even this proved inadequate time for the running of the necessary heats in the feature races that offered $75 to $100 for first place. In 1881 New Hunting Park in Philadelphia stretched its weekly meet over two days; and after the press reported "several hundred spectators" showing up there to watch the preliminaries, the other pop track stadiums soon began spreading their meets over the full weekend. The extra day was a boon to the promoters, since the capacity of their stadium grandstands was typically between 1,000 and 2,000, and not the size for much one-day profit.

Amusement-park track was decidedly working-class sport. Proper society had traditionally shunned such places. Fanny Kemble, for instance, had been struck by the absence of members of her own class at Hoboken's Elysian Fields amusement park, which she found crowded with "journeymen, labourers, handicraftsmen, tradespeople, with their families, bearing all in their dress and looks evident signs of well-being and contentment." What the liberal Ms. Kemble found rather a "lovely place" was deemed quite the opposite by less open-minded aristrocrats. The amusements at the typical park included "the gaming-house, the drinking-saloon, the billiard-room," and other attractions condemned by the respected New York minister Theodore L. Cuyler as "positively pernicious and poisonous." The long struggle to overcome such prejudices was suggested in the title of a history of Coney Island, *Sodom by the Sea*.

In that portion of the sporting press catering to the laboring classes, amusement-park track was considered an important addition to pedestrianism. In 1881 the *Police Gazette* applauded D. E. Rose for construction of his amphitheater near the Iron Pier at Coney Island, where "a large amount in prizes to both male and female pedestrians" would be given out "during the coming season." Applauding the spread of track for the masses, *Sporting Life* of October 1, 1883, noted, "Foot racing is reaching gigantic proportions in Connecticut," and the article went on to mention that the recent feature handicap sprints at the New Britain and Hartford amusement-park stadiums had each drawn nearly 120 contestants.

In historical hindsight it might appear as a rip-off to have youngsters chasing after a $75 prize, or for that matter, hopping around in a sack race for which they paid a 10-cent entrance fee in the hope of a $5 prize. Whatever it was, it was

for many young people with energy to burn their only opportunity to burn it off on a running track. And it was being
presented to them by those who could understand that need.
John Taylor, of Acton & Taylor's Pastime Park, was himself a
former sprint professional. Al Farrington, who ran Island
Park in Harrisburg, was a baseball player. The leading promoter of sprints out in St. Paul was city councilman John S.
Barnes, for many years the manager of the local Western
League baseball team.

The "dignitaries" who provided the purse for feature races
were not that wealthy. The Sam Allen 140-yard handicap at
Pastime Park, for example, was sponsored by a saloon keeper
who dabbled in sports and GOP politics. This particular race
was for a $75 first prize, a $15 second prize, and a $10 third.
It needed thirteen preliminary heats just to start the process
of elimination. The contestants in this handicap ranged in age
from fourteen years to twenty-six, with nearly half of them
being under twenty. Each of them paid a 50-cent race entrance fee.

Participatory track and the amusement park had by the mid-
1880s developed enough popularity for some track managers
to add $5 prizes for the winners of heats, and prizes to the
fourth- and fifth-place finishers in the finals. Other promoters
tried to capitalize on spectator interest by staging special
sprint meets to which only the best pros were invited. There
were now a half dozen 100-yard-dash men who could do it in
just under 10 seconds, and such runners were in much demand. To attract the stars Pastime Park upped the purse for
some of its feature races to $350, and Schuetzen Park in New
Britain went to $400. It was not only a bid for the topnotch
pros, but also an attempt to increase the small but steady flow
of ex-collegiate sprinters who were turning pro.

Bigger purses required higher admission prices and race
entry fees. To have lined up "all the best sprinters," as claimed
in an ad for an 1884 Pastime Park meet, required a substantially different financial outlay than did the usual all-comers
weekend affair. Professional sprinting had arrived at the point

at which continued growth hinged upon an appeal to a higher class of spectator. But the genteel of that Victorian age had their prejudices against sports of the masses, especially one like pro track. It seemed crude, not only in its connection with gambling, but also in the participation of women, and of many black Americans, native Americans, and fresh-off-the-boat immigrants. Pro track's image problem was an impasse which hit not only the promoters of sprints, but also the organizers of six-day walking marathons—the one form of pro track that came closest to attaining what could be considered true big-league status.

While amusement-park sprint races presented a commercialized version of participatory track, the six-day walking marathons in indoor arenas offered a grand, if rather gauche, commercialized spectator show. These exhausting endurance tests helped to launch many an indoor facility into the sporting limelight.

The six-day marathons were the creation of promoters eager to capture the public interest for cross-country walks and channel it through the turnstiles of a stadium or arena. In the first efforts along these lines, horse tracks had been rented for individual attempts to cover 1,000 miles in 1,000 hours or perform similar feats. But these shows hadn't drawn enough spectators to keep the walkers from claiming more than they had actually done. Hugh Donohue of Boston, for example, set out in May 1875 to walk 1,100 miles in 1,100 hours, and he claimed to have done it; but the New York *Clipper* was skeptical, commenting: "It is scarcely necessary to say that there is nothing to show that the walk was honestly performed." A carefully monitored marathon involving dozens of contestants was seen as a way to clean up confusion in distance walking, a confusion which extended to those who claimed records in walking from city to city. Even the greatest of all cross-country trekkers, E. P. Weston, was suspected of fraud, and the *Encyclopedia of Sport* footnoted his records with the comment that the routes were never officially measured. The claims of records and the counterclaims led to one-to-one walk-offs between the leading long-distance pedestrians, and the common form for these competitions became the six-day marathon.

The six-day marathon proved to be a lucrative capitalization upon public hero worship of cross-country walking stars. Marathoning was launched into the sporting limelight in the United States in contests featuring two of these folk heroes, E. P. Weston and Daniel O'Leary, the latter an Irish immigrant who had begun walking competitively in the early 1870s in his adopted hometown of Chicago. After handing Weston a series of defeats, O'Leary was able to use the savings from his winner's shares to finance the inaugural marathons in a number of cities.

In its financial aspects marathoning was a decidedly big-league operation in comparison with sprinting. When O'Leary first took on Weston in Chicago, in 1875, the announced stakes were $50,000, with the winning runner to receive a check for $5,000. A sleuth for the ever-vigilant New York *Clipper* discovered that the announced figures were exaggerations, but the actual take by the winner (O'Leary) was nonetheless sizable: half the net receipts of a $15,000 gross at the gate. A year and a half later, in a celebrated six-day walk at Providence, Rhode Island's, Agricultural Hall, O'Leary thoroughly beat Weston, and in the process established a new world record of 519 miles.

By the 1880s O'Leary had turned his attention to promotion of younger marathoners who soon stretched the six-day record to 568 miles, and by 1890 to 619 miles. O'Leary became the marathon promoter at Madison Square Garden, which had first featured marathons in 1878, when he was a contestant. At that time the promotion was in the hands of Joseph J. Doyle, owner of a gambling den, close personal friend of Tammany Hall boss John Kelly, and later a founder of the Brooklyn Dodgers baseball team.

It was marathoning which first established Madison Square

Garden as the premier spot for indoor track. The racing oval had been laid out in 1874 by P. T. Barnum when he refurbished the old abandoned railroad station at Madison Square. Barnum used the track for chariot racing, a fitting addition to the attractions in the place he called the Great Roman Hippodrome. Barnum held the lease to the Hippodrome for only a year before turning it over to a local bandleader, who rented the place out to a wide variety of users, few of whom were involved in sports.

For marathons at the Garden spectators were charged 25 cents' admission, and if they desired they could stay the whole time, sleeping on the boards of the bleachers. A special section in the stands was set aside for women and children, where no unaccompanied "gentleman" was allowed. Actually, there were few "gentlemen" at the marathon races. The crowd was more like that found today at the roller derby—a sport which was evolved in the 1930s out of the six-day roller skating marathons.

A description of Madison Square Garden on marathon days tells of the track being covered with loam and sawdust to ease the footing of the contestants. At the east end of the building the walkers were provided small wooden houses for use during their rest periods—they had to be on the track a minimum of twelve hours a day. Behind a picket fence on the infield of the track were a small army of officials. They were volunteers from the sporting world, and often politicians looking for a little public exposure. Among the officials were sheet scorers who made notations, as the lapmen in charge of sets of dials recorded the miles being covered. Another official recorded the progress of the individual runners on a large blackboard.

To the casual observer the marathon walks could appear little more than sadomasochistic exhibitions. Attendance was particularly high on the last day, when spectators had their best chance of seeing at least one walker collapse in agony and exhaustion. The six-day walks did seem to have something in common with the dance marathons of the 1930s Depression era, since they were inaugurated during the second worst economic depression of the nation's history, the one of the late 1870s.

The true fan of pedestrianism found more than a physical exhibition in the marathons. The contestants were a highly personalized group, in their reputation for cross-country walks, in their often flamboyant costumes, and in their various approaches to race strategy and walking style. The afficionados who brought their blankets and/or wine bottles and took advantage of the privilege of their quarter's admission to stay the entire six days certainly got to know the contestants in a rather personal manner. The true fan enjoyed knowing when the hero on the track was merely feigning fatigue in order to set up the opposition for the demoralizing sight of a fresh burst of energy. O'Leary was one of many who would trudge along in a twenty-minute mile and then more than double the pace for the next mile. The rules allowing contestants to "go as you please" made for all sorts of strange gaits which barely fit with what we know today as proper heel-and-toe walking.

When the six-day event at the Garden had proved profitable, the owners of the premises saw fit to up the rent. In 1881 O'Leary was charged the then enormous sum of $10,000 to rent the Garden for six days. The admission price had to be doubled to 50 cents, and at this price some gimmicks were needed to draw in sufficient numbers of spectators. To encourage attendance during the first days of the race, special prizes were offered to the runner leading at the halfway point, or at the end of the first 200 miles. The promoters in various sports of the 1880s were beginning to see the commercial value of making a fuss over statistical records, and at the marathons a distinct world record time was designated for each mile covered. Consequently the record book on marathoning includes pages of small-print detail revealing such facts as fastest 342 miles, "3d. 17h. 32m. 23s.," and fastest 343 miles, "3d. 17h. 44m. 9s."

Marathoning as a commercial venture came to experience, in a glaring way, conflicts between promoters and athletes which are covertly a part of most pro sport. Ideally, the promoters wanted the walkers to put out 100 percent effort 100 percent of the time. The athletes on the track, however, were in it strictly for the money, and it gradually became clear that the way to win was to save one's energy for the finish, even if that meant the pack was slowed to a virtual crawl. And winning meant avoiding the fan-pleasing style of alternating fast and slow laps. The promoters and paying spectators wanted more than a final sprint, so a new rule was put in, stipulating that contestants had to cover a set number of miles or there would be no prize. Four hundred and eighty miles was a common cutoff distance, below which even the first-place finisher wouldn't realize a dime. There were occasions when the athletes refused to get on the track until the cutoff distance had been lowered; and one such strike caused the cancellation of a professional bicycle marathon in Minneapolis.

The higher admission prices, and the new breed of walker who plodded along "with no style," caused a waning of interest in the marathon. Promoters now began going for six-day bicycle and roller skating races. Commenting on the first skating marathon at Madison Square Garden in 1885, Henry Chadwick, sports editor of the *Clipper*, compared the event with the six-day walks and concluded: "Throughout the tournament in the Garden last week . . . there was a lack of that wild enthusiasm which was characteristic of the surging masses of humanity who were wont to shout themselves hoarse in honor of Fitzgerald, Rowell, Hughes, O'Leary and the other bright lights of prolonged pedestrianism." The six-day "go as you please" marathon walks were still held once or twice a year at the Garden on into the 1890s, and then they faded from the sports scene, until they were briefly revived some three decades into the new century.

Marathoning had been the one form of pro track to develop a substantial cash flow, and it was relatively free from gambling scandal, but it was bound to fail. It was all too obviously a sport for the coarse and unrefined segments of society. The *Police Gazette* might employ polite language in reporting an

O'Leary-sponsored marathon handicap "intended as a test to
the relative endurance powers of men and horses," but the
fact remained that it was a crude contest pitting humans
against brute animals. In the opinion of proper Victorians
anyone reading the *Police Gazette* was of suspect morality, for
it was a paper carrying such distasteful news as the following
item in its April 21, 1881, issue: "SAN FRANCISCO. . . . There
is to be a ladies' handicap six-day pedestrian race, in which
Amy Howard gives Millie Young, Belle Sherman and
Madame La Chapelle 10 miles, and 20 miles to any other
contestant hailing from the Pacific Coast. The cash prizes aggregate $1,200, but no contestant who does not cover 320
miles, exclusive of handicap distance, will get anything."

One form of mixed pro and amateur track which developed
immense popularity was the track meet of the ethnic and occupational clubs. Such a meet was variously known as the
club's "games," "picnic and games," or "athletic meet." The
distinguishing feature of picnic track, as opposed to a mere
picnic, was that the competitors at top picnic meets included
the very best world class record-holding athletes; sometimes
it was the best amateurs, other times the best pros. There were
assorted running and jumping contests and "vaulting with
pole"; "putting the heavy stone"; "putting the light stone"
(16-lb. shot); dance contests; pitching quoits or horseshoes; a
tug-of-war; and at some meets, baseball-tossing or throwing the
caber (the trunk of a young tree). As a measure of their
popularity, it may be noted that picnic meets were often held
before capacity crowds at rented ball parks of major-league
baseball teams. Far and away the best-used facility for picnic
track in Brooklyn was the grass track at the ball park of the
team later known as the Dodgers. Running lanes were marked
by ropes rather than chalk, so as not to mar the grass.
    The picnic meets had been going on for years before the
newspapers noticed them and raised them to the level of
"sporting events." According to Frank Menke's *Encyclopedia*

of Sport, the honor of holding the first known track meet in the United States goes to the New York Caledonian Society for its games of 1867. But as reported in *Spirit of the Times*, this 1867 meet was actually the "Eleventh Annual Celebration" of the club; and it seems safe to assume that some of the many athletic contests held at this Caledonian picnic had also been part of earlier affairs. A decade or so later a large number of other immigrant clubs were beginning to get news coverage for annual meets revealed at that time to be their tenth, twelfth, or fifteenth.

Around 1880, in addition to more press coverage, there appears to have been a great proliferation in the number of clubs and organizations sponsoring track and field programs. In 1884 *Sporting Life* magazine in Philadelphia listed over three dozen of what it considered "fixtures," which were major East Coast track meets. There were those sponsored by Irish, Scottish, and German immigrant groups; the Printer's Union games in New York; military regiment meets; sprint meets at amusement parks; college meets; and the meets of clubs for wealthy gentlemen, such as the New York Athletic Club, the Manhattan Athletic Club, the Staten Island Cricket Club, and the Schuylkill Navy Athletic Club of Philadelphia.

The growing popularity of the track meet paralleled the phenomenal increase in the number of clubs and social organizations. Historian Arthur M. Schlesinger, Sr., has written: "For the average person no use of leisure so well suited his taste as that afforded by the ubiquitous fraternal orders which sprang up during the last quarter of the century." Clubs and societies were being created because "in the large cities some form of organized social commingling seemed called for to replace the spontaneous friendliness of small rural towns." The social organizations putting on track meets might be newly formed, or they might be older groups conducting a membership drive, but all could see the publicity value of a paragraph or two in the local sporting papers.

There were a variety of ways to elevate one's picnic and games in importance. To earn prestige organizations most closely connected to the working class tried to attract many thousands of people to their picnics. The crowds came not only to watch but to participate in events ranging from foot-races and other athletic contests to the dances, penny pitching, and pie tossing, and such incidentals as an "award for the best dressed gentleman," or lady. On the athletic field there were opportunities for both sexes and for many different age-groups to become winners, much as in the popular distance runs today, which have many categories of participants and winners.

To better the chances of press coverage, efforts were made to attract some star performers. Today the stars are often rumored to have received discreet payment of cash in return for showing up; a century ago there was not only appearance money but often such valuable merchandise prizes as pianos and grandfather clocks, and on many occasions there were outright cash prizes. Occasionally, a top pro agreed to appear at the picnic and merely give exhibitions, allowing the locals to seek the prizes. Duncan C. Ross, the noted wrestler, and world record holder in hammer throwing and weight tossing, made an agreement of this kind with the San Francisco Caledonian Club in 1885; he agreed to participate in three events at the Club's annual "picnic and games," and agreed to give any prizes he might win to the man finishing behind him. The appearance of Ross and a turnout of 6,000 people helped the Caledonians get national press coverage. Among the thirty-eight events mentioned in the *National Police Gazette* report there were races for men over forty-five, men over fifty-five, boys under sixteen (two races), girls under sixteen, "members' daughters under fifteen," and "married ladies," plus a sack race and a number of runs open to all comers. There was also field-event competition divided by age-group, and there were numerous dance contests. Almost all races were handicapped.

The sporting scribes had difficulty deciding whether picnic meets were pro or amateur sport. Some sporting papers reported the picnics under the heading "pedestrianism," which was commonly used for pro track, while other journals ran picnic results with the college-meet reports in the general section for amateur sports, usually titled "athletics." The typical picnic had one or more events designated "professional," while others were described in the words "amateurs only," or "for members only." Further complicating the pro vs. amateur issue, the sponsors of many of the biggest picnics, the Scottish-American Caledonian Clubs in particular, provided cash awards, be the event specifically for noted pros or merely a contest for novices. The *Sporting Life* report in its "athletics" section on the 1885 Philadelphia Caledonian picnic noted that by entering a number of events James Grant had gone home from the meet $75 richer; A. Scott had won $55; T. Aiken, $54; and half a dozen other contestants, more than $25.

Even the prestigious clubs of the wealthy gentlemen who insisted on amateur purity resorted in the early years to adding professional "exhibitions" to their club meets. However, in direct proportion to increased popularity and social prestige for track meets, the advocates of sports for sports' sake grew increasingly concerned over the professionalized aspects of these events. Meets with big-name pros and splashy cash prizes came to be seen as threats to the prestige of purely amateur track and field. The way the crusaders for amateurism handled this growing problem provides the next chapter in the track and field story.

3

Amateurism?

Organized running/jumping/throwing competitions began with the professional pedestrians and the loosely run picnic meets, but became detached from their original environments to become what we call track and field. By the early twentieth century amateur track and field had the modern Olympic Games, and international competitions arranged by the colleges and the AAU. Amateur track had taken the spotlight from the once well attended match races of the professional peds. It had eliminated from the sport the exploitative pitting of humans against horses or dogs. It had a promising future in the public schools, which were just then inaugurating athletic programs, as laws were passed abolishing child labor.

The development of clean, formalized track and field came at a price, however. Sprinting at the amusement parks was halted for lack of professional contestants. Women, who had shared a piece of the action from late medieval county fairs down through the picnic-meet era, were now rarely seen; nor was there room in tightly structured track for the forty- or fifty-year-olds. Black Americans had played a substantial role in pedestrianism; but in track and field the nurturing ground for talent became the colleges, and until the 1950s few blacks got to college, or even to a high school with decent track

facilities. Community groups lost out, too. The picnics of occupational and ethnic clubs had once drawn the top competitors, but by the turn of the century this was no longer the case,
and the athletic contests at picnics were rarely of good quality.
The best competitors went where they could find quality running tracks and coaching—to the colleges and a handful of
expensive clubs with private running tracks. Six-day marathoning faded from the scene. So, too, did cross-country walking, despite the efforts of the ageless Weston. He was still at it
in 1910, when at age seventy-one he trekked across the con-
tinent in 77 days. As running, jumping, and throwing became
structured and codified, the less formal events—the sack
races, wheelbarrow races, and tug-of-war—were dropped.
Track and field was called amateur, but it really provided less
room for the genuinely amateurish than did the wide-open
running/jumping/throwing affair that was the old picnic meet,
with its crowd of 10,000, its thirty to forty events, and its
evening dance party.

In the era of the picnics and pedestrianism massive numbers
of people had dabbled in competitive running and jumping, as
they did in bowling, or horseshoe pitching, or sandlot baseball.
But by the 1920s the athletic activities connected with track
and field had generally ceased to be something people dabbled
in.

Modern track and field took its highly structured, stratified
form because of economic factors, and because of the social
outlook of its early proponents: gentlemen like William B.
Curtis, athlete, sports handicapper, writer, and cofounder of
the New York Athletic Club. Curtis was a personable lifelong
bachelor with an unquestioned dedication to the amateur
cause.

In 1878 the thirty-nine-year-old Curtis dissolved a successful merchant business in New York to become editor of "The
American Gentleman's Magazine," *Spirit of the Times.* He
soon made the *Spirit* the nation's foremost journal for the
track and field of the colleges and athletic clubs like the
NYAC. The *Spirit* had covered "pedestrianism" for decades,

but Curtis now severely restricted this coverage, as he did the reporting on picnic meets of the working classes.

Curtis argued persuasively in the *Spirit* for the standardization of events at track and field meets. He criticized meet directors for running sprints over whatever distance fit the available straightaway, be it 85 yards or 120, and insisted that there should be a standard 100-yard distance. He ridiculed the proliferation of jumping contests and the invention of such events as "the stand, one hop, two strides, one hop, two strides and a jump." Curtis repeatedly made mention of alleged measurement irregularities in the makeshift running tracks at the baseball parks rented for picnic meets.

His concern with technical improvements ranged to discussions on the merits of stopwatches. He noted that only the very best were free of "a bounce" in the second hand. The best cost more than $100 apiece. He lamented the slow progress toward a watch with a tenth-of-a-second split, which could replace the fifth-of-a-second watch then in vogue.

The sport at the picnic meets, which was pleasantly reported upon at length in the mass circulation journals such as *Police Gazette* and *Sporting Life,* was sarcastically criticized when Curtis deigned to discuss it in the *Spirit*. He blasted the annual New York Clan Na-Gael picnic in 1881 for unruly spectators who "made themselves, in every way possible, thorough nuisances," while the "special policemen and other badge-wearers . . . made no attempt to preserve order, or keep the inner ring clear. About half the assembly amused themselves with eating, drinking and dancing, while the remainder swarmed all over the field." In other reports, Curtis criticized the Caledonian Society games for their noisy bagpipers and crowds of wild dancers, and he put down the games of a British immigrant society with the comment: "Many members of the society didn't bother to show up until the evening ushered in the music and dancing."

Curtis's snobbishness may have been what he believed necessary to entice society people into sports. Back in 1866 he had found few gentlemen interested in using the exercise gym set up in the rear of the Manhattan residence he shared with John Babcock, an industrialist and builder of the Third Avenue Elevated. The back-room gym was the first facility for the New York Athletic Club, created in 1866 with three members: Curtis, Babcock, and a weightlifter from Brooklyn, Henry Buermeyer. The three had been resting in the gym after a workout with the weights when discussion turned to the rapid rise in amateur sports then occurring in England. They decided New York deserved a club like the London Athletic Club, which was three years old at the time.

The hedonistic Gilded Age hadn't yet gotten into full swing in America, and special efforts were needed to attract high society to the joys of athletic participation. Frederick W. Janssen explained in 1885, in the first history of the New York club: "Those whose acquaintance with amateur athletics dates back but a few years can hardly appreciate the coolness with which these sports were at first received here, and the difficulty experienced by these three athletic crusaders in inducing recruits to rally around their banner." Curtis was able to organize some competitions among rowers in New York–area boat clubs, earning himself the title "father of amateur rowing." But running and jumping was another story. To launch amateur track, the NYAC men used the subterfuge of having boat-club competitors row across New York Harbor to the Hoboken docks near Elysian Fields, the traditional grounds for pedestrian races. The rowers ran some races of their own, and a second visit was made for runs at Elysian Fields; but then these grounds were rejected. As Janssen explained: "The Fields being then the people's pleasure-ground, much as Coney Island is now, the crowds of curious spectators were always annoying and sometimes aggressive."

The fashionable New York gentleman of the 1860s tried to model his sporting life after that of the English aristocracy, and from that perspective gentlemen's sport and people's playgrounds didn't mix. Shearman noted that the earliest "gentlemen-amateurs" in England had insisted that amateur sport belonged to their class. Centuries of feuding between rich and poor over hunting rights had helped instill this attitude. In the early 1800s there were more prosecutions for poachers invading gentlemen's estates for game than for any other criminal offense, according to John Ford in his recent history of English sports. The gaming laws were glaringly prejudiced, specifically making hunting illegal for any Englishman who did not own landed property. As defended in Blackstone's *Commentaries on the Laws*, standard reading for lawyers of Curtis's generation in England or the United States, the game laws were necessary "for the prevention of idleness and dissipation in Husbandmen, Artificers and others of lower rank, which would be the unavoidable consequence of universal license."

To attract society to sports, something had to be offered which contained higher purpose than mere conspicuous waste of leisure. By the 1890s a less puritanical social elite would see little wrong with conspicuous waste of time; but in the formative period of amateur sports gentlemen had to take care lest they appear no less a group of "great mischiefs" than the "inferior tradesmen, apprentices, and other dissolute persons, neglecting their trades, and employments"—this being one British-gaming-law description of poachers.

The New York Athletic Club's first official track and field meet, modeled after meets of the London A.C., was held in November 1868, after a lengthy search for suitable facilities. The roof wasn't quite finished over the track at the new American Institute building, but the uptown Manhattan location was excellent. The riding academy connected with the track was to become a prestigious spot for stabling the horses of the gentlemen and ladies who enjoyed riding through nearby Central Park.

For the first "amateur" track meet in the United States the New York club hardly had the level of world class athletes for which it would later be famous, but William Curtis made sure this 1868 affair was a memorable one. He arrived at the meet with the first pair of spiked running shoes ever seen in the United States, having recently purchased them from England, where the spiked shoe was becoming the rage among pedestrians. As he would later eagerly promote the best in running tracks and stopwatches, Curtis urged his fellows to try his spiked shoes in the events in which he was not entered, arguing that what was good for the English must be good for Americans. Others were eager to try, and put the shoes on easily, since they were of "generous proportions as best fitted their owner's ample feet." Curtis wore them for the 75-yard and 220-yard runs; others wore them for the quarter-mile, half-mile, and mile walk, and the hammer throw and shot put.

Amateur standing was loosely construed in 1868, and this first "amateur" track meet included a number of contestants from the New York Caledonian Club, an organization from which the NYAC would later dissociate itself because the Caledonians gave cash prizes to winners at their picnic meets.

The first cogent argument for carefully segregating amateurs from athletes seeking cash prizes was presented in 1872 in two small pamphlets written by William Curtis and John Watson, a journalist and member of the Schuylkill Navy Athletic Club of Philadelphia. The writers defended a definition of *amateur* which stated: "An amateur is any person who has never competed in an open competition, for a stake, or for public money, or for admission money, or with professionals, for a prize, public money, or admission money; nor has even, at any period of his life, taught or assisted in the pursuit of athletic exercises as a means of livelihood."

Curtis and Watson were writing in response to the public furor that arose out of the 1872 Schuylkill Navy Athletic Club rowing regatta, where the strict amateur standard had been applied, for what appears to have been its very first test.

The Schuylkill Navy, a club for young gentlemen of the Philadelphia area, had been putting on a regatta on the Schuylkill River since the late 1850s. In the post–Civil War period the regatta was becoming a major summer event for Philadelphians, in part because the rowing races were run along a stretch of river that had become a gathering place for the fashion-conscious. In a highly touted civic improvement project, the riverbank had been landscaped into a beautiful public park, and strolling the Schuylkill was an act of pleasure and civic pride. At regatta time thousands lined the banks.

Oarsmen came from all up and down the eastern seaboard to compete in the various races of the Schuylkill regatta. Gamblers and bookies were there too, along with sporting men who put up money for prizes. Each year the prizes went higher—to $1,000 in 1870 and then to $2,000 in 1871. The Schuylkill Navy offered winners a trophy cup rather than a cash prize, and as the prize money mounted the luster seemed to be wearing off the trophies. The Schuylkill club did the work of processing applications and acting as officials and scorers, and for this the rewards to the organization were minimal. The club's own gentlemen-oarsmen were no match for the muscular competitors who had gotten into the sport via their work on merchant ships or the docks.

Before the 1872 event the Schuylkill Navy announced that entry fees for all races in the regatta would be accepted from "amateurs only." Few if any were deterred, and the organization was deluged with the usual flood of applications, perhaps because virtually nobody worked at competitive rowing as a principal means of livelihood. Then, as one account tells it: "The Committee on Nominations for the Schuylkill Navy was almost ruthless in its rejection of applicants. It ruled out about half the men who had entered for the different events." When explanations were demanded the Committee tried to be tactful, refraining from calling the rejected ones professional; they were simply termed "not amateurs." The Committee declared ineligible any rower who was known to have competed anywhere in a race for prize money. Some of the rejected demanded reconsideration, because while they had competed for prize money they had never won any. The Committee did not reconsider. In their pamphlets, Curtis and Watson defended the Schuylkill Navy on the grounds that restricting amateur standing to those who had never competed for a cash prize was the only viable test of an athlete's loyalty to the ideal of sport for the love of sport—the amateur ideal.

Promotion of sport for the love of sport with total avoidance of monetary incentive was a luxury in the 1870s. If the competition was to be of more interest and drama than a pickup game of ball on the sandlot, there was unavoidable cost, first in the organizer's time, then in equipment and/or facilities. The leisure class, with time and money to spare, could far better afford amateurism as defined by the NYAC or Schuylkill Navy than could the sports-loving majority. And even the leisure class had occasional need to breach the amateur ideal. Most of the major "amateur" rowing regattas of the 1870s included special races by "non-amateur" oarsmen in order to draw larger crowds. Well into the 1880s the New England Amateur Oarsmen's Association was officially on record as allowing professional races at its amateur regattas. William Curtis' NYAC occasionally invited professional pedestrians to put on "exhibitions" at club meets; and in 1877 the New York club actually sponsored its own "Grand Professional Meet" in Madison Square Garden, with cash prizes to all winners.

Sports participation in this period was generally a pay-to-play proposition. In place of today's public baseball diamonds, watered and manicured by the employee of the city or county Department of Parks and Recreation, there were then the choices of the vacant lot or the private baseball diamonds rented by the game, or purchased outright by baseball enthusiasts wealthy enough to afford their own facilities. Good cinder and brick running tracks also had to be rented from some entrepreneur or purchased outright. This nineteenth-century situation has recently been experienced by many Californians, who have had to pay for public sports that were either free or at very nominal charge before the passage of the budget-cutting Proposition 13. "Can Little Leagues Survive Pay-for-Play?" asked the headline in a newspaper of the suburban California community of Livermore. The accompanying article explained how the Leagues were "being charged for the use and maintenance of fields as well as water and services. All those things the Leagues formerly took for granted as free are now costing big dollars." Commenting on

the spread of users' fees in the first twelve months of Proposition 13, Larry Naake, executive director of the California
Park and Recreation Society, declared: "We don't want to
turn parks and public swimming pools into country clubs for
the middle class and the rich."

The picnic meets of the late nineteenth century provided an
opening for working-class sports participation by handling the
funding problem in a manner befitting the age of Phineas T.
Barnum and torchlight parades. The track event was spiced
with dance music, raffles, and cash or merchandise prizes for
winning athletes. Big-name professional peds were invited to
add stature to the meet and to the competition of a group the
sponsors considered "amateur"—that is, the club members
and friends who ran and jumped for a prize at the games of
Caledonian Societies, Irish clubs, trade unions, benevolent societies, and businesses which sponsored annual picnics for
employees. An example of the latter is the McCreery dry
goods company's annual picnic in New York, which by the
mid-1880s had become a gigantic extravaganza open to the
running and jumping enthusiasts employed in any dry-goods
store in the city.

The picnic sponsors generally interpreted the amateur question in the manner then applied to the sport of baseball. In
the national game the accepted definition of a professional
of the 1870s was a player who worked at baseball for a salary
or attempted to live off the gate receipts of games. All other
players were free to consider themselves amateur, even if they
competed in tournaments granting substantial cash prizes to
winning teams. The Tammany Hall Democrats in New York
sponsored a number of baseball tournaments and other sporting events using the same definition of "amateur." In 1871
Tammany sponsored a two-week athletic festival for the benefit of the Union Home for Destitute and Orphan Children of
Soldiers and Sailors of New York. Among the featured events
was a "Mass Foot Race—Amateurs: No Professional runners
allowed in this race. First Premium, Amateur's Belt and $100;
second $75; third $50; fourth $25."

In the morally loose years immediately following the Civil War the formal and polite sport of Curtis and Watson, free of gambling and hucksterism, found little public support. The Protestant clergy, the crusaders for propriety, were little help. Holding fast to the Puritan traditions, the clergy opposed *all* sports. In arguing against prizes in sports, Curtis and company were in a sense even more puritanical than the clergy, for the churches had their raffles. Massive lotteries were managed from offices on Wall Street; bookmaking was legal; and city governments were funding civic improvements through lotteries advertised in the sections of sporting papers devoted to the sale of marked cards, sleeve machines, and the like. One such ad in the *Clipper* announced that the roving organizer of civic lotteries Charles B. Peters had sold a million dollars in lottery tickets toward the construction of the present Louisville (Kentucky) Free Public Library.

Around 1880 society life was spiced up by a breed of nouveaux riches with a penchant for conspicuous consumption and leisure. In time they would make their social focal point the suburban country club, but before moving to the suburbs they frequented the urban athletic club. For many of the new rich, sportsmanship was a quite secondary reason for joining an athletic club. But whether the new club members were athletes or mere socializers, their money and power greatly aided the efforts of Curtis and his athletic gentlemen friends in pushing forward their brand of pure amateurism.

In the late 1870s the leading clubs in the New York area, such as the New York, Manhattan, Harlem, and Staten Island athletic clubs, were composed almost entirely of athletes and contained only about fifty members each. By the mid-1880s, membership in the leading clubs numbered in the thousands, with long waiting lists of society people eager to join. The clubs which had been dedicated to sports now "seemed to develop an insatiable penchant for luxurious clubhouses and other trappings which symbolized wealth and success," say Queens College instructors Willis and Wettan in their historical study of the rise of New York–area athletic clubs.

Suddenly there was enough money for the best running tracks and the latest in exercise equipment—enough cash to fund the quality track and field desired by William Curtis and advocated in his *Spirit of the Times*. The clubs became quite competitive in their rush to opulence, adding one feature after another until the best of them had most of the following: running track, gymnasium, swimming pool, club rooms, dining rooms, bowling alleys, billiard parlors, rifle ranges, Russian and Turkish baths, sleeping rooms, ballrooms, and theaters. *Outing*, a magazine for the mod society crowd of the time, ran a lengthy series about the leading athletic clubs that provided ample illumination of beautiful grounds and the like but rarely a word about the clubs' prominent athletes. As Willis and Wettan note, invidious comparisons between clubs became common. The New York Athletic Club said it had "a club house such as no other athletic organization in the world can boast of." The Manhattan club, however, could boast that the value of its property was greater. At the height of the rush to add features, the property value of the leading clubs in New York ranged from $850,000 for the Manhattan and $800,000 for the NYAC to $100,000 for the Crescent and Staten Island clubs. According to Willis and Wettan, most club members were near the very top of the scale for occupational and social status.

The promotion of sports needing expensive grounds or equipment gave an added measure of prestige to the athletic clubs. Lawn tennis gained popularity in the 1880s through the work of enthusiasts at the Staten Island and Newport clubs, and with the help of William Curtis, who instituted a special tennis section in the *Spirit of the Times*. There was also a fad for court tennis, a sport with a long history of popularity among European nobility. (During the French Revolution it was outlawed in France because of its connections with decadent aristocracy.) Court tennis was played on a sizable field cluttered with walls and abutments. Even a modest court cost a small fortune. In the late nineteenth century budding American aristocrats like Jay Gould, Payne Whitney, and Clarence Mackay funded the construction of magnificent courts costing hundreds of thousands of dollars.

The athletic clubs and the colleges had a prestigious setting for track and field; but in comparative running time and jumping marks their athletes were decidedly inferior to the professional pedestrians, and were barely equal to the quasi-amateurs who performed at the massive picnics of ethnic clubs. The true amateurs were given prestige much the way the Wizard of Oz solved the problem of the cowardly lion by bestowing a medal. Curtis and company created a formal structure for amateur sports such as the professionals never attained in track. In 1876 the New York Athletic Club created a national amateur championship meet. In 1879, at the request of the New York club, the National Association of Amateur Athletes of America was created to supervise future championships and regulate amateur sport.

The Association promulgated a set of guidelines for the proper conduct of a track meet, and nonmember organizations, recognizing the value of structure, often announced that their meets would also be conducted according to these rules. However, it was not easy to gain membership in the Amateur Association. It began with eight clubs and kept membership to around a dozen a year, until 1888, when it was replaced by the new Amateur Athletic Union. The wealthy athletic clubs had no desire to expand their Association beyond their own restricted memberships.

Each year applications for membership in the Association were received from many groups. Most were rejected without comment, as were the applications in 1883 from the New York Printers Benevolent Society and the Caledonian Society, the holders of two of the biggest annual picnics in the city. Each year the Amateur Association published a list of "approved organizations" that were considered part of the amateur system but did not have voting rights. In 1882, for instance, the list included twenty-one athletic clubs, twenty colleges, and three finishing schools. Only three of these auxiliary clubs represented immigrant groups, and there were no laboring groups, nor were there any of the adventurous YMCA branches that were just then beginning to sponsor well-organized track meets.

By refusing auxiliary status to the track clubs of trade unions and most immigrant groups, the Association ensured that the athletes at its meets had the preferred appearance of "gentlemen sportsmen." Nonetheless, the Association's athletes generally lacked the financial standing of gentlemen, and to keep them in competition a loophole in the amateur code allowed them to sell their "amateur" winnings: their medals, silverware, gold watches, and furniture. As Henry Hall of the New York *Tribune* explained in 1887: "It is sufficient commentary on the spirit which actuates many men who remain in the amateur ranks to say that they take advantage of this loophole in the definition to derive profit from their success." The amateur code at this time also allowed the athlete to receive "compensation for services rendered as ticket seller or taker at any contest or exhibition of amateur athletics, or as secretary, treasurer, manager or superintendent of any amateur athletic club, or as editor, correspondent, reporter or manager of any paper or periodical."

The financial loopholes for track and field amateurs of the mid-1880s allowed a comparatively large number of post-college athletes to continue as amateurs, as well as allowing for participation by a great number who never got near a college. Among those working their way up the social ladder through track and field there was James E. Sullivan, in later years a noted sports journalist and longtime secretary of the AAU. He is remembered today in the annual James E. Sullivan Award for sportsmanship. Sullivan got his start in 1878 as a runner at New York City Catholic youth club picnics. In recognition of his talent he was granted membership in the Pastime Athletic Club and given the job of secretary. The noted amateur record breaker Lon Myers was working at his father's trade of bookkeeper when he was discovered. Myers became secretary of the Manhattan A.C.

Amateurism tailored to the financial needs of athletes was not to last, however. Shortly after the replacement of the National Association by the Amateur Athletic Union, in 1888, the assorted loopholes in the code were plugged; and they remained unopened until the 1970s, when such allowances were made as permitting amateurs television-commercial money, time off with pay for training, and the right to work professionally in one sport while remaining amateur in another.

The origin of the tight amateur system for track and field is a rarely told story. The few available accounts explain the reasons for it in terms of a reaction to the "unscrupulous promoters" in professional track. But today, when the traditional amateur system is under attack for failure to stimulate general participation, and failure to police itself, it is important to know that we are living with a system which was designed from the very beginning to eliminate the lower classes. The rules for amateur track standing have driven countless prospective stars from poor economic backgrounds to opt for the professional games. Others starred briefly in track and field and then were lost to the sport at the height of their ability, when they were forced by economic circumstances to turn either to pro sports or a factory job. The amateur system has restricted the financial options of promoters by prohibiting the "open competitions" which successfully mix amateurs and pros in tennis, golf, and other sports. And promoters have been hindered by the Amateur Athletic Union's selective use of its "sanction."

To understand the reasons for the creation of the AAU and its oppressive code, it is as important to know the founders and whom they represented as it is to know the abuses which they sought to correct. The founders were representatives of fourteen of the wealthiest athletic clubs. A powerful "social element" within the clubs showed disturbingly little interest in track and field, and to placate this element the founders of the Amateur Athletic Union were forced to make amateur track as classy and elite as possible.

The prominent athletic clubs of the Gilded Age were the powers-that-be for amateur sports, but they attracted to membership individuals with an outlook antithetical to democratic ideals of sports, such as the belief in equal opportunity for rich and poor alike to compete and receive credit for athletic excellence. The leading athletic clubs were functioning both as sports clubs and as an early version of the wealthy country club. The society people joining the Manhattan A.C. for its Turkish baths and banquet halls could not be expected to approve when their club's track stars showed up in large numbers at the New York Journeymen Plumbers Association picnic of 1883. That the Manhattan men won most of their events, and that club member Lon Myers came within two seconds of his world record time in the 880, was little consolation. The athletes were hobnobbing with plumbers. And in 1885, when athletes from the Manhattan, Staten Island, and Pastime clubs made an excellent showing at the Printers Benevolent Society picnic, it was still a success purchased at the price of competition with athletes wearing the colors of Typographical Workers Union No. 6. In the opinion of fashionable society, trade unions were worse than low-class—they were un-American.

The movement for an ever-stricter amateur code, one that would separate club athletes from picnic athletes, was part of a larger movement that found guards screening spectators at club meets, and a movement toward "invitation only" entrance rules for the grandstand. By 1890 this was the policy for the New York, Manhattan, and other posh clubs. The social exclusion policy for spectators was an extension of the trend to ever more stringent requirements for club membership. Explaining the importance of an applicant's "social position," a member of the Manhattan club stated: "I have no aspersions to cast on men who work for their living with their hands, but they are not exactly desirable members for a club which wants to establish itself on the plane of social clubdom."

Bitter resentment toward the promoters of "social clubdom" was expressed by old-liners who had joined the athletic clubs when they really were athletic clubs. Frederick Janssen, a former runner and founding member of the Staten Island club back in the 1870s, declared in 1885:

> The social element in Clubs is like "dry rot," and eats into the vitals of Athletic Clubs, and soon causes them to fail in the purpose for which they were organized. . . . It is like an octopus that squeezes the life-blood out of the organization by burdening it with debt. Palatial clubhouses are erected at great cost and money is spent in adorning them that, if used to beautify athletic grounds and improve tracks, would cause a wide-spread interest in athletic sports and further the development of the wind and muscles of American youths.

The year Frederick Janssen wrote caustically of the socializers in his history, *American Amateur Athletics*, a number of leading clubs in the New York area experienced bitterly contested elections for officers. Under the leadership of the old guard, the clubs had fostered an improved quality of amateur sport and had gained support from wealthy backers. But now the contributions of the old guard were becoming less impressive than the ability of wealthy socialite members to raise cash for fancy grounds and clubhouses.

The fierce contest in the famed New York Athletic Club became a major news story for the daily papers. Rival slates of candidates were run for the offices of vice-president, secretary, and club governors. William Curtis was no longer active in club affairs, but his younger brother Alfred was reigning vice-president, and also vice-president of the National Association. It was principally against Alfred Curtis that an opposition slate had been organized, a slate with the self-proclaimed title "the Stock Exchange ticket." A letter to the *New York Times* written by one of the old guard declared that should Curtis and his "regular ticket" lose, "the Club will sooner or later resolve itself into a social organization similar to the Racquet Club."

Running against Curtis was stockbroker A. V. DeGoicouria. While Curtis' defenders argued that he had made the club "the tops in the world in amateur sport," DeGoicouria's supporters emphasized the value of monetary contributions. A DeGoicouria supporter told the New York *World*: "When the new club house was being erected and money was necessary it was he who helped us. He got dollars where Mr. Curtis got pennies. He raised $40,000 while Mr. Curtis got $400." A writer to the *Tribune* said of DeGoicouria: "But for him the club-house could not have been built."

On election night the NYAC building was "a human beehive," said the *Herald*. The *Times* noted a scene of "unusual animation," and the *World* reported Curtis defenders complaining of unfounded gossip and rumor being spread against their man by campaigners of the Stock Exchange ticket. Nearly 1,000 of the 1,500 club members voted, and the tabulating took until 3:00 A.M. the morning of March 11. A large crowd was still on hand, and the overwhelming victory of the DeGoicouria ticket "was enthusiastically applauded, and a few brief speeches were made then and there." Curtis had garnered only 237 votes to 725 for his opponent. The *World* reported that the elections were "the talk of the town. . . . Merchants old and staid gossiped about it. Bankers ceased to discuss the price of exchange or the silver question." The *World* noted that when DeGoicouria appeared at the Stock Exchange the next day it was the signal "for a noisy demonstration. 'How is DeGoicouria?' somebody cried out. A hundred voices answered in chorus, 'Oh, he is all right!' and three cheers were given for the successful candidate." Later in the year Alfred Curtis was replaced as vice-president of the National Association, too.

Divisive battles for control contributed to the collapse in

1885 of two clubs which had for years rivaled the NYAC in amateur athletic prowess. The American A.C., founded in the 1870s by runners and jumpers from the YMCA, split apart, with the athletic faction going off to form the Olympic A.C. As described by Janssen: "At present the Olympic is an Athletic Club, pure and simple, with none of the social element that slowly but surely causes a club to become athletic only in name." The bitterness between rival slates of candidates for offices in the Williamsburg A.C. contributed to its financial collapse, and it was reorganized under the name Brooklyn Athletic Association. Hard feelings lived on, however, and spilled out in a scandalous incident. The runner Austin Remsen, disgusted with the socializers in his club, coaxed a group of his athlete friends into invading a meeting of club ladies, where the athletes proceeded to sing "objectionable songs." Remsen was subsequently expelled from the club.

The huge financial stakes and often alarmingly large debts contributed to the tension in struggles for club control. Early in 1887, for example, the Boston Athletic Club borrowed $221,000 for land and a new clubhouse; and at the end of that year the club borrowed on the mortgage an additional $150,000. A few years later the club had to undergo a financial reorganization, reemerging under its present name, the Boston Athletic Association.

As the "Gay Nineties" approached, the prospects appeared dim for track and field remaining a major sport in more than a handful of urban athletic clubs. Janssen had been of the opinion in 1885 that most of the performers in the sport were being priced out of membership and were being replaced by "the wealthy young man whose sole claim to athletic distinction is his connection with a 'high-toned' club." Competition in installing facilities had made sporting glory expensive. The returns seemed to be negated by the cash flow. The Manhattan club, by the early 1890s, was spending $300,000 annually on sports—for payments on construction, upkeep, trainers, grounds crew, and the like.

There was one powerful inducement for maintaining high-quality track at the athletic clubs. Status-hungry members had discovered that sporting events as well as balls and dinner parties could be given on an "invitation only" basis. And championship-quality athletes made the invitation a more prestigious commodity. Preferably, the champions at the "invitational meet" would represent the same class of people as those who got invited to the grandstand. But social separation on the playing fields was not easily attained, given the temptation of a sure winner in the person of one of the numerous superior athletes from the laboring classes.

The desire to create a more powerful policing organization for amateur sports was one of the purposes of a meeting of club representatives held in the boardroom of the NYAC on the evening of October 1, 1887, following the club's fall athletic meet. From this gathering would come the Amateur Athletic Union, which was officially launched, after careful preparation, in February 1888.

The October meeting at the NYAC was called at a time of apparent mounting chaos in the amateur ranks. Charges were flying back and forth that top clubs were enrolling professionals under assumed names, and ignoring occasional runs for money by some of their well-known amateurs. New York and Manhattan were among the accused clubs. The signing on of pros was an extension of feverish hunts for amateur talent, which reached into Canada and across the Atlantic Ocean. The Manhattan club received sports page headlines late in 1887 when it signed on a nineteen-year-old Irish distance-running prospect.

The economic pressures towards professionalism were unrelenting. There were so many club meets and picnics that the better, more popular athletes had little time for paying jobs. Enlarging the "amateur" prizes from pots and silverware to grandfather clocks, pianos, and carriages helped the athletes to survive. Under-the-table appearance money was common. Frank Menke, in his historical sketch of the origins of the AAU, describes a type of promoter who, "advertising a 'strictly amateur' meet, would donate a trophy to the winner in full view of the spectators, after which promoter and victorious athlete would meet in some sheltered spot. The winner would give back the trophy and get cash, and the promoter would start shining the trophy to award to some other 'amateur' at a later promotion."

An alarming report from the Games Committee of the National Association in August of 1887 had said of the situation in New York: "Amateur athletics are getting to be a byword in this city. Amateur athletes rush around to all the picnics, compete under assumed names against nobody knows who, and capture whatever kind of prizes are offered, if they can." The new AAU would take steps to stop this practice by creating the first national register of legitimate amateurs.

Within the big clubs the pressure from debts, and from the social element, made a championship showing ever more necessary. As the National Association's Games Committee report said of the Manhattan Athletic Club: "The club is very enterprising. It has just established a big club house on Fifth Avenue, and in its desire to attract new members to help pay its necessarily large expenses it gobbles up every good athlete it can find without inquiring at all into his standing so long as he is certain to win prestige for the club by his performances."

The decision of the NYAC to lead a drive for a new organization was sparked, in part, by its own professionalism problem. Just ten days after the meeting which would lead to the founding of the AAU, the NYAC had to attend a formal hearing of the National Association's Executive Committee investigating charges that one of the club's best distance runners had competed professionally. The hearing was chaired by the NYAC's archrival, the Manhattan club, which interestingly enough had not been invited to the NYAC for the memorable meeting of October 1. A number of other clubs in the National Association were also uninvited, and in response to complaints a spokesman for the new movement told a reporter from the New York *World*: "True it is that clubs, members of the present Association, were not asked to send delegates, but it was business policy on the part of the projectors of the new association, to act in this manner."

Their policy was to enroll a majority of clubs from outside the New York–Philadelphia area, where the old Association had been largely based. The statement to the *World* explained that the new organization would be truly national, and would act as a regulatory body not only over track and field but over gymnastics, swimming, rowing, and many other amateur sports. It also intended to be more purely amateur, and the code declared by the AAU in February 1888 showed this clearly in its prohibition of the indirect financial aid allowed under the National Association through jobs at the club as office help, ticket taker, grounds keeper, and the like.

The Amateur Athletic Union opened for business, under the initial title American Athletic Union, with membership of thirteen clubs and one college. The rival National Association, led by the Manhattan A.C., carried on with a membership of nine clubs, and the nearly two dozen colleges of the IC4A. Throughout 1888 debate raged in the press as to which organization deserved to rule amateur sports. The question of which organization had the big-league show was often asked. William Curtis said it was the new AAU. In July, just after a major National Association track meet, Curtis sarcastically wondered out loud if the old Association "still exists," and he answered: "The Manhattan A.C. . . . owns and controls the N.A.A.A. of A., and . . . as long as the Manhattan A.C. finds pleasure or profit in keeping up the N.A.A.A. of A. that institution will continue to have a more or less normal existence, for the astute manager can always find enough dummy clubs to maintain the semblance of an organization."

Each side attempted to show more purity of amateurism than the other. The issue was complicated in the fall of 1888, when seven midwestern clubs formed their own short-lived Western Association of Amateur Athletes, an organization with such a rigid definition of amateurism that according to Curtis, "a strict enforcement of this definition in the East would decimate our athletic world." The westerners had banned anyone who had ever "sold or pledged any prize or token won." Curtis noted: "Many prominent amateurs have medals, in the pawnshop." In 1890 the Manhattan club decided to throw in with the AAU, and the National Association was shortly thereafter dissolved.

The Amateur Athletic Union decentralized the administration of amateur sports through regional bodies and distinct associations for each sport, this structure being adopted at the suggestion of Abraham G. Mills, former president of baseball's National League, and a member of the NYAC. Nonetheless, the organization of the Amateur Union allowed a handful of prominent clubs to monopolize the decision-making processes. Between the annual meetings, policy was made by a board of managers composed of representatives of the bigger clubs. A description in *Sporting Life* of the AAU managers at work made it appear like a board meeting of a corporation. The managers "carry through their measures by voting their proxies. As each member of the board had several proxies concealed about his person it was an easy matter to hurry things up, but it was decidedly unsatisfactory to the representatives of the small clubs, which had no delegates in the board of managers." Voting rights within the Amateur Union's various other bodies were reserved to a few full-member groups, while the majority fell into the category of "approved organizations" and had no voting power, by proxy or by any other means.

Under the AAU, track and field at the top levels was classier than ever before. The 1890s witnessed a great many international meets. Timing of races became quite sophisticated, and there were even experiments in the nineties with electronic timers providing twentieth-of-a-second splits. But despite the best apparatus and new, improved composition running tracks, there was a decline in the level of performances. Talented young prospects were turning to other sports. Whereas from 1883 through 1892 American amateur records in 19 events had been broken 62 times, for the next decade, from 1893 through 1902, only 21 new records were established, and the next five years produced only 7 more.

Sportswriters perceived their readers to be far less interested in track than they had been in the 1880s. During the 1890s previously sizable sections on the sport were shortened and then eliminated entirely in such widely read journals as *Sporting Life*, *Sporting News*, the *Clipper*, and the *Police Gazette*. It may not be surprising when the elevation of a mere game or exercise into a sport is marked by press coverage, but the decline in track and field coverage was a rare chronicle of a sport dying. It was certainly dying at the amusement parks, whose owners were putting in Ferris wheels and the like where there had once been running tracks.

The picnics ceased to be newsworthy, in part because competitors from the elite athletic clubs, the top amateurs, could no longer participate at the picnics and maintain amateur standing unless they used false names. To compensate for their absence, the promoters made picnics more of a circus show, adding features like weightlifting, wrestling, fencing, and boxing matches.

Ironically, the triumph of clean, pure amateur track and field was little help to the big-league athletic clubs. The social element had discovered golf and the attraction of quiet and fresh air at the suburban country clubs. Bankruptcies of leading athletic clubs became common during the 1890s. The Manhattan A.C. had, in 1891, been able to hold a gala athletic meet attracting 15,000 "invitation only" spectators. Two years later this mighty club went into receivership. In 1894 a disheartened James E. Sullivan, secretary of the AAU, commented in *Spirit of the Times*: "Every month witnesses the death of several athletic clubs, but they fade noiselessly away like morning mist and have no public funerals. It is only a few of the more prominent clubs whose plunges into the pool of bankruptcy make a splash loud enough to attract attention." With the collapse of the clubs, many fine athletic facilities went entirely to waste; while in other cases buyers were found who at least saw a use for the club's banquet rooms and Turkish baths.

The colleges took the track and field limelight during the 1890s, but college track was then almost a monopoly of schools on the eastern seaboard. The expansion in the decade was not so much across America as across the ocean. Yale took on the Oxford track team at the Queen's Club in London in 1894, and Cambridge came to Yale a year later. The U.S. team at the first modern Olympics in 1896 was composed exclusively of athletes from Princeton, Harvard, and the Boston Athletic Association.

Track and field was becoming an activity identified with young gentlemen, or at least with athletes of any class who had the manners and decorum of gentlemen. The gaudy showmanship of professional pedestrianism was out of place, and professional track declined rapidly in the nineties and was all but extinct by World War I. It had been sorely hurt by the accumulated years of attack on its morality, such as William Curtis' comment that "professional jumpers are, as a class, the scurviest of all tribes known to modern sport, and their life seems to be spent in trying to avoid the possession of money honestly earned or won."

At its height in the 1880s track and field had been one of the sports containing the qualities of color and schmaltz, which are brought out by wildly cheering fans, promoters with a touch of Barnum in their character, and athletes who come from the uncultured part of town and are not ashamed of their roots. The success of such a sporting mix is always threatened —on the one hand, by the drift into the theatrical showmanship of the roller derby or professional wrestling; and on the other hand, by the three-piece-suit types who would clean up the show in order to sell it to the high-priced box-seat minority. Track and field caved in because both these trends hit it at once.

*　　*　　*

The story of the rise and fall of popular track and field requires a postscript on the athletic records of the professional pedestrians. Their outstanding abilities were widely recognized in their day. Their appearance increased the gate receipts, not only for picnics, but also for the athletic clubs that chose to have a well-known pro put on an "exhibition" at one of their meets. Even the caustic William Curtis would on occasion acknowledge the pros, as when in 1882 he compared the great amateur Lon Myers with the professional Hal Hutchins and declared: "Hutchins is the most wonderful sprinter ever known, and can give Myers long starts . . . and Myers would not have the slightest chance with him at any distance under 300 yards."

Today the professional pedestrians are forgotten and their marks are missing from the lists recording humanity's steady progress in feats of running, jumping, and throwing. During the era of the pedestrians, sports annuals of the *Clipper*, New York *Tribune*, and *Police Gazette* did provide comparative lists of accepted professional and amateur marks in track and field. As was to be expected, the well-trained professionals were superior to the amateurs in almost all events. The degree of superiority, however, is noteworthy. W. G. George set a 4:12.4 standard in the mile in 1885 which went unmatched by an amateur until 1915. J. H. Fitzpatrick crossed the 6'6" barrier in the high jump in 1889, and the first amateur over this height came in 1912. The remarkable George White set a professional 6-mile standard in 1863 that stood until Pavlo Nurmi topped it in 1930; and the professional 10-mile mark set in 1899 stood until 1945. It was in sprinting that the professionals were most impressive. Hal Hutchins set marks in the rarely run 300- and 330-yard sprints which apparently have never been broken. Professional marks set in the 1880s for 50 yards and 75 yards, by H. M. Johnson and James Quirk respectively, stood for nearly four decades. Johnson lowered the professional 100-yard time to 9.6 in 1886, twenty years before the first amateur attained that speed. By then, the professional time had been lowered to an amazing 9 seconds flat, by the most remarkable of all the professional pedestrians, Richard Perry Williams.

This totally forgotten individual began his athletic feats in 1896 with a time of 47.2 seconds in the quarter-mile, which stood until Herb McKinley topped it in 1948. Williams then reached the 25-foot barrier in the long jump, two decades before the first amateur. In 1904, 1905, and again in 1906 Williams ran the 100 yards in 9.2 seconds. Disbelievers were numerous, and as explained by Frank Menke, Williams was asked to run an exhibition 100 "on a truly measured track and against absolutely perfect watches. He agreed and made his world's record on June 2, 1906. Five businessmen who were sprinting enthusiasts and expert timers each timed him—and each watch showed 9 seconds for the full 100 yards. A while later, when Williams had regained his breath, he tried to shatter that mark, but the best he could do in his second try was 9⅕—the fourth time in his brilliant career that he was clocked at that mark." It was nearly six decades later when the first amateur clocked 9.2, and almost seven decades before 9 flat was reached.

Richard Perry Williams was a graduate of the University of Pennsylvania, and at the time of his 100-yard-dash accomplishments was athletic director for the New London, Connecticut, YMCA and public schools. The stereotype of professional peds as poorly educated and easily bribed showmen didn't fit Williams, nor did it fit many other professionals either. But the image was a strong one and contributed to the tragic denial of recognition for athletic abilities. Williams was last acknowledged in Menke's *All-Sports Record Book* of 1931.

BASEBALL

4

The Roar of the Crowd: Baseball and the Ungodly Politician

When Alexander Cartwright of the New York Knickerbocker Club set down the basic rules for baseball in 1845, the public attitude toward ball games was that they were children's pastimes. The excuse for grownups playing a ball game was the license held by the upper classes to fill up their leisure time. So early baseball took on the appearance of a "gentleman's game," and was played with rules prohibiting swearing and loose behavior unbecoming a gentlemanly amateur sportsman.

A variety of games involving a ball, bat, and bases were played around the country, but the nine-inning game with nine men to a side played on a diamond was the one termed "The American National Game of Base Ball" in an 1856 *Spirit of the Times* headline. The accompanying article noted: "We have been . . . inundated with communications in reference to the mode of playing the game of Base Ball," and in response the *Spirit* published a diagram of the regulation field, and mailing address for obtaining the rules of play.

The gentlemanly teams with their uniformed players looked impressive, but play was ragged since the techniques were just beginning to be mastered. A good catch or throw drew applause from both sides, and became a highlight of the report on the game in the sporting weeklies. Scores were high and routs were common, but hard feelings were rare. It was customary for the host club to provide the visitors with post-game dining and entertainment. The Knickerbockers had a well-established reputation for quality entertainments. A report on an 1858 match between the Knickerbockers and the Excelsior Club from Brooklyn notes that, gracious in defeat, the host Knickerbockers escorted the Excelsiors to Odd Fellows' Hall, where the victors were "entertained in splendid style, covers being laid for over 200 gentlemen. Dodworth's Band was in attendance to enliven the scene, and all the arrangements were exceedingly creditable to the taste and liberality of the committee who had charge of the festive occasion."

The Excelsiors embarked in 1860 on baseball's first extended tour, traveling through upstate New York. The press noted that after winning in Troy the Excelsiors were "well entertained at the Troy House." After winning 50–19 over Niagara the Excelsiors were escorted to Bloomfield's Hotel, "where a splendid supper was provided." Returning to Brooklyn, the Excelsiors were scheduled against less amiable opposition, the Atlantics.

The decidedly ungentlemanly Atlantic Club, 200 members strong, with ties to the local Democratic party, was the best of a number of working-class clubs which had assumed a prominent place in the New York–area baseball world of the late 1850s. The Atlantics tried to follow the code of polite behavior on the field and provide post-game entertainment for the opposition, but they represented a radical break with tradition. Their fans got carried away, and booed and hissed at the opposition and the umpire; and the large crowds at Atlantic games attracted gamblers, and in one case, enough pickpockets to inspire an anti-pickpocket riot.

The Atlantics and similar clubs were an outgrowth of unorganized sandlot ball, which in the New York area had reached such proportions by 1856 that *Spirit of the Times* stated: "Games are being played on every available green plot within a ten mile circuit of the city." At first the working people were hesitant to organize clubs and take on the leisure-class outfits. The origins of the Eckfords, a club of Brooklyn dock workers, were explained to the *Spirit* by Eckford second baseman Francis Pidgeon: "Being shipwrights and mechanics we could not make it convenient to practice more than once a week; and we labored under the impression that want of practice and the fewness of members from whom to select our nine would make it almost impossible for us to win a match if we engaged in one." Deciding to give it a try, the new Brooklyn team found the better-known clubs reluctant to take them on. Finally, the Unions of Morrisania (a.k.a. the Bronx) gave the Eckfords a chance. The Unions do not appear to have been very ritzy themselves, since their team captain of many years later became state chairman of the Workingmen's party. The Eckfords beat the Unions 22–8. From this victory in 1856 the Eckfords went on to become a fixture on the baseball scene, and in the 1872 season they played in baseball's first professional league. The Atlantics were in this league too, as were Tammany Hall boss William Marcy Tweed's New York Mutuals, begun in 1857 as a team of New York City firemen.

The baseball boom, which was so notable in the New York area during the late 1850s, was marked by the large and unruly crowds at games between the Atlantics and the Excelsiors —the best of the blue-collar outfits against a top club, self-defined for the *Spirit* as a club of "merchants and clerks." At one of the two games the Atlantics played (and won) against the Excelsiors in 1858, the overflow of spectators could be seen on rooftops and also perched at the top of the masts of ships docked at the nearby Brooklyn wharves.

The three-game Atlantic-Excelsior series in 1860 was a memorable one. There was little love lost between the two teams. They hadn't met since '58, when the Atlantics proudly attributed their victories to the hardiness their players obtained from having outdoor jobs. The Excelsiors did have one noted outdoor laborer, however. For the 1860 season the club had signed on James Creighton, the pitcher *par excellence* of the period, for a promise of pay for play. Creighton was thus baseball's first professional player, which was not publicly known at the time. The Excelsiors claimed to represent the best in the gentlemanly amateur tradition.

Creighton's speed ball kept the Atlantics in check and his team won 23–4 in the series opener, played before one of the biggest crowds yet to see a baseball game—10,000-plus. The second game drew upwards of 12,000, and there were 70 policemen on hand to keep order. The Atlantics won 15–14, since Creighton was ill. For the finale the number of spectators was estimated at 15,000 to 20,000. Police Inspector Foulke had another small army of cops on hand. Atlantic supporters included "roughs," also known as "a gang of toughs," who had stated before the game that they would not allow the Excelsiors to win a close contest.

In the showdown game the Excelsiors were leading 8–4 when the Atlantics came to bat in the bottom of the fifth, which turned out to be the last full inning these two teams ever played against each other. The Atlantics rallied for two runs and appeared on the verge of making it a new ball game, but then the umpire's decision on a close play at third base ended the inning. Some reports claim that the play was not that close, that the Atlantics' runner clearly overran third and was tagged out. It was nonetheless close enough to anger the Atlantic faithful. They hooted and shouted for the removal of the umpire in a manner most unsuitable for a gentleman's game. The venomous jeering got worse in the top of the sixth after a close play at first was decided in the Excelsiors' favor. The final batter of the day then hit what appeared to be a sure double-play ball. The lead runner was cut down at second, but on the return throw the Atlantic first baseman dropped the ball.

It was too much frustration for the Atlantic fans to bear. Vituperation against the umpire and the Excelsiors reached such a crescendo that the Excelsior captain threatened to remove his team from the field, and Police Inspector Foulke sent his men into the crowd to quiet them down. Quiet was not restored, and the Excelsiors left the field. Umpire Thorn declared the contest a draw. Thorn later explained, in a written statement for the press, that in his opinion the behavior of the players on both teams was proper and "without disputing which an umpire could take umbrage at." And as for the fans, Thorn said: "It made no difference to me how many remarks or how much noise there was made, so far as I was concerned."

The game ended by the roar of the crowd marked the beginning of the end of polite baseball. Over the next few years clubs like the Excelsiors and Knickerbockers played "friendly" matches with one another, but public interest in such games waned, and the quality players followed the crowd and joined the teams that played before "the fanatics"—"fans," for short. By the time General Lee surrendered to General Grant, gentleman's baseball was a lost cause.

The gentlemanly amateur game might have survived had it attracted a social elite on the order of the "Stock Exchange ticket" that won control of the New York Athletic Club in 1885. But baseball came upon the scene a good quarter of a century before the Industrial Revolution created a close-knit, self-indulgent high society. The Knickerbockers established a genteel game at a time when the Whiggish element in society was into Sir Walter Scott novels, poetry, and whatever else of "high culture" could be borrowed from Europe.

Gentlemanly baseball was more the work of the middle class than the upper class. In Washington, for instance, the two superior clubs of the pre–Civil War period were both organizations of government clerks. Historian David Voigt notes: "By any standards, some of the men in the Knickerbocker ranks were would-be gentlemen." A check of names on the club roster from 1845 to 1860 shows seventeen merchants, twelve clerks, a number of professional men, and among others, a "segar dealer," a hatter, a cooperage operator, a stationer, and a U.S. marshal. Alexander Cartwright, head of the committee which wrote the baseball rules for the club, was a member of the city fire department. The Knickerbockers played their home games at Hoboken's Elysian Fields, that "people's pleasure ground" which was renounced by the elite sportsmen of the New York Athletic Club—as seen in the discussion of track and field.

The more pretentious clubs tried to avoid matches with the rowdier outfits, and yet the more elite clubs neglected to build for themselves the isolation of their own enclosed ball parks—either for lack of cash or some other reason. The first such enclosed park was opened in 1862 at the refurbished skating rink of entrepreneur William Cammeyer. The principal user of Cammeyer's field became "Boss" Tweed's Mutuals.

The influence of the Knickerbockers was already slipping in 1857 when some two dozen clubs joined to form the National Association of Base Ball Players, an organization spawned to further the game in the interest of a group calling itself Young New York. The Knickerbockers were frozen out of all officers' positions in the new Association. Nor did they get a spot on the committee created to pressure city government, in the name of baseball, for "a Plot of Ground in the Central Park." A statement from the committee noted that changing the plans for the proposed great park to include sports facilities might "be offending the nice prejudices of our over-refined people," but then, "Young New York would not object—why should the 'Old Fogies'?"

The Old Fogies with their Victorian moral standards were a group to be reckoned with, and they had an influence which dissuaded many a proper gentleman from associating with the baseball crowd. The initial plans for Central Park were not changed to include the "Play-ground" requested by the baseball buffs. In Cleveland, where the town common was being heavily used for ball games, the Old Fogies tried in 1857 to get the city council to ban baseball from that park. Demanding enforcement of public-nuisance laws, a writer to the editor of the Philadelphia *Public Ledger* complained that "the police seem oblivious" to the way youngsters were congregating downtown and "using the broad pavement as a ball ground." The YMCA of this period was on record as opposing baseball, on the grounds that it attracted an un-Christian element similar to that associated with billiards and prizefighting.

The continued growth of baseball was in the hands of street-corner society, rather than proper society. The social hangouts for ball players and fans were the saloons, the cigar stores, the bookmaking establishments, and in the case of the Brooklyn Atlantics, the large billiards emporium of club member and Democratic ward heeler A. R. Samuells. To street-corner society the game was more than a pleasant time-killing diversion. It brought the neighborhood together, as was the case for the many teams of the late 1850s representing political wards —such as the Americus Club of New York's Ninth Ward and the Mazeppas of the Eighth. Baseball provided a social focus for occupational groups: the dock workers of the Eckfords, the mechanics' team of Newark, and New York clubs for policemen, firemen, bartenders, and schoolteachers.

The Civil War put a damper on baseball at the home front, but expanded the game in other respects. Baseball became a popular rest-and-recreation activity for the troops, who introduced the game in areas of the country previously untouched by baseball mania. The top nine of one regiment were pitted against the all-stars of another in games attracting enormous crowds. One such contest in 1862 was witnessed by some 40,000 troops, the largest single-game attendance of the century. Among the players learning the sport in the war was Abraham G. Mills, later to become president of the National League; he remembered packing his bat and ball with his field equipment, because he found as much use for them as for his musket.

The post–Civil War baseball boom had many contributing factors, such as greater urban concentration enhancing the prospects for spectator sports, and better rail travel facilitating intercity competition. But why these opportunities were so dramatically channeled into sports, and baseball in particular, has long perplexed students of baseball history. The phenomenon is probably best explained in reference to psychologist Harold Beisser's argument that identifying oneself with the local ball team can be effective therapy for lonely people in a strange city. (Beisser's test case is a neurotic, withdrawn teenager who, upon moving to Los Angeles in the 1960s, became a Dodger fan and in short order became talkative and more self-confident.) The Civil War traumatically dislocated millions of Americans, who if asked "Where were you when President Lincoln was shot?" could respond: "In a strange city."

The mobile American was common, too, in antebellum years, but in that period he had little need of sports for obtaining a sense of belonging. His employer could introduce him to everyone in the town or village. But it was the cities rather than the villages which attracted the veterans and other displaced people of the war. The standards for being somebody were different in the city. One had to fit into a crowd, at the bank office or union hall, at the saloon or temperance meeting, at the yacht harbor or ball park. The latter crowd was easily enough joined. While admission charges for a good game went from 10 cents at war's end to a quarter by 1870, it was still affordable. A little reading through the sporting papers could make a new fan sound like a native so far as knowledge of the team was concerned. And the presence of the gamblers, combined with the opposition to the sport from the Old Fogies, added a risqué touch; the knowledgeable baseball "crank" became the prototype of the "hipster."

The postwar migration to the cities found businesses as well as individuals searching for public recognition. Teams representing business concerns became common. In Chicago such teams included one for the Palmer Hotel and another for the Field and Leiter department store. Levi Leiter was one of the first of a great many Jewish merchants who helped promote nineteenth-century baseball. In their case, the use of the game as a means of assimilation in a new city in a new land is apparent. In much the same manner baseball sponsorship integrated into community life many a merchant who was not an immigrant from abroad, but was a newcomer to the city by way of emigration from the rural America of antebellum times.

The enthusiasm for the game was not restricted to men. The *Ball Player's Chronicle*, July 25, 1867, reported: "The Base Ball Disease has attacked the women, the young ladies of Pensacola, Fla., having organized a baseball club. One of the rules is that whenever any member gets entangled in her steel wire [hoopskirt] and falls, she is to be immediately expelled from the club. A young ladies' base ball club has also been organized at Niles, Michigan."

The widely prevalent "muffin" games provided a whimsical form of baseball for the unskilled beginner. Players burlesqued the game, making their lack of skill a feature of play, running bases backwards and putting a keg of beer on second as an incentive to hitters. From these beginnings a "muff" became baseball jargon for a bad play.

Increased popularity created pressure on the better-known clubs to carefully recruit as good a nine as possible. In 1866 the Philadelphia Athletics openly admitted they were achieving this goal by paying for the services of their four best players. "Shall we play ball as gentlemen, or shall we hire men to win?" asked an angry letter writer to the Philadelphia *City Item*. The clubs that wanted to play in the new enclosed stadiums where admissions were charged were choosing the latter course. Clubs that neglected to reorganize on a more professionalized basis were doomed to be relegated to the sandlots. The "Railroad Union 9" of Cleveland had been one of the very best teams in the Midwest in 1867 and 1868. The Atlantics of Brooklyn went to Cleveland to play the railroad workers' club and were soundly beaten, much to the delight of 3,000 screaming Cleveland fans. But the union club refused to modernize and recruit. When a consortium of entrepreneurs, led by a Cleveland minstrel show promoter, raised $10,000 to organize a professional team in the city, the days of the Railroad Union 9 were numbered. The fans wanted to watch the best, and the best was the new professional Forest City Club.

Economic necessity forced many a team to go professional.

For the Washington (D.C.) Nationals it was a need for paying customers to cover the debt incurred in building their own enclosed ball field. The club was founded in 1859 by a clerk in the Pension Office, the doorkeeper of the House of Representatives, and a post office messenger; and they initially played in an open lot that became part of the Pennsylvania Railroad yards. The club then played a number of years in the "President's Back Yard," the White House Ellipse. Then the testy secretary to President Andrew Johnson ordered the Nationals off the Ellipse, and the club had to secure its own field—no easy task for a collection of clerks. To attract customers they had to have a winning show, and toward this end the Nationals signed up the future Hall of Fame shortstop George Wright, who in 1869 jumped to Cincinnati, where he helped the Red Stockings establish pro ball in that city.

Before pro baseball could become the organized sport we know today, it had to undergo a period of trial and many errors. Recruiting players, securing grounds, obtaining travel funds, and a host of other problems confronted the teams as they went pro. They needed all the financial breaks they could get—for example, the decision of the Chicago aldermen to build a municipal park and rent it cheaply to the White Sox, enabling the team to move from its demeaning home field, the inner grass at the Dexter racetrack.

That the successful players, managers, and club officials often made their own breaks is demonstrated in almost any available baseball history. But the growth of the game was much more than a sporting story; it involved the breaks, lucky and unlucky, out of which modern urban America was evolving during the late nineteenth century's Industrial Revolution. The impingement of daily life on the affairs of the national game is a subject to which we may now turn.

The famous Cincinnati Red Stockings of 1869 were successful on the playing field, provided recognition and prestige for their city, and showed a grand profit of $1.26 for the season.

Nineteenth-century baseball in general was a failure so far as team ledger sheets were concerned. Between 1869 and 1900 over 850 professional franchises were launched; 650 of them went out of business in two years or less, and only 50 lasted six years or more. Teams came and went with such frequency that to this day there is no comprehensive list of nineteenth-century professional teams, even though baseball is a sport with a record and statistic for just about everything subject to addition, subtraction, multiplication, or division.

Considering the failures, professional baseball's attraction for investors is unexplainable in the strict context of "a commercialized amusement business"—historian Harold Seymour's definition of the pro game. There had to be more than a business angle to pro ball for Albany, New York, to run through ten different pro franchises between 1877 and 1898. One of these was organized by the itinerant promoter Ted Sullivan, who in a thirty-year span left a trail of bankrupt franchises through eleven states. *Sporting News* considered Sullivan one of the best organizers in the game. Cities were proud to get his services. The question is, what was he serving up?

In 1885 Ted Sullivan went south to help organize the original Southern League, which inaugurated pro ball in deep Dixie. The entire league failed, and was reorganized and failed again eleven more times before the turn of the century. Apparently, the deep South was still too rustic for the urban game of pro baseball. Significantly, the investors in the early Southern Leagues were individuals who had a stake in modernizing and urbanizing the area. A surprising number of club officials were Jewish merchants and professionals. A key figure behind the 1885 Atlanta franchise was Henry W. Grady, the publisher of the Atlanta *Constitution* and the foremost exponent of the "New South," modern and industrialized.

Sullivan spent a number of years in Texas and in the Plains

states, organizing ball teams in the boom towns advertised by civic boosters as the nation's next major metropolis. The ball team, ornate opera house, and a trolley line running the entire mile-and-a-half length of town were signs of the future glory.

Sporting News and similar journals usually identified the club officers and directors of a team as "leading citizens"— and to the degree to which such people are part of the business community, the early pro game appears to have been a business concern, albeit a foolish one. But a good third of the club officers and directors of this period were workers rather than businessmen, according to their occupational listings in city directories of the period. Salesmen and clerks—in particular, government clerks—were the most common occupational groups in the running of the pro game. Working people, along with neighborhood merchants, saloon keepers, and the like, were especially prevalent in leadership of the earliest pro teams, many of which were not companies at all, but sports clubs.

Baseball's promoters didn't have to be corporate or professional people to earn the "leading citizen" title. In the late nineteenth century, politics provided prestige positions to a very large percentage of the populace. Baseball blossomed at a time when turnouts of 80 to 90 percent on Election Day put many a workingman in public office. The Haymakers of Troy, New York, were first run by a prizefighter turned congressman; then by an ex-policeman turned sheriff; and then by a brushmaker who was chairman of the city council in nearby Lansingburgh.

Funding the "home team" could mean votes, and for some it was an adventurous way to launder the profits of political graft, which was rampant during that age of Industrial Revolution and the rise of the city. In cities big and small, and in all parts of the country, a political connection of one sort or another can be found for virtually every nineteenth-century professional team with a list of its board of directors published in the sporting papers. Nearly one out of every two club officials had an active role in politics, and the number is probably much higher since the available information for many cities includes only officeholders and not those who ran without success or were behind-the-scenes party functionaries.

Baseball's politicians were generally from the lower ranks, but there were 56 mayors and 102 state legislators. There was also Garrett A. Hobart, U.S. vice president under William McKinley, and president of the Paterson, New Jersey, team at the time he took office in 1896. This was a period of political bosses running powerful urban machines. In one way or another, all of the big-city organizations exposed in muckraker Lincoln Steffens' *Shame of the Cities* were into baseball. On occasion the game drew financial backing from the advocates of political reform; but in general the reformers were aligned with crusaders against liquor and gambling, who had little love for the sporting world.

Perhaps it is the presence of infamous graft takers and ballot-box stuffers that has kept the political angle something of an untouchable subject in the standard works on early baseball. The politics of backers is rarely mentioned. Regrettably, the omission leaves out of the baseball story one of its more intriguing features. There is much to be learned about both baseball and politics in exploring their relationship. At the very least, the contest for baseball supremacy in Philadelphia has an added dramatic touch when viewed in terms of the Republican-backed Athletics vs. the Democratic-backed Phillies; and similarly for the Democratic Dodgers vs. the Republican Giants, and the rival teams for each party which existed for a time in St. Louis, Boston, Cincinnati, and Cleveland.

The political connection illuminates those aspects which made baseball more than a game, a national pastime, and a distinct addition to American culture. Nineteenth-century baseball was made more than a game, in part, because it was promoted to express social issues of that time. In New England of the 1870s an ongoing public debate over the relative merits of cricket and baseball was more than a sporting question. Cricket was British. British culture dominated in New England, and yet the population in the fast-growing mill towns was heavily Irish. The Irish-Americans became rabid baseball fans. Alderman Jeremiah Crowley of Lowell, Massachusetts, solidified his base with Irish voters when he organized a powerful professional team for his city. In later years Crowley got to be mayor, and eventually he went on to the state Senate.

In St. Louis, the colorful Democratic committeeman Cris Van der Ahe appealed to the city's sizable German community with a combination of baseball and the Germans' favorite brew. He put a team in the American Association, known as "the beer-ball league." It allowed clubs to break with the puritanical National League stand against selling beer at games, and German-American brewers and saloon keepers backed many a team in the beer-ball league.

The baseball fever which swept the nation after the Civil War coincided with a period noted for temperance crusaders, Sabbatarian crusaders, and blue-nosed law-and-order societies. The politician defending the people's pastime might be called upon to take a stand on a law banning Sunday ball, or on a proposed zoning change that would require the local stadium to be torn down. To sponsor or attend baseball games was to side with Chicago White Sox second baseman Robert J. Downing, who played under the alias of Robert J. Glenalvin, so that his minister father would not know his son toiled in such an ungodly profession.

The rise of baseball was intimately tied to the establishment of a thriving pop culture. Many a ball player worked as an actor or circus hand in the off season. Teams were financially backed by theater owners or managers. A loan from a circus promoter enabled a former minstrel-show banjo player to obtain a one-third interest in the Philadelphia Athletics of the 1880s. For a time, the most widely circulated baseball journal in the land was the New York *Clipper: Sporting and Theatrical Review*.

In the opinion of the ministry and the purveyors of "high culture," the ball games and variety shows frequented by the masses were hardly more reputable than the goings-on at brothels, known as "sporting houses." The distinction between baseball games and legitimate theater, on the one hand, cock-fights and bearbaiting at a tavern, on the other hand, was clouded by a centuries-old Puritan tradition.

By 1900, however, baseball was well on its way to achieving sufficient respectability for a minister's son to play without using an alias. Modern business techniques were beginning to pay off. Franchises lasted much longer. The new box-seat sections at the ball park were attracting a higher class of clientele than the game had known previously. But baseball was not taken away from the people and turned into an exclusive show of fashionable clubs and elite colleges, as was, for example, track and field. The tie between the national pastime and the common people was ingrained in folklore, and indelibly authenticated by the sporting scribes.

In the sponsorship of baseball for the masses, Democratic party boss William Marcy Tweed had a singularly important role in New York City, and his involvement provides a good example of processes at work in advancing the game in most other cities. Born in 1823, Tweed was raised in the tenement districts of New York, and as a teenager led a gang of rather notorious delinquents. Tammany Hall Democrats were active workers among the Irish-Americans in his neighborhood, and in time Tweed became a local "ward heeler." As the emissary of the machine in his neighborhood he was responsible for getting out the vote and endearing the party to the locals through such favors as bail for the indigent in trouble with the law and aid to newly arrived Irish in obtaining naturalization and jobs.

Tweed was a city councilman in the 1850s when the reigning Tammany Hall boss, Mayor Fernando Wood, was caught at corrupt practices and forced to retire from leadership. In the ensuing power struggle within the party Tweed had the grass-roots connections, but he lacked the respectability and financial clout of a rival faction, whose leadership included

State Senator August Belmont, prominent businessman, sports enthusiast, and founder of Belmont Park Race Track.

In 1857 Tweed gathered "a number of local politicians" and they founded the New York Mutuals Baseball Club, later to become the first openly professional team in the city. A historical sketch of the team notes that founder Tweed was "the leading spirit of the Mutuals for several years." In 1871 the directors' list of the Mutuals read like a *Who's Who* of the infamous Tweed Ring, which systematically plundered the city treasury of more than $30 million through faked leases, padded bills, false vouchers, unnecessary repairs, and kickbacks. The club officers in 1871 included a number of aldermen, six state legislators, two judges, the city coroner, the sheriff, and a future sheriff. There was also the mysterious Aubry C. Wilson, Tweed's courier of the booty fleeced from city hall.

A portion of Tweed's loot was regularly reinvested in measures designed to bolster his political power. He lavishly distributed to charities, and provided free coal to the indigent in wintertime. It was his custom, just before elections, to load his followers on excursion trains for an outing at Coney Island or some other pleasure spot. His assistance to baseball came in many forms. There was a Tammany Hall Junior League, and there were Tammany Hall "amateur baseball" tournaments, usually for substantial cash prizes. Local ward heelers were encouraged to form teams at the precinct level. August Belmont had his prestigious stable of horses, but Tweed probably had the better vote-getting ploy in baseball.

In 1862 Tweed's crony William H. Cammeyer remodeled his sizable ice-skating rink into the city's first enclosed ball park. The Mutuals were one of the first teams to use the park. Games went for ten cents' admission at first, but within a year important matches required a quarter from the spectators. In 1865, under the direction of the Mutuals' president, Coroner Wildey, a wooded area adjacent to Hoboken's popular Elysian Fields was cleared and a sizable enclosed baseball park was constructed. By the late 1860s Tweed had the city government underwriting the growth of baseball. His aldermen justified one appropriation of $1,500 from the city treasury on these grounds: "It has been the custom of the municipal authorities of several cities in the United States to encourage, by legislative action, such pastimes and pleasures among their immediate citizens as tend to their physical benefit and education." This particular appropriation was apparently used as prize money for tournaments, which for baseball of that time were the game's best spectator attraction.

From the beginning the Mutuals played a more extensive schedule than did most other teams. Since the players were employees of the city government and Tweed's people ran the government, it was an easy matter to arrange substantial free playing and practice time. To facilitate this step toward professional baseball, the city jobs of players were changed. Originally the team had represented firemen of Hook and Ladder Company No. 1. Later the Mutuals were generally employed in a branch of New York city government where workers are proverbially never on the job—the street-cleaning department.

The Mutuals were never baseball's champions, perhaps because they threw too many decisions for the benefit of the gamblers. Charges of fixed games involving the club were numerous, and involved some of the first recorded instances of fraud in the game. The Mutuals' reputation for fraudulent performances was no doubt on the mind of the critic who declared, upon hearing that Tweed had personally invested $7,500 in the club, "He probably got it all back again."

In 1871, when the Mutuals became charter members of the National Association of Professional Baseball Players, the first professional baseball league, Tweed was at the height of his career. The amiable, rotund, well-dressed frequenter of opening nights at Broadway theaters had connections with the most flamboyant of self-made millionaires of the period. For his attorney Tweed had one of the finest legal minds of the time in David Dudley Field, who was also the mouthpiece for the wheeler-dealers "Jubilee" Jim Fisk and Jay Gould. Dudley

Field notwithstanding, in 1872 Tweed would be in jail. He died in jail in 1878.

Events leading to Tweed's downfall shed light on the social divisions around the sport of baseball. Tweed's control of Tammany Hall never did extend to democrats of proper breeding. His days were numbered when some of his supporters, led by three state legislators in the Mutual Club, aligned themselves with more respectable elements in the Tammany society. Then Tweed's hand-picked sheriff, angry at not getting his share of the graft, took to the *New York Times* documents detailing Tweed's methods of fleecing the city treasury. The *Times* bravely launched an all-out attack on Tweed, most other papers fearfully remaining on the sidelines.

Tweed's entire operation came under the careful scrutiny of the *Times*, including his uninhibited use of city employees in electioneering. Under the headline "Base-Ball Sinecurists," the *Times* demanded to know when the ring "first commenced to subsidize the Mutual base-ball club of this city[.] How long have the members of its first nine been on the city's pay-roll? What is the aggregate amount paid them up to the present time? What is the character of the services thus remunerated?"

It can be noted that the *Times* was a newspaper read by gentlemen, and it drew distinctions between what it considered clean amateur sport and crass professional sport. The *Times* opposed professional baseball from its inception on throughout the 1870s, no matter who was running it. According to the *Times* the pro game was not sport; it was "a purely business transaction." The professional ball player was characterized as "a shiftless member of the laboring class, prone to drink, having a loose moral code, and preferring to avoid an honest day's work by playing ball." In another *Times* piece the game was described as being "patronized by the worst classes of the community, of both sexes; and moreover, many of the gatherings have been characterized by the presence of a regular gambling horde, while oaths and obscenity have prevailed." Will Tweed goes down in history as an utterly corrupt individual; that he ever gained political power in the first place owes something to his good fortune in having such self-right-eous snobbish opposition.

In urban politics of the late nineteenth century the two great political factions were not so much the Democrats and Republicans as what could be called the Party of Vice and the Party of Reform. Widespread success for the former was at-tributable in part to a Victorian definition of vice which in-cluded almost all pleasurable activities. Avid moralists of the period drew little distinction between a brothel, a bribe, and a baseball game. The enterprising political boss could link him-self publicly with baseball, variety shows, and amusement parks and declare that these were part of his package of quasi–social welfare: the soup kitchen, the public works job, influence with a judge, and so on. Disguised as "the people's choice," the political boss was free to do the bidding of the industrialists who paid the bribes. In return for graft payments the bribers got cheap city land, favorable zoning regulations for their plant and unfavorable ones for competitors, and a sufficient amount of police muscle when the workers went on strike, which happened with great frequency in this period.

Political sponsorship of the local professional ball team was an extension of the local ward heeler's effort at creating a team for youngsters in the precinct. To the baseball-bitten of this period there seemed little wrong with such politicalization of sport. "A Gubernatorial Nomination to be Decided by a Base Ball Series," ran a *Sporting Life* headline in 1883. The planned series was between teams composed of Democratic committeemen from Essex and Hudson counties in New Jer-sey. The New Jersey Democrats felt sure the nominee for gov-ernor would come from either of these counties—either Leon Abbett of Jersey City or Andrew Albright of Newark. *Sport-ing Life* explained: "The friends of both these gentlemen re-cently entered into an agreement, it is said, to play three base-ball matches to decide who should be the choice of both counties as the candidate for Governor."

Baseball and politics shared a tie with the gambling crowd, wagering on political contests being one of the many popular

pastimes of this corrupt age. On state and national elections
the handle was enormous. A national election-wagering operation was run from Troy, New York, by Jim Morrissey, ex-
congressman and founder of the Troy Haymakers baseball
team. He appears to have gotten wind of the impending fix in
the 1876 Hayes-Tilden presidential contest a good month before the infamous meeting in the Washington hotel where the
Democrats sold the presidency to the Republicans for the
price of ending Reconstruction in the South. "Presidential
Race—Bets Declared Off," read a New York *Herald* headline
of December 8, 1876. The report noted that Morrissey had
also canceled the betting on the Oregon governor's race, due
to charges of stuffed ballots.

Philadelphia was second in importance only to New York
in the development of baseball. A Republican machine did for
Philadelphia baseball what Tweed's Tammany Hall did for
New York. One of the Philadelphia GOP's accomplishments
was the refusal to enforce Sunday "blue laws," from the late
1860s until 1874, when the Christian Victorians launched a
massive petition drive to close down the city on the Sabbath.
The petition drive was followed closely by writers for the sporting papers. The open Sunday had been a boon to many a
backer of baseball teams. The Athletics and Phillies had
among their directors during the open-Sunday period thirteen
involved in saloons, billiard parlors, and liquor stores, and
seven others in theater.

The Athletic Club was run from the 1860s until its demise
in 1892 by a procession of Republican stalwarts. From 1866
to 1879 its directors included three legislators, six councilmen,
the city comptroller, the receiver of taxes, the receiver of de-
linquent taxes, five tax clerks, the U.S. marshal, and a number
of judges and commissioners. For a number of years the Athletics' manager was City Councilman E. Hicks Hayhurst. The
rival Philadelphia Phillies had James McColgan, a city councilman of the rival political party, as manager in 1876. The
Phillies, created in 1873, were the team of the Democratic
loyal opposition, which in this city was an exceedingly loyal

opposition. Political independents led the reform cause in Philadelphia. The list of Phillies directors was as heavily political as that of the Athletics, but the former's politicians rarely got elected.

In most years the Athletics also had a better won–lost baseball record than the Phillies. Then as now, superiority on the playing field was related to the amount of cash club officials had on hand to recruit the superior players. Backers of the two Philadelphia teams were equally nondescript in relation to the world of commerce and industry; but in the financial power that came from political office the Republican Athletics had a decided advantage. The Athletics were one of a number of prominent baseball clubs around the country that had close ties to the lucrative business of tax collecting.

An inordinate number of baseball club officials held office as city or county treasurer, tax collector, comptroller, or assessor. Baseball also had an abundance of clerks and deputies working with city finances, such as Deputy Tax Collector Edward J. Flynn of Brooklyn, who was said to have funneled sizable sums of cash to the Atlantic Club. It was a short step between deciding to gamble with the law and gambling the graft on investment in professional baseball. There were enough baseball/tax people caught or publicly charged with having a hand in the till to suggest it was a general practice. City Treasurer David A. Gage, a key organizer of the first professional club in Chicago, was run out of office amid charges of embezzling between $100,000 and $300,000. Three kingpins of St. Louis baseball, including City Treasurer Frederick J. Espenschied, were indicted on charges of schemes netting hundreds of thousands of dollars. A bloody riot of Cincinnati citizens led to the downfall of longtime baseball backer, political boss, and fleecer of the treasury John R. McLean.

A number of tax men backing baseball had rather humble positions before taking office but left these positions with sufficient cash to buy into banks and manufacturing concerns. Illustrative of such social mobility was David F. Houston. In

1872 he was employed in the office of a boilermaking factory in Philadelphia. He worked hard that year for the election of the Republican ticket and was rewarded with one of the more highly sought after political plums, a position as customs collector. In 1875 he was elected to the board of directors of the Athletics Baseball Club. A few years later he left his customs post and moved to Lynchburg, Virginia, where he purchased a bank, an iron-smelting concern, and a number of other businesses.

Policemen, sheriffs, police commissioners, and judges were as active in late-nineteenth-century baseball promotion as tax people, and their reputation for taking kickbacks and other forms of graft was just as infamous. Of course, there were some honest officers of the law, but they didn't seem to be the ones funding ball teams. Baseball got Sheriff Davis of Jersey City, who was, according to the *New York Times*, the head of an "infamous ring." And there was Cleveland's police chief John N. Frazee, who was, according to the Cleveland *Ledger*, a kingpin in "the ring" of that city. Concerning judges, the attempt of infielder Charlie Fulmer to win election to the seat of Philadelphia police judge in 1883 created much interest in the sporting world. Fulmer had declared before the election that if he won he would quit his playing job with Cincinnati, because sitting on the police court could "earn me much more than I earn now"—a statement which may be taken to reflect negatively on the pay scale in baseball and/or to reflect positively on the potential for raking it in as a Philadelphia judge. (Actually, with Fulmer's meager .247 batting average, he probably earned between $800 and $1,000 playing baseball, while a position on the police court, the bottom rung in the judicial system, netted from $1,000 to $1,100, officially. Fulmer won the election, and played one more season anyway. His batting average dropped to .177.)

Players running for office were rare, but there were enough ex-players in politics for sports editor Henry Chadwick of the *Clipper* to publish each November a roundup of how the heroes and ex-heroes of the diamond had done in election contests. In some years Chadwick mentioned only half a dozen cases; in other years, more than twice that number. As members of the working class, there was a tendency for players-turned-politicians to appeal to the labor vote; and some, like Tom Foley of the Chicago White Sox and N. A. Carsey of New York, were in the Workingmen's party—a party which carried many a local election during the 1870s and 1880s. But joining a labor party wasn't all that necessary for a politician claiming to represent the masses. The zealous Victorian opposition to popular culture, including baseball, made championing popular culture a rather cheap way to garner working people's votes. A survey of the opinions about the masses expressed by the Victorian clergy, intellectuals, and society people helps explain why there were so many politicians in baseball, particularly politicians of party machines catering to the labor vote.

Sports in America seemed to increase in popularity in inverse ratio to the decline in the power and influence of organized religion. Ball games, picnic track meets, rowing regattas, and prizefights were facets of the "Gilded Age," a time when city wage earners were staying away from church and alarmed ministerial groups were speaking bitterly of the "unchurched masses" who were accused of having abandoned the faith. Then, too, there were the ever-increasing numbers of immigrant Catholics. In the opinion of many a Protestant minister, the immigrants hadn't had the faith to begin with, a view expressed by the eminent Republican parson who, in a slap at the Irish in New York, called the Democrats "the party of rum, Romanism, and rebellion."

In antebellum America churchmen had commanded attention by reason of the important role of the church in American life from colonial times, and by reason of the inseparable connection of the clergy with the genteel cultured folk who

had represented what passed then for high society. The post–
Civil War period, however, found public notice shifting to
pugnacious rascals like "Boss" Tweed. Declining interest in
the traditionally long Sunday sermon matched faster approaches to life in general—cross-continental train travel,
more headlines and shorter stories in the newspapers—and
such cryptic analyses of the religious issue as the quip of robber baron Jim Fisk, "I worship in the Synagogue of the Liber-
tines." With much resentment the ministers and the genteel
intellectuals watched the public slip away from the Sunday
evening lecture on transcendentalist philosophy to attend P. T.
Barnum's circus.

Sports spectacles stole attention from the church, especially
if the spectacles came on a Sunday. Sports were more exciting,
and sports were for the living, for the here-and-now, rather
than the hereafter. Compared with the mysteries of meta-
physics, the playing rules and statistical compilations of sports
had an orderly rationality which paralleled the mechanical
accounting and ordering of modern economic life. At the
same time, both religion and sports offered escape from the
pressure and insecurity of daily life. As Paul Hoch noted:
"Five generations ago Karl Marx called religion the opiate of
the masses. Today that role has been taken over by sports." In
a secular age, sports provide the more potent fix.

Protestant religion, for better or for worse, had once held
unchallenged influence over cultural and social life in America, and religious chieftains such as the Massachusetts Puritan
Cotton Mather would have nothing of sport in the theocracy.
Similarly, in the Connecticut colony gaming, sports, and frolics of almost any sort were strictly proscribed by the blue laws.
In Quaker Pennsylvania such diversions as balls, masques,
plays, cock fights, bullbaiting, cards, and dice were declared to
be "inventions of the vain, idle, and wanton minds to gratify
their own sensualities and raise the like wicked curiosity in
others to imitate the same by which nothing but lust and folly
are promoted." Indulging in the above pleasures in early

Pennsylvania earned the guilty fines or imprisonment in the workhouse.

In the Gilded Age of industrial revolution, organized religion was confronted with a nation apparently gone alcoholic, debauching itself at amusement parks, sporting events, risqué vaudeville shows, burlesque houses, and dens of prostitution. There were, of course, some legitimate concerns here, but the pious moralists all too often failed to separate dislike of vice from a dislike of poor people in general. Until the surfacing of the liberal "social gospel" in the 1890s, the attitude of Protestant divines toward the exploited industrial worker was unmistakably hostile. The *Congregationalist* journal editorialized as follows on the unemployed in 1878: "They are profane, licentious, filthy, vermin-swarming thieves, petty robbers, and sometimes murderers, social pests and perambulatory nuisances." Another organ of the Protestant press said of striking workers in Pittsburgh in 1877: "If the club of the policemen, knocking out the brains of the rioter, will answer, then well and good; but if it does not promptly meet the exigency, then bullets and bayonets, canister and grape—with no sham or pretense . . . constitute the only remedy and the one duty of the hour." The *Christian Advocate* demanded that action be taken to "legislate Trades' Unions out of existence." One of the period's great preachers, the Episcopal bishop Phillips Brooks of Boston, expressed a widely held ministerial view upholding the desirability of social inequality: "The fact of privilege and inequalities among men . . . makes a large part of the interest and richness of human existence . . . I believe that the more we think, the more we become convinced that the instinct which asks for equality is a low one, and that equality, if it were completely brought about, would furnish play only for the lowest instincts and impulses of man."

This argument was an old one, which in early New England had been presented to a captive audience. Modern city life freed the captives for other activities than sitting through such sermons. Declared one Sabbatarian of the Gilded Age: "To

the masses of the workingmen Sunday is no more than a holiday . . . it is a day for labor meetings, . . . for saloons, beer-
gardens, base ball games and carousels." Many a minister,
looking down upon the half-empty pews of his church, declared that the absence of the masses was good riddance. Said
one: "Let the fact be recognized, then, that as the church
includes the better classes of society, it will be disliked by the
worse classes who are yet outside."

But to others, preaching salvation to the heathen was part
of the calling. To get them to listen, war was declared on the
assorted diversions associated with the urban masses. There
was the Women's Christian Temperance Union, and Carrie
Nation taking her ax to the saloon; there were the law-and-
order societies; and there were the Sabbatarians.

The battle to close the town on Sunday contributed heavily
to the politicalization of baseball. In the often-expressed opinion of the sporting press, the Victorian moralists seemed to
make the war against Sunday baseball second in importance
only to the crusade for temperance. In some cities baseball
was closed on Sunday while the saloons were allowed to remain open, as were gambling dens, burlesque theaters, and
other alleged evils.

The defenders of Sunday ball wondered out loud why the
national pastime was singled out. A sportswriter for the
Brooklyn *Union* said to the bluenoses who were trying to stop
Sunday baseball at Coney Island: "It seems to me that it
would be more within the bounds of consistency to first put a
stop to the Sunday evils of gambling, dance halls, pool selling
and other violations of State laws on Sunday at Coney Island
before troubling what is comparatively a venial offence." In
Cleveland the Sabbatarians went so far as to make a political
alliance with saloon keepers, a deal for city council votes
whereby Sunday baseball games would be prohibited but saloons could stay open. Saloon keepers would thus enjoy the
luxury of selling booze on Sunday without the competition of
baseball.

The proper people in any historical era can be found trying

to keep the poor out of sight. Let them gather in a dance hall or a saloon, but not in a mighty cheering outdoor throng. In one court case, a professional team in Michigan was given a judge's permission to play on Sunday, provided there was no loud cheering from the spectators. From the 1870s to the turn of the century there were hundreds of court and legislative battles involving Sunday sports, and the fight continued in many cities well into this century. The issue of a Christian Sabbath vs. "the Continental Sunday" took on the rhetoric of class conflict. A *Sporting News* editorial was headlined "Base Ball on Sunday: It is the Only Day on Which the Masses Can Enjoy the Sport"—true enough, considering the prevailing six-day work week. *Sporting News* had strong words for "some rich men who have plenty of time during the week to attend the national game," while they "think it is a sin that their less fortunate fellows should devote Sunday to 'rooting' for their favorite players."

Sporting News gave ample space to the opinions of "a popular Eastern divine" who had come out in favor of Sunday ball. The rebel minister noted that in response to his views

certain members of my congregation will raise their hands in horror. Yet they are equally as bad. After hearing my morning sermon they will prepare for a Sunday excursion to Long Branch, Glen Island or some other summer resort and there spend the balance of the day.

Now the poor people cannot afford to go on these Sunday excursions. It so happens that the national game is within their reach. They go and watch their favorite team play ball. . . . They enjoy themselves as much as the men who are strolling on the sands at the seaside resorts. . . . Again, there are thousands of young ambitious boys who are cooped up in shop, mill and factory and office during the week. They have athletic tastes. Six days of their time is given to their employer. What more natural than that they should meet on the green turf and indulge in friendly contests. You cannot drive these boys to church. Without needed exercise they would rust. . . . Preaching against the game will not reform it. If those who are fighting it would recall the fact that they were once young and poor, though now they may be rich and powerful, they would withdraw their opposition and say, as I do, that . . . those who work six days out of seven should have the privilege of selecting their own styles of amusement.

The whole issue was, of course, of rather small consequence in relation to the more pressing problems faced by working people; but it was the kind of issue which enlivened the debate among the shallow-minded politicians of the day who ran the major parties. So it was that the politicians behind the "beer-ball" American Association were Democrats, and those behind the "dry" National League were Republicans; the Association played on Sunday, but the National League did not.

The Sunday baseball desecration of the Sabbath packed the ball parks, attendance on that day running from three to five times the weekday average. During the 1870s the playing of professional ball on Sunday had been relegated to a few midwestern cities with a large German-American population, a group in tune with the Continental Sunday and the feeling that any outing was an occasion for the bringing along of a bucket of beer. In the 1880s, there were promoters to be found scheming to arrange Sunday baseball in every area of the country, except New England. The sporting press described many teams being founded on the hope of Sunday attendance providing the margin for a profitable season. *Sporting News* carried an optimistic report from a promoter in St. Joseph, Missouri, who expected Sunday games to provide more fans than would come from the combined total on all the other days of the week. He explained: "There will be fifteen Sunday games played, and placing the attendance at 3,000 each game that will be 45,000 people. The sixty-nine weekday games, averaging them at 600 people each, will make 41,000 more, or a total of 86,000."

To take advantage of Sunday profits, one of the minor leagues put a franchise in Chicago in 1888. Minor leagues don't often compete in major-league territory, but since the Chicago Nationals were not going to play on Sunday, the minor-league team thought it had a good chance. Its first Sunday game set a city attendance record. According to the reminiscences of old-time ball player Fred Lange, it was the greatest crowd he had ever seen; sections of the outfield had to be roped off to accommodate the overflow. In 1892 the National League changed its rules to give clubs the option of Sunday games. The Chicago club took this option. Sunday ball was again an immediate success, attracting over 13,000 fans to the first game. At the time, the local Sabbatarians gave little opposition, since they were then devoting their complete attention to fighting the proposed Sunday opening of the Chicago World's Fair.

The profit potential for playing on the one day when the masses could get to the ball park led to a variety of peculiar arrangements for taking this advantage. When local law stopped Pittsburgh of the American Association from playing on Sunday, the schedules were rearranged so that the Pittsburgh club was playing at some other park each Sunday, even if that meant leaving Pittsburgh Saturday night and returning for a game on Monday. While Cleveland was in the Association, it adopted a similarly taxing travel schedule to ensure its cut of the Sunday profit. The leading black American club, the Cuban Giants, received an offer in 1885 to join the Eastern League, which had a number of franchises in New England and did not play Sunday ball. The Cuban Giants refused the offer rather than give up their lucrative Sunday games at their home park in Hoboken, New Jersey.

The opposition to Sunday games was led by militant organizations such as the American Sabbath Union, the Sunday League of America, the Lord's Day Alliance, the Women's Christian Temperance Union, various law-and-order-societies, and various clergymen's alliances. They ran petition drives and had street marches. They lobbied for blue laws in city councils and state legislatures. More often, they were pressuring for enforcement of laws long on the books. Suggestive of this line of attack was the letter to the editor of the Philadelphia *Public Ledger* complaining that "the police seem to be oblivious" to the habit of youngsters congregating downtown in front of "public buildings" and "using the broad pavement as a ball ground."

In city after city the fights against Sunday baseball were bitter ones. *Sporting News* reported that the baseball fraternity in Syracuse was up in arms over the arrest of a visiting team of newsboys from Detroit; they had been practicing on a Sunday when the police descended upon them and, reportedly without a word of warning, spirited them off to jail. Generally, it was the professionals the police went after, and there were numerous instances of police marching onto a playing field to arrest whole teams of pro ball players.

On one April Sunday in 1887, sixty deputy sheriffs in Queens, New York, made a sweep of a number of games; then they got to the one at Atlantic Park, where the Cuban Giants and the Newarks were playing before an estimated 4,000 spectators. The *Clipper* reported that Police Captain Kavanaugh and his deputies "were surrounded by the crowd and for a time it looked as if there would be trouble. Six innings were played, the Newarks winning 4 to 1." At Toledo, and again at Des Moines, there were cases of players being put under arrest at the ball park, paying their bail on the spot, and going on with the game. The ominous presence of the sheriff and his deputies helped Syracuse to win a game by forfeit from Louisville in 1890. The Syracuse manager figured that no arrests would be made until the first pitch had been thrown. He stationed his men in the field and then demanded that the umpire declare a forfeit because the Louisville players, eyeing the sheriff, refused to come up to bat.

The ministers and the temperance crowd employed many creative strategies in their cause. In some places they managed to close down streetcar lines on Sunday to ensure that there would be few people at the ball park. Church groups would rent the local baseball park for Sunday and hold all-day religious services there. Where there was no blue law to be enforced, the Sabbatarians took ball teams to court under public-nuisance statutes, and argued that the unruly and uncouth crowds at games depreciated property values in the surrounding neighborhoods. In an apparent bid for labor support, a clergymen's group in Saginaw, Michigan, added to their petition against Sunday games the suggestion that local industry adopt a Saturday half-day schedule in order to provide the workers with time to attend games. *Sporting Life* noted that the Saginaw petition would probably go unheard, since "Mayor Baum was recently elected on a wide-open platform." In Alabama the bluenoses tried to outlaw the game entirely, and managed to get a bill through the lower house of the state legislature that would have prohibited professional ball on any day of the week.

The issue remained a hot one through the turn of the century. In 1899 a Ft. Wayne, Indiana, minister was bodily thrown out of a ball park one Sunday when fans noticed he was roaming the stands writing down names. Police took the minister to jail, where, a judge told him, he would have to remain for the rest of the day. When the minister asked why, the judge told him his detention was necessary to avoid a riot. The anger of New York's baseball fraternity was aroused in 1889 when it was learned that the Sabbatarians had quietly been working to convince the commissioner of public works to extend 111th Street—a move which, had it been carried through, would have flattened half the grandstand of the Giants' home park, the Polo Grounds.

To avoid municipal ordinances, ball teams played Sunday games outside the city limits. The Cincinnati Reds got around a state blue law by playing Sunday games across the Ohio River in Covington, Kentucky. The ball club in Newark, New Jersey, had difficulty escaping the religious crusaders. When the Law and Order Committee stopped Sunday ball in Newark in 1888, the team moved the games to South Orange. But the Law and Order Committee didn't give up. It tried to get the residents of South Orange to bring a public-nuisance complaint against the team. This failed, but the residents of East Orange, three miles away, were willing, and in July 1890 the Newark club was ordered by a court to stop its Sunday ball. The *Clipper* declared that over the previous two seasons "the big attendance at these games is all that saved the club from financial ruin. . . . The club will probably disband if the Sunday games are discontinued." The club did disband; and Newark went four years without pro ball.

The financial necessity of Sunday games forced many a ball club into lengthy court battles. The fight was particularly fierce in Columbus, Ohio, where the local YMCA got into the fray by refusing to allow the local ball club to use its gymnasium for spring practice activities. When Columbus and Brooklyn players were arrested in 1884, the Brooklyn club wanted to plead its players guilty and be done with the issue. The Columbus directors, however, said that without Sunday ball their club would fold, so they were going to fight for it by entering not-guilty pleas and making a test case out of the law. The lawyers for the Columbus club were prepared to argue—unsuccessfully, as it turned out—that contrary to constitutional safeguards baseball was being singled out for punishment, while the Law and Order Society that brought the complaint did nothing to stop the saloon business on Sunday.

Similarly, during a trial of players arrested in Cleveland the defense raised the argument that the local ordinance specifically prohibited "playing" but not "working" on Sunday; and according to the defense lawyer, baseball was a business and the players salaried workers. Therefore, if the players were to be fined for their activity on Sunday, so should every factory laborer in Cleveland who had the misfortune to draw a Sunday work shift. The judge saw otherwise. At a trial of Sunday ball players in Lincoln, Nebraska, the defense noted that the law did prohibit common labor as well as sporting activities on

Sunday; the defense contended that "if this law was strictly enforced it would close the doors of nearly every church which had a janitor at work on Sunday, had a paid organist and a paid choir, people engaged in their usual vocation."

The judge in this case acquitted the players on the grounds that baseball was neither common labor nor a sporting activity in the terms by which sports had been defined in the statute; "as baseball was not played for any wager, or stakes, but was merely an exhibition of skill and agility, it could not come under the heading of sporting." The argument that baseball was not specifically mentioned in the law, and was a special entity all its own, proved a successful defense in an increasing number of cases, according to L. A. Wilder in a study of baseball and the law published in the lawyers' magazine *Case and Comment*.

The fight over control of Sunday pitted the sporting crowd against the religious establishment, but then, too, there was involvement in the controversy on the side of religion by social groups that felt threatened by professional baseball on quite secular grounds. These groups represented the athletic establishment of the upper classes, found in clubs like the Staten Island Cricket Club, the St. George Yacht Club, the New York Athletic Club, the Detroit Athletic Club, and so on. In theater, art, and music, their high culture held its prestige rating in the face of the mass culture of vaudeville and ragtime. The masses might still envy the rich for their collection of classical paintings, or their front-row tickets to see the great Edgar Booth or one of the Barrymores at a first run on Broadway. But in sports, baseball had come to be a threat to the prestige of the wealthy. Who needed their tennis, golf, polo, yachting, and badminton when one could have baseball?

The popularity of baseball upset the design of the ruling classes to hoard what Thorstein Veblen termed "conspicuous leisure" and "conspicuous consumption." The desire of the fortunate few to flaunt their privileges worked well in social affairs. The banquets and balls of "high society" received lengthy newspaper "box scores" in the form of columns of names—lists of who attended whose illustrious gathering; there were no social box scores for the gatherings of ordinary people. But in the sporting sections, the box scores of baseball games took up far more space than the reporting of yachting contests and similar sporting affairs of the rich.

Baseball upstaged the sports of the gentlemen, and in many instances obstructed the development of rich folks' athletics. The Detroit Athletic Club had been created for the initial purpose of promoting boating among those "of sedentary habits," meaning the local middle and upper classes. According to the history of the club in *Outing* magazine, the prospects for the boating crowd seemed bright, but then "the organization of a baseball club and its admission to the National League diverted some of the enthusiasm which had been given to boating, and the city became 'ball-crazy' at once." Professional baseball was described as pirating interest and spectators from the college rowing regatta at Springfield, Massachusetts, and from the regattas on the Charles River in Boston.

The belief that professional ball clubs attracted disreputable crowds which disturbed the peace and quiet and lowered the property values of the neighborhood led to a crisis for one of the nation's wealthiest athletic clubs, the Staten Island A.C. Over a sixteen-year period the club had expanded and developed facilities on grounds of "picturesque beauty." Then in 1887 one of the members of the club, Erastus Wiman, turned class traitor, and set about constructing on adjacent property an amusement park and baseball stadium, which he planned to use as the home park for the New York Metropolitans of the American Association, which he owned. The Staten Island club sold its property and moved elsewhere rather than stay on where the noise of the fun-loving common folk of New York might disturb the members' sensitive natures.

The *New York Times*, which voiced the sentiments of "respectable" people, had looked forward to the collapse of baseball, commenting editorially on August 30, 1881: "There is reason to believe that base ball is gradually dying out in this country," and "probably the time is now ripe for a revival of cricket." Delving into history in a manner revealing of the editors' prejudices, the *Times* explained: "About twenty-five years ago there was an effort made to induce Americans to play cricket, but it failed. We were not, at that time, worthy of the game, and in our ignorance and indolence we said, 'Give us something easier.' It was then that . . . the base-ball conspirators said to their fellow-countrymen, 'Here is an easy game which everybody can learn. Let us play it and call it our national game.' "

For the *Times*, proof that the game had been adopted by brutish elements was seen in the number of injuries suffered in baseball. "It is estimated by an able statistician that the annual number of accidents caused by base-ball in the last ten years has been 37,518, of which 8 per cent have been fatal; 25,611 fingers and 11,016 legs were broken during the decade in question, while 1,900 eyes were permanently put out and 1,648 ribs were fractured." The editorial concluded that baseball "was in the beginning a sport unworthy of men, and . . . it is now, in its fully developed state, unworthy of gentlemen."

Henry Chadwick responded to the *Times* piece, calling it "silly and pernicious." He took issue with the accusation that baseball was a sport of ignorant brutes. Said Chadwick: "Surely, it is an . . . honorable game—calling for a clear brain, quick perception, and mental exercise, as well as muscle, endurance, and physical training. . . . It is much more than mere bodily strength or agility. The ball-field offers opportunities for all the brain-work which is needed to give character to any game." Chadwick also took issue with the claim of the *Times* in this editorial, as in earlier ones, that the professional game was crooked and run by gamblers. Historically, the social elite can be found in all too many cases pinning the labels of brainless and fraudulent upon the sports favored by the laboring classes.

*   *   *

The struggle between the Victorian "Old Fogies" and the political defenders of mass culture is one part of the story of early baseball. Another part is the struggle within the baseball fraternity over the question of the game's economic organization, the subject of the next chapter.

Start of a six-day marathon at the first Madison Square Garden in 1879, showing the tents where the marathoners took their rest periods.

Schoolboys in a walking race, 1897.

Litho of men at the start of a sprint, in 1887, shows the handicap start and how the contestants had a variety of starting styles.

Turn-of-the-century women sprinters at the starting line.

From *Athletics and Football*, by Montague Shearman, The Badminton Library.

A shot of runners in action. The running lanes were divided by ropes so that a track meet could be conducted at rented grounds without smudging the field with chalk lines.

Ladies running at a California picnic meet, 1911.

From *Playground Magazine*

Hurdling in the 1890s. Hurdles were made from sawhorses then.

Many of today's "new games" were the rage back in the first years of public playgrounds. Here, a 1910 version of today's "earth ball" at a Philadelphia playground

The immortal game on the streets of New York, 1914.

A march for the cause of public playgrounds—photographic evidence of how public sport had to be fought for and did not come easy.

The Atlantics of Brooklyn, 1865.

The Excelsiors of Brooklyn, 1860. Hired pitcher Creighton is shown holding the ball.

From Leslie's Illustrated Weekly

*his fanciful 1888 picture of baseball fanatics
ggests why some people felt ball parks depre-
ated neighborhood property values.*

From Leslie's Illustrated Weekly

*fore radio, New Yorkers gathered
inning-by-inning telegraphed re-
rts outside the New York* World
ices.

The New York Giants playing at the Polo Grounds in 1888.

The rooftop gym of the famous University Settlement House, 1909.

5

Commercializing
Professional Baseball:
The National League Coup

The corporate structure for professional sports was an invention of midwesterners. Whereas in the Northeast the majority of ball clubs that paid players were still membership clubs well into the 1870s, the pay-for-play game in the Midwest was almost from its inception the work of "stock companies." Apropos of this development is the comment of one citizen of the Windy City, circa 1870: "In Chicago the first thing to do toward any achievement is to form a stock company. In Chicago nobody builds a church, or pickles a winter's stock of cucumbers without first forming a joint stock company under the general statute."

The Midwest was experiencing population expansion and urbanization. Chicago was mushrooming toward the one-million figure, while Cleveland and Milwaukee went from less than 50,000 people on the eve of the Civil War to more than 100,000 a decade later. In measuring social standing, the size of one's bank account substituted for the easterner's ties to a traditional family. Any action to ruin a competitor was acceptable so long as it was within the law; and as seen in the young John D. Rockefeller's practices in the oil industry, the law was often circumvented. Of course, the Midwest had its socially responsible citizens, but they were often no more in control of affairs than were their counterparts in the gunslingers' cow towns on the prairies.

The stock-company format provided a business structure for the organization of baseball which in time would become the accepted mode. But in the beginning there were many who saw the baseball corporation as quite unnatural. The Chicago White Sox of 1870 were one of the first teams organized as a stock company, and due to the novelty of the idea the club couldn't get legally incorporated until 1871. Illinois law didn't acknowledge the legitimate existence of such a thing as a baseball corporation. The club finally used a statute allowing the incorporation of benevolent, educational, literary, musical, and missionary societies. Since baseball seemed to have little in common with the aims of this statute, the White Sox soon became the subject of jocular inquiries, questions as to just what this organization was. Was it "a benevolent society for the benefit of the stockholders and players"? Was it perhaps "a missionary league to carry the Gospel of baseball to more benighted communities"? Or was it "a corporation for the mutual improvement of the gamblers"? The *Illinois State Journal* of March 29, 1871, interpreted the incorporation as an ominous new departure. While the club had paid the players salaries the year before, the *Journal* felt that creating a corporation was something else again, and that the White Sox had now been put "on a thorough gambling basis, to be used like a race-horse or a bull terrier in the hands of experienced sportsmen, for the purpose of making money. The respectable public should give no countenance to the game of base ball when it is perverted to such bad ends." The White Sox were soon to be put out of business, not by the respectable public but by the great Chicago fire—which is to say, one sporting adventure was ended by another, for as the sporting crowd knew, the great fire was not caused by Mrs. O'Leary's cow, but by one Louis Cohn, who was shooting craps in O'Leary's barn, got overexcited, and knocked over the lantern.

Economic competition between eastern and western cities played a role in generating the pro game in the Midwest and in giving it there a stronger following among businessmen. The economic strength of the budding metropolises of the Midwest was untested, and their businessmen felt that they had something to prove to their eastern counterparts, the long-recognized commercial leaders of the nation. A well-financed and winning baseball team was one vehicle for symbolically, at least, displaying the mettle of a new commercial and industrial stronghold. "Glory, they've advertised the city—advertised us, sir, and helped our business, sir," exclaimed one citizen of Cincinnati about the triumphant nationwide tour of the 1869 Red Stockings.

Touring the country from the Atlantic to the Pacific, the Red Stockings of '69 had taken on all comers, gone undefeated with one tie, and earned for Cincinnati the distinction of being the town where professional baseball was born—because this was the original stock-company team, the first team to give all players announced salaries; in effect, the first club to be run expressly as a commercial rather than social venture. The Reds were an all-star aggregation which had been recruited largely from the East, lured to Cincinnati by fabulous offers of from $600 to $2,000 for a season of play. The audacious notion that a team composed entirely of outsiders could be identified with the city paying the team was the secret of the Red Stockings' success; as the *National Chronicle* explained: "Had the Cincinnati Base Ball Club depended upon home talent it would never have been heard from outside its own locality."

The image of professional baseball springing forth as the creation of enterprising Cincinnati capitalists is a strong one, and it has helped obscure from view the social and political angles to the creation of so many other clubs, since this is *the* early club above all others which gets the scrutiny of the baseball historians. The picture drawn is of creator A. B. Champion bringing together businessmen, enrolling over 300 members in the club, some of whom, according to a local newspaper, were among the city's wealthiest citizens. Champion also enrolled the city's leading Democrats, including boss John

R. McLean. Champion was a lawyer and Democratic National Convention delegate. Next to Champion the most important organizer for the Reds was Alderman Albert Goshorn; and when Champion stepped down as club president in 1870 he was replaced by alderman candidate A. P. C. Bonte. The histories neglect the political side to the Red Stockings, but they do reveal interesting sidelights to the financial picture which suggest that the club had less input from financial leaders than has been assumed.

Supposedly, $15,000 worth of stock in the club had been sold to outfit and recruit the team. But it seems there were some mere token payments toward stock purchase, and the announced amount of stock sales was highly inflated, and quite unreal, as would be the announced sums for countless later professional nines of this period. Historian Seymour found that the financial condition of the Red Stockings on the eve of their nationwide tour was not at all clear. One report had it that the team set out for the East in such precarious straits that a rabid fan donated his wife's $300 savings to ensure train tickets and other last-minute expenses. Another account recalls that the start was made with "no bands, no enthusiasm, no send off." Aside from tickets through to Boston, the team had only $24 in hand, and the players were apprehensive and in many instances drunk. So began "the miraculous task of transporting this insubordinate band a couple of thousand miles on $24 and chance."

The gate receipts were barely enough to get the Red Stockings from one town to the next until they got to Philadelphia and New York, where enormous crowds turned out to witness the Reds defeat the Mutuals, Atlantics, and Athletics. With the profits from these games the Cincinnati club was able, later in the season, to take its tour to the West Coast. The Reds finished the year with a net profit of $1.26 on an outlay of salaries, railroad fares, and the like totaling $29,724.87. The club had certainly brought fame to Cincinnati, but this was insufficient to entice capital from local business leaders. The Red Stockings had tough financial sledding the next season, and lost whatever significant financial resources they might once have had. A forlorn committee attempting to put a team together for 1871 was a decidedly undistinguished group, the identifiable among them being a railroad ticket agent, a clerk, and two shopkeepers.

Breaking even in the season of '69 was fine with Champion. He got credit for advertising the city. At the team's, homecoming parade he had the opportunity to ride through the city streets waving to the crowd—a dream for any politician, and Champion was a politician. Alderman Goshorn benefited too; he went on to make a career out of advertising Cincinnati, through promotion of industrial and fine arts exhibitions. He went to Europe to promote his city and had himself knighted "Sir Albert" by the queen of England. Lawyer Champion finally did make some financial profit out of it all, through his sale of '69 Red Stockings memorabilia: bats, balls, uniforms, emblems, ticket stubs, and so on. Somebody else got something out of it too, for among the pioneering features of the Reds club was the mail order sale of team lithographs.

Whatever Cincinnati could do, Chicago could do better, said the boosters and sporting crowd in the Windy City. Realizing that the secret of the Red Stockings' achievement had been recruitment, the Chicago club aimed to up the ante for grab-off of ball players. Where Cincinnati had offered players an average of $1,000 or more for the season, Chicago would make it $1,200 or more to play for the White Sox in 1870. In addition to the promised salary, White Sox backers, who were a genuinely impressive group of "leading citizens," doled out cash advances of up to $500 to convince top players to move to Chicago—the White Sox were taking their players from the principal clubs of the East. A reported $20,000 had been raised by the Chicago club, and in this instance the stated amount was probably an accurate one; the president of the White Sox, City Treasurer David A. Gage, had at his disposal some $100,000 to $300,000 personally embezzled from his office, according to the indictment brought against him in 1873. Put in a positive light, the backers of the White Sox exemplified the innovative use of sports by individuals who were creative in the business and professional world. There was future mayor Joseph Medill, whose journalistic techniques would make the Chicago *Tribune* the outstanding newspaper of the Midwest. There was Potter Palmer, owner of the remarkable Palmer House hotel, and well known in theater, billiards, and horse racing circles. Future senator Charles B. Farwell backed the team; he had organized one of the first department stores in the nation, and his sales techniques were carefully studied by representatives sent out from Macy's of New York. Among the many political allies of Farwell backing the team there was William Tucker, vice-president of the Union Stock Yards. It can be noted that Chicago had not yet cornered the market on meat-packing, and a ball team that helped advertise Chicago as the metropolis of the West could help the cause of those like Tucker who were attempting to concentrate the meat-packing industry in their city.

The White Sox and the Red Stockings established precedents for the commercial use of baseball which were, for the most part, slow to be adopted elsewhere, and at first subject to open criticism. The Chicago club became a subject of widespread journalistic abuse, and its officers were generally held to be anything but honorable gentlemen. The raiding of the rosters of established clubs in the East seemed particularly offensive. The Boston *Herald* of November 14, 1870, took to task the tactics of the White Sox backers. "Last Winter a few sporting men clubbed together and raised $20,000" in Chicago, "with which to employ a nine that should 'sweep the board.' Players were picked from the Eckfords, Haymakers and Athletics. . . . The White Stockings are merely a money making concern. They care nothing for the welfare of the game, except that it enables them to rake in on an average from $2,000 to $3,000 a week, which goes into the pockets of the men who run the machine, a party of speculators." Unlike the complaints found on the pages of papers like the *New York Times*, the Boston *Herald* was not arguing with the idea of paying players to play the game, but with the use of paid players for the commercialization of the sport. The *Herald* urged the creation of a "well-run" professional club for Boston, the writer believing that such a club would "perk up interest in the national game in the Boston area."

According to the eastern scribes, there had been more to the White Sox recruiting than just high salaries. It was alleged that Sox manager Tom Foley obtained some of his players by getting them drunk and then, while they were pleasantly mind-blown, advancing them sums of money. To suggest the illegitimacy of the White Sox venture, the club was called "Foley's What-is-it," and it was noted that the team played its home games not in a ball park but on a baseball diamond in the infield of the Dexter Park horse track.

The way the White Sox set about massacring local amateur teams couldn't help but build some resentment in their own city; representative scores were 75–12, 48–2, 41–1, and 36–8. Traveling to Memphis, the White Sox humiliated the Bluff City's club 157–1, something of a record rout. Upon going east the Chicago club was beaten by the Mutuals and had rough going with a number of other teams, some of the scores in these contests arousing suspicions that the White Sox were in cahoots with the gamblers.

During the controversy over the White Sox the advocates of amateur ball had taken the offensive, demanding in 1870 that the obviously professional nines of both East and West be expelled from the National Association of Amateur Base Ball Players. By this time the old "amateur" organization was being run in New York by the pros of the Mutuals and Atlantics; in Pennsylvania by the Athletics; and in Illinois, of all clubs, by the White Sox. When these leading clubs refused to expel themselves, and won the votes of many "amateur" clubs through promises of lucrative playing dates, there was nothing left for the amateur purists to do but pull out of the Association. The Knickerbocker Club led the walkout in the summer of 1870. The Knickerbockers called together a meeting of clubs for the purpose of forming a new and truly amateur organization. It was a pitifully small and disorganized gathering, termed by the *Clipper* "A What-is-it Convention."

Baseball as a vehicle for organizing and perpetuating elite social clubs was dying out; the status seekers had been in the game to gain fame; the professionals were monopolizing the fame; and the clubs that didn't go pro were losing their prime reasons for being in the game. Early in 1871 the *New York Times* described the trouble in terms of the gamblers and other sporting types who were turning the national pastime into a mass spectacle for the mob. "Hence, we have seen club after club once prominent among the most reputable of the base-ball organizations, either become defunct altogether, or so dormant as to cease to exist as an active club." The game was being stratified—professionals at the top, and far below them the pickup games of laborers. Actually, the demise of the clubs didn't mean less people pitching and hitting baseballs. In ensuing years the pro game would grow by feeding off an ever-expanding pool of talent developed among factory, mine, and mill hands, playing in vacant lots and in the streets, with taped-up broken bats and with balls that lasted until they were lined through some nearby window.

The formalizing of the division of baseball into pro and amateur segments came in March 1871, when representatives of ten clubs met at Collier's Cafe on lower Broadway in New York. As recounted in one history: "There, in a smoky gaslit hallroom adjoining the Cafe [saloon], pro baseball suffered its real birth pangs, for that meeting established the National Association of Professional Base-Ball Players," the first professional league. The delegates drew up a set of rules, but no fixed schedule. Each club was to play the others a best-three-out-of-five series, and the team with the best record at the end of the season was entitled to fly the championship streamer, called the "whip pennant." The Association's entry fee was a mere $10, but even this appeared too much to risk in the opinion of the delegate from the Eckfords; his club withdrew, believing the organization was too shaky to survive a season.

The remaining clubs were the Mutuals, the Athletics, the White Sox, the Haymakers, the Olympics of Washington, the Forest City Club of Cleveland, the Bostons of Boston, the Forest City Club of Rockford, Illinois, and the Kekiongas of Ft. Wayne, Indiana. The one thing these had in common besides a hope for profit was politicians on their boards of directors. Their economic arrangements varied widely, reflecting differences in the class composition of the club backers. At the top of the scale was the stock company of the White Sox; at the bottom were the clerks and salesmen who ran the Ft. Wayne club and offered their players, in lieu of a salary, a share of the gate receipts.

The National Association was in many respects a league run by ball players. The Kekiongas of Ft. Wayne typified a majority of the clubs that were to play in the Association during its life span of 1871–75: clubs organized on a shoestring, with players having a key role in financial affairs, scheduling, and the like. The league president for 1872 was the Atlantics' third baseman Bob Ferguson. The poorly financed Eckfords of Brooklyn joined the Association in 1872. During the playing season the affairs of the Association were handled by periodic meetings of club managers, many of them players as well. The clubs in the East which had evolved out of social and political organizations granted players positions on the all-important Finance Committees, and players made up the majority on the Audit Committee of the Athletics.

The first professional league was hardly a financial success; very few teams turned a profit, and if any one group made out well it was the ball players, at least two dozen of them going on in later years to become directors or owners of ball clubs. A number of others became successful in the sporting goods industry. This is as it should be, considering the American ideal of equal opportunity for any hardworking citizen to go from rags to riches. The Association helped the players and also helped to spread the professional game. Association clubs became drawing cards, and through "exhibition" games with outside clubs helped bring fans to ball parks in many cities.

Two interrelated problems plagued the NA. A handful of clubs had wealthy backers and bought off the best players, making the rest of the teams in the league noncompetitive; the worst off were the "cooperative nines," which offered players only a share of the gate receipts, and these teams developed a reputation for making side money through connections with gamblers, i.e., by throwing games. Every season the *Clipper* had at least one long editorial on "fraudulent play," or "Hippodroming," as it was called. By 1875 the lack of competitive balance and the infestation of gamblers had brought the Association into ill-repute. Debate over these problems within the Association reflected the differences between the rich and poor clubs; the former claimed gambling was the key issue, the latter said it was the hoarding of quality players—a clash of the business vs. the sporting interests.

Conflicts over the control of baseball pitting the poorer elements against the richer would mark the course of the national pastime from 1871 on, until the climactic showdown in the season of 1890—the year of the Players' League, also known as the year of "Baseball's Great Rebellion." First, the amateurs having been routed, the question arose, Could a team run cooperatively by players and ne'er-do-wells of the sporting crowd exist in the same league with the likes of the White Sox corporation? The corporation types were unable to win within the Association, so in 1876 they pulled a "coup d'etat," in the words used by the *Clipper*'s Henry Chadwick to describe the creation of the National League. Now it was the National League, created expressly for stock companies, against the player-run International Association. After the players had lost this three-year battle, a new champion of the lower orders appeared—the American Association, "the beer and whiskey league," offering as attractions top players, cheap tickets, beer, and Sunday games. Next into the conflict came the Union Association of 1884, created, so its promoters said, to do battle with that hated invention of the National League, the reserve clause. The following year the players formed their own trade union, and in 1890 they struck. Organized baseball was shaken to its foundations as tensions that had festered throughout the entire evolution of the professional game finally exploded.

On February 2, 1876, a group of professional club representatives met behind locked doors in a room of New York's Grand Central Hotel. So far as the public and the sporting press knew, the meeting had been called to draw up reform proposals covering three areas: punishments for players caught fixing games; rules for the financial organization of professional clubs; and changes in the playing rules. The announced objectives were only a ruse to cover a more important objective, unknown even to some of those who found themselves locked inside, with chairman William A. Hulbert of Chicago holding the key in his pocket. The secret meeting was to organize a new league, the National League, having a controversial lineup of teams and adopting financial regulations that would create a storm of protest. Had the grand design been known in advance, the resulting outcry no doubt would have frightened off a number of delegates.

The justification for the closed-door meeting was based on a wide consensus that the pro game was in a chaotic state and badly in need of reform. The gambling issue aside, there were the so-called amateur clubs that seemed to be "poaching" on pro turf by paying players with gate receipts and offering them a chance to rake in hundreds of dollars in prize money in allegedly amateur tournaments. Players of top professional quality were in a number of these "amateur" outfits, circus man P. T. Barnum's Bridgeport, Connecticut, nine being one of the best of such clubs. Barnum's baseball act was in jeopardy, however; the roster of his club would be raided by the pros, two of his stars going into the new National League.

The concern of the clubs that played for gate receipts, be they "amateur" or pro, was that someone like a William Hulbert would come along and further stratify the game. The fears mounted when it was learned that for 1876 a reorganized Chicago White Sox had $30,000 in capital, a new Cincinnati club $20,000, and clubs in St. Louis and Louisville a similar amount. These were to become charter members of the National League; they bolted a National Association which had already developed a glaring discrepancy in pay scales—salaried players on stock-company teams averaging $1,200 a year, and the players on "cooperative nines" making approximately $300 a year in their gate receipts, along with the consolation of having the honorable role of helping to run their clubs. With the season of 1876 approaching, pressures mounted for some move to stabilize the working conditions of the performers in the game, and any decisions were bound to be controversial. The drama of this historic moment in baseball history was summed up succinctly by one of the National League founders, Albert Spalding: "It was, in fact, the irrepressible conflict between Labor and Capital asserting itself under a new guise."

A key objective of the National League founders was the elimination of players from any position of authority in club or league financial affairs. This also meant the planned extinction of the cooperative nines and similar clubs run by petty merchants and by white-collar as well as blue-collar workers —those clubs that barely raised the cash to rent a ball park and paid players by a share of the gate.

The new league upped the entrance fee from the old $10 to $100 and tagged on an additional $100 in annual dues. The NL constitution excluded coop teams and any club that did not organize into a stock company. In later years it would appear, in light of the established baseball monopoly, that the National League had discovered the only way forward for the pro game. At the time, however, the coops and other clubs of modest financing had been looking forward to the annual meeting of the National Association with arguments prepared to show that there were now enough clubs of their kind to create a competitive level among themselves—and their season could be augmented with games against the stock-company outfits, to everyone's benefit. The poorer clubs were prepared to argue that the problem of competitive balance was really the problem of the rich clubs that hoarded the top players. Boston seemed to have most of them in 1875, going 71–8, being virtually unbeatable by stock-company or coop teams. For the coming 1876 season a reorganized White Sox club in Chicago had (like its burned-out predecessor) raided the East to gather a superior aggregation—Chicago had bought off all the top stars from Boston and had bought future Hall-of-Famer Cap Anson from the Athletics. The poorer clubs were prepared to argue, if balance was the goal, that the White Sox should be expelled from organized baseball.

White Sox president Hulbert nipped this in the bud with his National League coup d'etat in February. He had told Spalding: "I have a scheme. Let us anticipate the eastern cusses and organize a new association before the March meeting, and then see who will do the expelling." Hulbert was able to pull it off in the hotel meeting by arguing persuasively about modern business principles, sure profits, and a higher respect for the national game that would come from having the new league be above reproach when it came to the gambling issue. Besides, he had the key in his pocket and wasn't going to open the door until he had an agreement. Hulbert had come to the meeting with the votes of western club delegates. Those invited in from eastern clubs had been selected for their receptivity to arguments which, in Spalding's recollection, were designed to awaken in them an awareness of where they stood on the issue of labor vs. capital; an awareness that "like every other form of business enterprise, Base Ball depends for results on two interdependent divisions, the one to have absolute control and direction of the system, and the other to engage [in]—always under the executive branch—the actual work of production."

The National League's actual contribution to the game is not what comes down through baseball folklore, but the league did accomplish three things. First: It created a layer of ball clubs run on business principles, so that if and when prosperity came, as it did in the late 1880s, the profits would fall into the hands of a few promoters. For example, in 1889, when the Boston franchise cleared approximately $90,000, it was profit to be divided not through a few hundred "club members," nor even through two dozen members, such as the Boston stock company had had in 1876; it was profit for a triumvirate which had bought out the lesser stockholders, the buying out of the small-fry being a natural progression in stock companies. Second: By removing the players from financial decisions the National League ensured that when the prosperous period came the players would get a drastically reduced share of the net receipts, not to mention the club profits. Comparing 1876 with 1889, the players would have in the latter year roughly 30 percent more in pay, on a rough 300 percent raise in the net receipts, out of which the club officials made previously unthought of profits. Third: The National League's talk about clean, honest play was tied to a desire to flush out from the grandstand the allegedly foul-mouthed, odorous, and tacky-looking working class and replace them with a higher class of people willing and able to pay double the standard ticket price: a half-dollar instead of a quarter. To this end the League resorted to puritanical measures: no beer at the game; no Sunday games; no cussing and excessive drinking by ball players; plus assorted innovations catering to the bourgeois notions of conspicuous consumption, such as the cushioned box seat.

The original sales pitch given to attract a more bourgeois clientele was the argument that the National League represented eight distinctively first-class clubs—sort of an exclusive attraction, comparable to first-run Broadway theater. Any team not in the League was supposedly either second-class or a bunch of crooks.

Press reaction to the new League was generally unfavorable, and press opposition could be found even in cities with a National League franchise. The League's stand on the gambling issue appeared hypocritical. Supposedly its eight member clubs were the eight most honest clubs available. But the Mutuals were in the National League. In the opinion of the St.

Louis *Globe-Democrat* of February 4, 1876, this club was obviously included for its "gate receipts . . . alone. This club has been accused of more crooked playing than any other in the arena." The Hartford *Times* and New York *Clipper* strongly protested that the National League's exclusion policy branded players on unaccepted teams as crooks unworthy of employment. The New Haven *Register* found the League hypocritical in saying it was only open to stock-company organizations and then admitting the New York Mutuals, who had become a player-run cooperative after the breakup of the Tweed Ring that had supported the team.

In the opinion of the New York *Herald*, "no more baseball gambling" was a worthy goal; but the new league seemed to go beyond this in its constitutional provisions granting territorial monopolies. The *Herald* noted with alarm that "according to the Constitution," when the White Sox or Red Stockings came to the New York area no club except the Mutuals was going to be allowed a game with the visitors—a ruling granting no exceptions "even with the consent of the other members of the League."

Hulbert had taken special precautions to keep Henry Chadwick of the *Clipper*, the most influential sportswriter in the nation, from knowing in advance the real purpose of the meeting in the Grand Central Hotel. Hulbert figured correctly that Chadwick would side with the baseball majority, the excluded clubs. The National League bombshell caught Chadwick by surprise and he responded with a caustic editorial in the *Clipper*. He deeply resented being lied to, having been told the meeting had been called to discuss reform.

Chadwick declared that the League founders must have known their plan had little public support or they wouldn't have resorted to "closed doors and a star-chamber method of attaining the ostensible objects in view." Chadwick was committed to the continued expansion of the professional game, and he interpreted the policies of the National League as being anything but expansive.

Chadwick's *Clipper* was the one widely distributed national

sporting magazine of the time emphasizing baseball; and it
became the principal organ of the press for opposition to the
National League, an opposition Chadwick helped to organize
into a rival league, which he championed until its demise in
1879. Chadwick was an Englishman by birth, who had come
to the United States at the age of thirteen. In 1858 he joined
the staff of the *Clipper*, which was then primarily a theatrical
journal, as it is again today under the title *Variety*. Chadwick
built and expanded the *Clipper*'s sporting section, while on the
side editing sports annuals and writing for numerous newspapers. He is the only member of Baseball's Hall of Fame
enrolled for work as a sportswriter, his contribution through
this medium earning him the title "Father of Baseball." The
clippings in the scrapbooks of his personal papers show him to
have had a wide range of interests: theater, history, and politics as well as sports. He was fifty-two years of age in 1876,
and his reactions to the National League were those of a man
from a generation that had known an America without cor-
porations and monopolies. He represented an opposition to
monopoly having little in common with trade unionists, but
standing instead on bourgeois ideals of open competition in
the marketplace and in sports. His was the consensus view-
point. The tactics of the robber barons were live news then;
the public wasn't confused when it came to whether or not J.
D. Rockefeller was a good American. It said right there in the
paper that Rockefeller was going to be righteously thrown in
jail if he set foot again in Pennsylvania, where he had swin-
dled hardworking oilmen out of their land and wells. And
when a judge overturned this indictment, the papers noted that
he had been appointed by a governor who was a friend of
Rockefeller; the papers made such connections in those days.
During the Industrial Revolution damnation of the "pluto-
crats" and "monopolists" found favorable response, not only
among workers and craftsmen but among storekeepers and
professionals. The highest politicians in the land spouted the
antimonopolist creed. President Grover Cleveland, a conservative as Democrats go, was nonetheless the stump speaker

who declared: "Monopoly is ruining our land, robbing the nation of its wealth and the citizens of their spirit, and all in the pursuit of an absolute domination that all righteous Americans must oppose."

In terms of the future of American professional sports, the most far-reaching innovation of the National League was probably the idea of territorial rights, which would become a bulwark of the professional system, accepted by the public as one accepts the axioms of geometry and the law of gravity. But when first instituted by the League the idea of territorial rights did strike many Americans as an odd notion, and it created a suspicion as to the purpose intended, which caused the instigators to cloak their design. The National League's public explanation for choosing for membership only one club in Philadelphia, the Athletics, and excluding the Philadelphia Phillies, was that the latter team, allegedly, had crooked players. Chadwick retorted that the National League was afraid of the public reaction to a straightforward application of its territorial rules, and consequently a "glaring inconsistency . . . is apparent in the throwing-out of the Philadelphia Club for its 'irregularities'—that is the mild term, we believe—while another club in the League is countenanced in its engagement of players guilty of the very 'irregularities' for which the former is punished."

In spite of its careful planning, the National League barely survived the season of 1876. The Chicago all-star team won 79 percent of its League games and was apparently the only club to turn a profit. The Mutuals and Athletics didn't have the funds to finish their schedules, a breach of the rules for which they were summarily expelled from the League. That the League survived at all was due in no small part to the extensive scheduling of exhibition games with excluded teams. Here were grudge matches filled with a special tension. The stereotype of old-time baseball fans as epithet-screaming maniacs was probably never more accurate than in these contests. The League clubs lost thirty-seven of these games, as tabulated by Chadwick. The League apparently won many more than that number, but Chadwick doesn't list their wins, an omission that can be attributed to his prejudices on the matter.

The NL teams supposedly had started the season in possession of sufficient funds to buy up whatever high-quality talent was available; high-salary lists were considered one cause of the League's financial difficulty. As Chadwick noted, the League, for all its money, had still left plenty of quality players spread throughout the half a hundred professional clubs on the outside. Apparently, many pro players preferred to take less in order to play for their hometowns. Then too, in baseball, as in the theater of this time, there was not yet any stigma attached to playing to small-town audiences.

The big metropolis was, however, coming to be seen as a threat to the social and economic health of many a middle-sized urban community. The 75,000-population minimum for National League cities was, for example, a threat to the prestige value of ball clubs in towns of lesser size, just as the corporate economic power of the metropolis was a threat to the independent small-town businessman.

The battle on the sporting front took a new turn in February 1877 when representatives of eighteen clubs met in Pittsburgh to form a new association to replace the old National Association which Hulbert, Spalding, and Company had killed. In a foreword to their constitution the delegates at Pittsburgh condemned "serious abuses" of the character of baseball and declared that "many true and tried friends had become so thoroughly disgusted with these irregularities that they determined to eradicate the abominations. As a result, the International Association of Professional Baseball Players was fully organized in the interest of reform." The New York *Herald* reported the delegates leaving Pittsburgh "elated" over the new organization's "strong representation and substantial evidence of prosperity."

The new association couldn't openly condemn the League without jeopardizing the profitable grudge matches between the two organizations, which both sides were going to need in the ensuing struggle. It would be a battle between two organizations created amid flowery rhetoric about "reform" while the fundamental differences between the two groups were glossed over by both sides.

The International Association was obviously based on the assumption that in baseball, at least, power could be shared with those engaged in "the actual work of production." Pitcher Candy Cummings, inventor of the curve ball pitch, was elected president. Cummings was also president of the Lynn Live Oaks club; the president of the Association's entry in St. Louis was a player–saloon keeper; and a player had organized and brought in the Rochester entry.

The Association clearly stood on the premise that in baseball small cities and big ones could compete in the same organization. During its three years of existence the IA had teams in dozens of cities, including such cozy towns as Lynn, Lowell, Holyoke, and New Bedford, Massachusetts; Utica and Auburn, New York; and Allentown, Pennsylvania. They also had franchises in St. Louis, Pittsburgh, Buffalo, Brooklyn, and Washington, D.C. The International Association not only admitted to membership clubs from cities of whatever size; it put no restriction on the number of clubs competing for its pennant race, aside from an added dues fee, which was paid by seventeen of the more than two dozen clubs which held membership in its first year. Whereas the National League was operating according to Hulbert and Spalding's concept of an exclusive top-quality sports show in the major metropolitan marketing areas, the International Association was aiming to run a version of pro baseball after the fashion of present-day college basketball, which has competition among colleges big and small in cities big and small. If Peter Axthelm is right in calling college basketball the last bastion of hometown spirit, then the International Association of Professional Baseball Players was the first bastion.

The Industrial Revolution in the United States was transforming the community and in the process setting the stage for

mass culture. On the sporting front, the International Association's strongholds were the small towns of New England and
upstate New York—traditional, tightly knit communities that
were built around a town square rimmed by the brick buildings of the merchants and the whitewashed frame of the favored church. In the age of industry and the new metropolis,
identification with one's community was sorely tested. The
prestige value to the smaller city of a baseball team that could
compete with the metropolis must be seen in the light of both a
growing centralization of economic power and an incredible
demographic transformation. Farms were being abandoned by
the thousands. The rush was to certain urban areas and not
others. In Ohio of the 1880s, 755 out of 1,315 townships
declined in population; in Illinois, 800 out of 1,424. The
boom-and-bust phenomenon was by no means exclusive to
Wild West cow towns and mining camps. Everybody seemed
to be on the move. Even staid Boston was affected; 80 percent
of those in the Boston census of 1880 did not have their names
on the city census of 1890.

The International Association had its metropolitan clubs,
but what it really represented was the organized expression of
an immense popularity of baseball in the smaller industrial
city. These are the places stereotyped today as "Dullsville";
they were quite something else in the late 1870s. Flooded with
refugees from the farm and immigrants from Europe, their
social fabric seemed to be coming apart at the seams. At voting time in International Association towns like Lynn, Lowell,
and Fall River, Massachusetts, and Binghamton and Lansingburgh, New York, there were as many people choosing the
socialistic Workingmen's party as the Republicans or Democrats. With the coming of the factories and the mills there
were, on the one hand, new social clubs for the families of
industrialists, and on the other hand, the fledgling trade unions
for the industrial proletariat. The leftovers, those standing in
the middle, tended to be the ones who got their names on the
officers' list of the new professional ball club.

Of 129 known officers of clubs in the International Association, the biggest number, 52, were white-collar workers, typically in retail sales or city government; there were 13 blue-collar workers; 11 players; 35 members of the mercantile class such as shopkeepers, hotel keepers, theater owners, contractors, and the like; and 11 factory or mill owners, 4 of these backing the New Bedford, Massachusetts, team.

Rallying the populace for some scheme to boost the old hometown is a specialty of the politicians, a group which the International Association had in abundance, including the mayors of Worcester, New Bedford, Manchester, Albany, Springfield, Lansingburgh, and Columbus. There were also five future mayors, the son of a mayor, and one who ran for mayor and didn't make it; and there might have been other mayoral candidates too, but the voting records in a number of cities are too obscure to unearth them.

The season of 1877 opened with fifty-four professional clubs in operation. Remarkably, there wasn't a one in New York City, the now-defunct Mutuals having given the game there a vile reputation. Baltimore, then the fifth largest city in the nation, didn't have a club either; nor did Washington, D.C. The National League entered the fray with six clubs, located in Boston, Hartford, Cincinnati, Louisville, St. Louis, and Chicago. The unwieldy International Association had taken $10 entrance fees from nearly two dozen clubs, but only about half that number expected to play a full IA schedule.

The season provided the first among a number of cases in the history of American pro sport where one organization, run strictly for financial profit, was pitted against another run not only for the money but also for the social and political profit to be gained from hometown glory. It was a season in which confusion reigned in the IA, with incessant arguments over whose games counted in what standings. There were New England and New York State subdivisions in the IA—in effect, leagues within leagues. In the NL gloom prevailed from the beginning of the season to the end. In June the Cincinnati franchise folded, briefly. It was out of business just long enough for President Hulbert of Chicago to send out an emissary to buy up three star players from the Cincinnati club. The outcry against this action forced Hulbert to give back one star, and he would be punished for his greed. Publisher Joseph Medill of the Chicago *Tribune* found the pirating act so disgusting that until Hulbert's death in 1881 the *Tribune* refused to run stories, or even the scores, of Chicago White Sox games; and the *Tribune* had the biggest, most widely read sports section in the Midwest.

The Chicago club was the only one in the League to turn a profit in '77, one western paper estimating the combined losses of the other five clubs at $17,300. Hartford, St. Louis, and Louisville folded—the latter collapsing in part because of the scandal surrounding the expulsion from its team of four players found selling games to gamblers. With the failure in St. Louis, added to the previous loss of New York and Philadelphia in 1876, the National League was now without clubs in three of the nation's four biggest cities. At this stage in the battle between corporate and cooperative baseball, the cooperative nines appeared to be winning. The pro game was kept alive in St. Louis by the player-run cooperative of the International Association, and in Philadelphia by an independent coop, the Athletics. The majority of the clubs in the Association were cooperatives, paying players through gate receipts rather than salaries; the Association had proven impressive enough in '77 to attract many additional clubs for the '78 season.

Considering baseball as a spectator sport, the loosely constructed Association was spreading the game, becoming a success. It was, however, up against an organization predicated on turning the sport into an amusement business, and doing so regardless of the negative consequences. By the season of 1880, the consequences would be the extinction of the International Association and a reduction in the number of regularly scheduled professional teams from over fifty to a mere twelve, eight of them in the National League.

This collapse of the pro game was in part related to the severe economic depression which the nation suffered through during the late 1870s. However, the economy was already depressed in 1877 when the number of professional nines almost doubled, and the economic bottom was reached in 1878, a year which saw a further increase in pro ball teams. The principal effect of the depression was in delaying the takeover of the game by the National League; since its clubs were run as businesses, it was going to be hurt more by a business slump than would be cooperatives run on a shoestring and prayers. The difference here was between one type of club trying to meet player salaries of $1,000 to $2,000 and another type of club in which players were generally paid from the gate receipts and got by on a few hundred dollars a year. For example, when Cincinnati's NL club folded briefly during the 1877 season its players reacted immediately with an offer to finish out the schedule as a cooperative.

For the League to achieve its ultimate objective of monopoly it had at first to move most cautiously against its International Association opposition. What one historian termed "the more relaxed atmosphere" of the Association had made it attractive to a good percentage of the better ball players, and the League had to be careful or it might lose others as well. One reason for choosing the Association was that it gave the working athlete a hand in running club affairs. The idea that a craftsman of any trade deserved a measure of control over the workshop was then quite strong. Labor studies have shown that a high percentage of the strikes of the 1870s and 1880s were related to opposition of workers to their proletarianization; that is, opposition to the instituting of shop foremen, to the division of labor that reduced the control of a given worker from, for example, the making of a whole shoe to a simple, repeated task of gluing, stitching, leather cutting, and the like.

Albert Spalding knew well the threat of the IA. When he first heard that a meeting was going to be held in Pittsburgh to create a rival association, he set to work to appease the opposition with statements about friendly competition within the baseball fraternity, and explanations that National League

clauses concerning territorial rights didn't mean League clubs
would refuse to visit non-League cities, or not allow non-
League clubs to visit and play League clubs in return. He did
insist, however, that when and wherever the League played
the ticket price had to be 50 cents, the ball used had to be the
League ball, the umpire a League umpire, and so on. The
League issued a statement that it would respect player contracts of Association teams, and they were generally respected
during the season of 1877, at least.

In 1877 the League lost no fewer than seventy-two times
to outside clubs; and discounting games with amateur outfits
and pickup nines, the League appears to have won barely
more than half of its games played against outside professionals. Despite its high-priced tickets and other classy features, the League was no more than the equal of the 1877
International Association in playing talent, with the players in
the top six IA clubs having more past and future years of "big
league" baseball among them than had the six clubs of the
NL.

In 1878 the National League moved openly to financially
squeeze out the small-town clubs. The League office issued a
decree prohibiting outside clubs from playing in League ball
parks. The League teams had stadiums with gate-receipt potential far beyond that of most IA clubs. Under the new arrangement Boston of the NL was free to play the Lowell club
in the latter's 2,000-seat ball park, but not in the former's
park, which had a capacity of 10,000. The Boston directors
angrily protested the League ruling. In 1877 Boston had
drawn quite well in home games against small-town teams
from New England. The Bostons had even agreed to a special
showdown series with the New England Association champions—Lowell—which Lowell had won.

The Association still had a dozen clubs competing for its
championship and another dozen nominal members, this leaving a sizable number of independent clubs which the National
League was gradually enrolling in a "League Alliance," an
organization whose members were promised a number of

dates with League clubs and given a form of territorial rights. These really didn't amount to much; an Alliance club was assured it was the only one in its area that would get a game with a League team, but the League still had the right to come to town with two League teams which would play each other, these "neutral court" games being rather common. The prime function of the Alliance was in helping the League to divide and conquer the small-town competition. Alliance clubs were invited to send in applications requesting a franchise in the League, and in 1878 some Association clubs were found also among those asking for a franchise. The clubs which by reason of town size, and weak financing, had no possible chance to ever get into the National League roundly condemned the breaking of ranks. Among the protestations was a circular sent to every club in New York State by the secretary of the Auburn Club, prison clerk Underhill, who urged them to "stick together and kick together." Shortstop Dave Force of Buffalo, upon hearing that his IA club was toying with the idea of joining the League, exclaimed: "I heard that we was going to Join the League. I hope & pray not for if we do we are gone financially . . . for there is nothing in it."

Distrust and suspicion as to the designs of club officers seemed to infect the players. During the 1878 season players were found scheming to get out from under their contracts in alarming numbers, so as to make themselves available in the raids of rich clubs for the players of poorer ones; according to Chadwick both the League and the Association were guilty in this respect. Still, those who jumped were generally "ye olde revolving ball players" habituated to the practice, such as Ross Barnes; he had been one of those who jumped from Boston for a fat contract with Chicago in 1876; and in 1878 he jumped into the International Association. A number of those who jumped clubs were players with seamy reputations. Cincinnati got one of these from Syracuse in Will Geer. He had begun his professional career in 1874, playing some suspiciously inept outfield for the New York Mutuals. He was next found in upstate New York, the organizer and manager of the

Ku Klux Klan Club of Oneida (race prejudice was apparently rampant everywhere). His club didn't last, and he moved on to receive notoriety in September 1875, when he was arrested, along with his roommate in the New Haven club. The two were charged with burglary. It seemed that as the New Haven club traveled from city to city there were a suspicious number of guests at the hotels used by the ball club reporting missing property. As reported in the press: "The players were noticed on the tour in various cities, leaving their hotels with extra baggage. Detectives were put on the tail of the players leading to the arrest of them on the stealing . . . charge." The roommate was reported winning an acquittal in court, but what happened to Will Geer is not known, other than that he was out of circulation for a couple of years.

The pirating of playing talent in 1878 seemed to stem from desperation on the part of club officials. Keeping fans in those economic hard times was difficult enough; and the situation was made worse by the League's ban on hosting outside clubs, and by a decision on the part of most IA clubs, in turn, not to host League teams. Consequently, clubs were unable to draw spectators by offering many different attractions; so they had to put more emphasis on winning in contests treating the hometown faithful to repeated showings of the same opposition. To be a winner means to have top players—hence the increase in talent hunts. To appreciate the gravity of the situation facing baseball in this year, one has to keep in mind that many of the come-ons drawing fans to ball parks in the twentieth century were missing back then. There was no World Series; there was no batting-title hoopla; there were no fifty-year records to shoot for; sanctimonious utterances about "the big-league game" carried little or no weight; the whole idea of professional sports was suspect in many people's opinion. Then, too, the notion that the fan should be content to watch his or her team play only six, or eight, or a dozen teams a year had yet to become an axiom of natural law.

For the 1878 season there would be few winners in financial terms. Lagging attendance figures were all the more agonizing in view of the special costs of stealing players. Apparently no club wanted to risk lawsuits by grabbing a player under contract to another club. Special inducements, therefore, had to be offered to players to get them to agree to the tactic of purposely playing so poorly they would be given their release from the contract; at this point, much to the disgust of many in the baseball world, the player would be immediately picked up by the club that had wanted him in the first place. Among the NL clubs, Chicago was once again the only one to turn a profit. Milwaukee and Indianapolis folded, the owner of the latter team losing so much money that he was forced to flee the state to escape his creditors. A good portion of his debt had been incurred before the start of the season on his trip into Canada, from which he returned with most of the talent on the Guelph (Ontario) Maple Leafs of the IA.

The ace in the hole for the National League in its struggle for survival was its ability to get the more financially profitable clubs of the Association to accept a franchise and start charging 50 cents a game in accordance with League regulations. Providence had deserted the IA–related New England Association for the NL in 1878. In '79 the League took in Buffalo, the IA champion; Syracuse, the runner-up; and Troy, the New York State Association powerhouse. A new club from Cleveland was also added, giving the League an eight-team circuit for the first time in three years. In the case of Troy, admission to the League seemed to make the club attractive to a higher class of backer, including a clothing manufacturer and an alderman who was soon to open a savings bank.

Surveying the coming season in the March 2, 1879, *Clipper*, Chadwick declared that "there has never been a better opportunity" for putting the International Association "on a permanent foundation." Actually, his favored organization was in desperate straits. He had championed its cause because he believed it to be the protector of the pro game in all its forms, the only "truly national professional association," whereas "none but clubs competent by their wealth as stock companies . . . can enter the League. Hence it is not a national association in the proper and thoroughly representative meaning of the term." Should the IA fail, Chadwick foresaw a worsening of the "chaotic condition" facing the "cooperative professional clubs," these still being found in sizable numbers, particularly in the smaller industrial cities. Were the deterioration of these clubs to go unchecked, Chadwick feared, they would be driven to suspicious showboating and ties with the gambling crowd, spreading "the very evils the League . . . aims to put a stop to."

The Father of Baseball had little in the way of a workable solution for saving the coops and the other non-League clubs. His shortcoming in this regard was much the same one found among the small businessmen fighting corporate monopoly—they were not in a position to force self-regulation in industry, and they couldn't accept government regulation, although many of them in this era did accept the idea of government regulation of monopoly. Henry Chadwick wasn't going to argue for legislative or court regulation of baseball. If he or one of his fellow sportswriters wasn't going to argue the case, nobody else was either. Organized labor—judging by its journals of this era—didn't see fit to bother with the professional sports crowd one way or the other. Pro ball was, after all, a business, in a dog-eat-dog business world. As for Chadwick, realizing that those who survived in baseball did so by forming stock companies, he now conceded a need for the International Association to have all clubs competing for the championship pennant organized into stock companies. He urged, however, that beyond a well-knit dozen or so clubs playing for the pennant "it is absolutely necessary that the terms for simple admission to membership [in] the International Association should be of the most liberal character." In no uncertain terms Chadwick warned the Association that it courted disaster and hurt the game as a whole if it chose to be picky about scheduling games with clubs that might be below its members' level. That is the way of the National League, which, Chadwick noted, "was dangerous alike to the pecuniary and to the popular interests of the League clubs."

The business angles of the game were still open to question, but they were getting a grudging acceptance, even among the workers in the industry. The loyalty to the Association which the players had displayed in 1877 was gone entirely in 1879. The luster of being in on club management was gone when the club could no longer put bread on the table and keep the rent paid. If the officers of Association clubs were so free to jump at a chance for a National League franchise, then, reasoned the players, why shouldn't they jump to get a National League salary? There was another inducement having little to do with economics. The League had pirated enough talent to field an impressive lineup of teams, and since the number of their games with outside opposition was limited, the talented players on the outside were not getting the opportunities they had once had to go up against others of known talent. In 1879, for the first time, to play in "the League" was coming to be something of a status symbol.

The small-city outfits began to fold and their better representatives jumped to the National League (which didn't seem to mind overlooking its requirement of a 75,000-population minimum to take in the likes of Troy, Syracuse, and then Worcester, which was the IA champion in 1879). In 1880 and 1881 the number of teams outside the League playing a regular schedule of games could be counted on one hand. Hundreds of players had been driven back to the factories, mills, or pool halls from whence they came.

The problems for professional baseball were made worse by the rising tide of blue-nosed Victorian opposition to sports, gaming, and booze. In many places the moralizers had succeeded in having pool halls taxed and regulated, driving many of them out of business, and in the process cutting off professional baseball from one of its sources of financial aid.

It appeared to some representatives of propriety and morality that baseball was about to die out. In their view it had never been more than a fad in the first place. The *New York Times* concluded in 1881 that the world of baseball was in such sorry shape that cricket might soon replace it as the national pastime, in the process restoring sports dominance to "gentlemen" and abolishing crass professionalism once and for all.

One of the curious things about professional baseball in this period was the failure of both the NL and the IA in many of the most populous metropolitan centers, where the idea of a one-team baseball monopoly was slow to take hold. During the late 1870s and early 1880s, six of the eight biggest sports-marketing areas in the nation were lacking organized intercity-league professional baseball. Pro ball hadn't completely failed in New York, Philadelphia, Brooklyn, Baltimore, and for a lesser period St. Louis and Pittsburgh. It was the idea of territorial monopoly that failed. Ball fans in these metropolitan cities supported many unaligned teams, most of them being run as cooperative nines. Each club developed its own constituency, often through politics, as was the case for the Republican Athletics and Democratic Phillies, the Democratic Atlantics and Republican Eckfords. In New York, Tammany Hall had a sizable "Junior League" of semi-pro outfits which played before large crowds. In places like the Prospect Park grounds in Brooklyn large crowds gathered, for free, to watch a day-long succession of semi-pro and so-called amateur teams. In enclosed stadiums the top teams drew crowds that paid a dime to a quarter to watch contests which led to showdown games in the fall for the city championship. The National League claimed that its six-year absence from metropolitan New York and Philadelphia was due the rampant dishonesty of the pro game in those places; the game there allegedly wasn't respectable enough for a respectable league. The League would have been more honest itself if it had acknowledged that it would have had difficulty getting up a stock company in New York, Philadelphia, or Brooklyn. The financial prospect of a National League franchise, and its concomitant 50-cent charge for an exclusive showing of the visiting League nines, just didn't look all that appealing. That is, it wasn't going to be all that appealing until the League had managed to corner the market on talented players. Then it

could successfully advertise a sports exclusive, and in the burgeoning metropolitan cities "big league ball" could become the
choice of the hip sports fans, who had earlier given their loyalty to a club of more intimate acquaintance, the one whose
players hung out at the fans' favored pool hall, saloon, or
ward heeler's office.

For professional leagues, the experience of the first decade
showed that the unifying of players', fans', and sponsors' interests was most readily accomplished in the smaller urban centers, places where the words "our town" evoked a community
spirit which could be easily channeled into support for "our
team." Other pro sports would begin by establishing footholds
in similar towns. "Big league" baseball for the period 1871–
1890 had franchises in many of the same places that would
later put the National Football League and National Basketball Association on the map: Rochester, early NFL and NBA;
Providence, early NFL and NBA; Hartford, NFL; Syracuse,
NBA; Toledo, NFL; Ft. Wayne, NBA; and Columbus, NFL.
Consider "big league" baseball in Troy, Worcester, Keokuk
(Iowa), Altoona (Pennsylvania), New Haven, Richmond,
and Middletown (Connecticut); and consider football's Hammond, Pottsville, Newark, Canton, and Massilon; basketball's
Ft. Wayne, Sheboygan, Anderson (Indiana), and the Tri-
Cities, and it becomes apparent from these few examples
among many that professional sports have to first establish
themselves where "hometown" spirit can be generated before
the sports become self-sufficient amusement businesses in the
metropolitan centers with their major television marketing
areas.

During the Industrial Revolution of the late nineteenth century, the popularity of baseball in the small industrial city was
not a product of a dead town looking for thrills, but stemmed
rather from an excitement brought on by rapidly changing
social patterns, and by intense conflict on the labor front.
Baseball thrived in places which are today lucky to draw a
crowd for a Fourth of July celebration, and which were then
the scene of repeated parades and mass demonstrations by

trade unionists. The impact of labor in industrial towns of the 1870s and 1880s can be seen from a cursory glance at the delegate lists for national conventions of the largest labor organization of the period, the Knights of Labor. The lists are dominated by representatives from places like Lynn, Lowell, Binghamton, Reading, and other International Association–type towns.

In towns where a parade of striking workers was as common as the periodic parades of temperance crusaders or political parties, a parade organized to promote the opening of the new baseball season was a natural addition. Included among the promoters in the towns were sporting types such as were found in the big city. The sportswriters, poolroom keepers, and sponsors of rowing regattas and sprint races were hometown boosters with a special purpose—selling community spirit and unity where diverse social groups seemed to be at one another's throats: old residents and new, immigrants and old-stock Americans, industry and labor. There was a liveliness in all this, and at all levels an intense competitiveness in regard to the economic, cultural, and social threat of the big metropolis—an across-the-board hostility to the metropolis giving added weight to the ranting of small-town baseball promoters when they proclaimed that their players could "knock the stuffing out of the old Leaguers."

The vibrance of the towns in this period of the nation's history could be seen in regard to the theater. The national theatrical as well as sporting journal was the *Clipper*. Its advertising pages were cluttered with notices for small-town theaters which claimed to have excellent profit potential for visiting troupes of actors, vaudeville and minstrel shows, circus acts, and the like. In turn, the leading acts advertised for a chance at getting into the town auditoriums. Take, for example, the ad for Buffalo Bill from the *Clipper*, November 24, 1877:

Receipts in Manchester
$1,543.65

THEY WERE THERE. EVERYONE OF THEM
SQUEEZED IN, PACKED IN . . .
Receipts in Portland
(notwithstanding a severe rainstorm the first night)
$1,430.63
Augusta Me.
the city all managers condemn and avoid visiting, styling
it the poorest show town in America . . .
$773.35

"Augusta Me." didn't have a professional ball team in this period either, nor did this "poor show town" have much of a rating on government lists of labor strikes.

Among the advertisements in the *Clipper* were those from ball clubs wanting to book games. The Lowell club of 1875 took an ad to announce it had a new enclosed park with a 2,000-seat capacity; the ad noted that Lowell was close to Boston and that any pro club visiting Boston would find it worthwhile to make the short trip for a game in Lowell. Then there were the ads placed by ball players, reading much like those taken out by actors: "W. Terry would like to engage in some professional nine for the season of '76. References A. F. Child's Washington; A. Allison Hartford." Teams advertised for players too: "A Pitcher and Catcher are wanted for the Cricket Club of Binghampton. Both must be First-Class."

Ball players often took acting jobs in the off season, and the identification of baseball with the theater didn't exactly enhance the reputation of the game among the respectable circles that saw actors as a decidedly immoral lot. And, too, mixed in with the "sporting" ads of the *Clipper* there were those for state lotteries, and for concerns like the "Sporting Man's Emporium," which featured among its paraphernalia "Marked Cards—The Greatest Variety, Latest Styles. . . . We Can Enable You to Win At Every Game."

The club owners of the National League had a vested interest in giving their baseball attraction a stature that was elevated above the game one saw in mill towns, just as first-run

Broadway theater was eventually to become elevated above
small-town summer stock. In both the sport and the theater
the means to this end was the star system, the elevation onto a
pedestal of a few talented heroes. There in the limelight they
would be shilled by sycophantic promoters extolling the rare
gifts of their prize actors or athletes. For the promoter to make
the most out of a star attraction it is best that the star be
owned, as one would own and display the only living dodo
bird, or the treasures of King Tut's tomb, which the Egyptian
government recently put on tour for much-needed currency.

Of course, owning a human being is prohibited in this country by the Thirteenth Amendment to the Constitution. When
theater promoters tried to hold their star players to contracts
binding them to one financial source for life, these reserve
clauses were rather quickly struck down in the courts. The
player reserve clause in baseball would prove to be a different
story—a source of conflict and hot debate extending over a
century from the National League meeting in Buffalo on September 29, 1879, when it was first voted into being. This date
coincided with the collapse of the International Association,
the only obstacle then in the way of giving the League a virtual monopoly on the professional game.

CHAPTER

6

The Promoters and Players of the 1880s

The 1880s were baseball's "Golden Age." The professional game mushroomed from one eight-team league at the start of the decade to seventeen leagues at the start of the 1887 season. It reached from Maine to the California League of the San Francisco area; from deep Dixie to the Red River League of the Dakotas. The decade also spawned a Colored National League and a Southern Negro League. Teams in the hinterlands rarely lasted more than a year or two, but there seemed no shortage of investors willing to create a new club where the old one had just failed.

The 1880s gave the game much of the flavor it still carries today; the period inaugurated the post-season World Series, the exhibition season in the sunny South, and the Western Union telegraph company inning-by-inning reports. Standard equipment for the grandstand spectator came to include a beer, a sausage, and a scorecard. Ernest Thayer immortalized mighty Casey of the Mudville nine.

The sandlot game expanded and became organized, with the better amateur teams renting the ball parks of the pros on the latter's off-days. "The Paregorics of Morrison, Plumber & Co., defeated the Castor Oils of Lord, Stoutenburg & Co., 21–13," noted the Chicago *Tribune* in its list of game reports

for July 9, 1882. By the end of the decade Chicago baseball
included a Wholesale Grocers League, a Commercial League,
a Mercantile League, a Market Street League, and a number
of other sandlot organizations.

Playing the game was affordable for everyone. While a regulation "professional league" baseball sold for $1.50 in 1886,
balls of lesser quality could be had for half the price; and then
there were the spheres known as "popular base balls," which
looked like the real thing, and even had stitches, and went for
a dime—or in the case of the "O.K." brand, for a nickel. Low-
cost equipment was a by-product of mass-production techniques in the expanding sporting goods industry, which was
one of the first American industries to use the assembly line.
Scientific American described the Overman Works in Chico-
pee, Massachusetts, where bicycles and baseballs were manufactured, as "nothing but a huge machine."

Sports in the eighties benefited greatly from the enlarged
daily newspaper. Technical improvements, including a high-
speed printing press and the Mergenthaler linotype machine,
made a cheap and sizable daily paper possible; and innovative
publishers such as Joseph Pulitizer of the New York *World*
showed how increased column inches devoted to sports, and a
distinct "sports section," would increase circulation. Cheaper
printing costs led to a flood of new periodicals, including such
baseball magazines as *Sporting Life* in 1883, *Sporting News* in
1886, and *Sporting Times* in 1887. Sports earned a page in
the history of printing in 1887 when the New York *Tribune*
brought out *The Tribune Book of Open-Air Sports*; as explained on the frontispiece, "This Book is Printed Without
Type, being the First Product in Book Form of the Mergenthaler Machine which Wholly Supersedes the Use of Movable
Type."

Voigt and others have linked the sports boom to an increase
in people's leisure time, a byproduct of the Industrial Revolution. The increase in leisure, however, was minimal, the average industrial workday being reduced from twelve hours in
1870 to ten and a half hours in 1890. Perhaps a more impor-

tant factor was the structuring of time, both on and off the job. The monotonous labor of the factory hand and office clerk led them to seek a meaningful use of leisure. The organizing of ball teams went along with a movement for the creation of new social, economic, and political associations. Americans had long been noted as a nation of joiners, but never so dramatically as in the 1880s. The decade gave birth to the American Federation of Labor and innumerable trade associations of businessmen. The Salvation Army arrived in 1879 and spread widely in the ensuing decade. Older fraternal groups such as the Elks and the Knights of Pythias went from minuscule to national organizations, and well over a hundred new secret societies were formed, including the likes of the American Order of Druids and the Concatenated Order of Hoo-Hoo.

Baseball's Golden Age coincided with greater respectability for many forms of popular amusement. In previous times the purveyors of leisure for the masses had had difficulty separating their show from that of the bawdyhouse and gambling establishment. But popular amusement was cleaning up its act. As reflected in the sports and theater magazines, the advertisements for gambling equipment, love potions, prophylactics, and "French deck" picture cards, which had adorned the pages of the journals in the seventies, were now rare.

As baseball became more respectable so did the legitimate theater. Between 1880 and 1900 the number of actors increased from roughly 5,000 to nearly 15,000. Baseball promoters and theater owners and managers were often the same people, and many a ball player was engaged with an acting troupe during the winter. The circus reached the height of its popularity in this period, and for a time there were nearly forty touring companies, including the pace-setting Barnum and Bailey, who had combined their separate shows in 1881. In the field of musical theater, there was Gilbert and Sullivan's *Pinafore*, which arrived in the United States in 1878; during 1881 there were five simultaneous New York presentations of this comic operetta. Ethnic theater thrived on Manhattan's

Lower East Side in the form of Irish plays, performed on stages which a generation later would ring with the words of Yiddish playwrights.

Circuses, Gilbert and Sullivan, baseball, bicycling, roller skating, and other fads and fancies of the period were given added stimulation by a new breed of entrepreneur, the advertiser. Before the Civil War, advertising had been relegated to billboard posters and to newspaper notices in microscopic agate type. As of 1867 the total national expenditure on advertising was only about $50 million annually, but by 1900 the sum had risen to $500 million annually. The expanded newspapers and magazines did then what the electronic media have done for the ad industry in more recent times. By the mid-1880s advertising was being used extensively to promote sports, and sports in turn was used to promote business, as in the Michigan Central Railroad advertisement stating that this was "The Way the League Clubs Travel," and the ad noting that the United States Hotel was "Boston headquarters for all League Clubs."

Baseball's Golden Age occurred at a time when the American economy was moving in an upward direction and consumers' purchasing power was increasing. A number of League clubs were beginning to sell enough of their 50-cent tickets to turn a profit, and then in 1882 the American Association came along with its bargain 25-cent ticket and far outstripped the profits of the League. The rush was then on to put pro baseball in just about every sizable town with a mainline railroad connection. Nevertheless, it was still a highly speculative business, attracting more than its share of eccentric individualists and fly-by-night operators. How the flamboyant club owner became a fixture in the baseball scene is a story around which the particulars of the game in the 1880s may be described.

Baseball in the eighties was for the most part classical free enterprise, unlike the modern closed system in which the major-league clubs own or control most of the lesser clubs, and the big-league owners are almost guaranteed a profit. The club owners of a century ago were speculators and took the risks of speculators. With a handful of exceptions they all ended up run out of the game, even those in the National League. There were the many who left the game bankrupt; there were the few who took a handsome profit and got out while the getting was good; and there were others who were driven out on various larceny charges.

The mystique of baseball is built not only on the triumphs of its heroes but also on their fall; the Babe Ruth story is in part his 60-home-run season for the 1927 Yankees and in part his miserable 1935 finale with the Boston Braves: 6 home runs and a .181 batting average. A century ago the club owners as well as the players had their rise and fall.

From the point of view of business efficiency, pro baseball a century ago was all too chaotic. But it did develop elements of stability. Between 1880 and 1887 the Chicago White Sox, led by Cap Anson, won five National League pennants and became the prototype for the later New York Yankee pennant-consuming teams. The role played by the Philadelphia Phillies was of equal importance. The Phillies entered the National League in 1883 and did not win their first pennant until thirty-three years later. The repetition of championships by sports dynasties unavoidably creates the pathetic melodrama of the perennial losers: the Phillies, the St. Louis Browns, the Washington Senators, and more recently the Chicago Cubs.

Minimal fan support for the doormats is essential for the league system, which when operating at maximum efficiency presents a continuing sports soap opera of the same franchises operating from the same cities year after year. During the 1880s the National League had to drop lower-division franchises in eleven cities. Teams jumped leagues frequently during the eighties, creating the kind of excitement generated in recent times by big-league expansion teams. The forerunners of the Dodgers went from the Inter-State to the American to the National. Shifting franchises, new leagues, and expansion minimized the doormat problem, and for the clubs that did get in the rut there were other remedies.

For the suffering fan of a lousy team the promoters of the 1880s hit upon a number of inducements to attendance which are still part of the game today. A long season assures at least a few victories for the doormats, and the longer the season the greater the chance of catching one of the top teams on a day when it is not putting out 100 percent effort. In 1880 the National League played an 84-game schedule. In 1884 it went to 112 games, in 1886 to 124, and in 1888 to 132 games.

Sportswriters of the eighties played up stars of the diamond the way theater reviewers were personalizing and selling the stars of the stage. Boston finished fifth in the National League in 1886 and again in 1887; but attendance was way up the second year, thanks to the acquisition of the batting champion and base-stealing specialist Mike Kelly.

Attending a game became a pleasant ritual. For some it was an opportunity to swill beer and act silly; most of the new teams of the eighties sold beer at games. Some fans enjoyed keeping score; the Harry Stevens scorecard dates from this decade. A big opening-day crowd has become customary in baseball, even for doormats. It is a custom developed in the 1880s, when the opening-day game was usually preceded by a parade down Main Street. In the long run the aspects of ritual and showmanship were as essential to the system as the hard-boiled economic policies of the National League—policies which have received all too much applause from baseball historians.

The National League–oriented cost-accountant's history of baseball puts great emphasis upon the League's invention of the player reserve clause, which among other things dramatically reduced the cost to the owners in players' salaries. However, all the other leagues and associations began without the use of the reserve, and as of 1887 only the National League and the American Association were using it. As Francis Richter of *Sporting Life* noted in a critical piece on the League, it did not grant the Minors "the right of reserva-

tion" until 1888, and preferred instead to maintain its own
privilege of pirating the top players of the Minors with im-
punity.

Specifically, the reserve clause was an extension of the anti-
tampering provision prohibiting owners from negotiating with
a player on another League team for that player's services in
the subsequent season. The clause gave management the right
to "reserve" the player's services for the next season. Since
each annual contract included the reserve stipulation, the
player was bound to that team for life, unless there was an
outlaw league around for him to jump to.

The reserve was initially instituted in 1879 by private
agreement among the owners, and then for the 1880 season
the clause was inserted in the players' contracts. Until 1883
only the top five players on each League team were reserved.
An often-published survey of Boston players' salaries for the
1879, 1880, and 1881 seasons shows that the salaries of the
reserved players dropped substantially. While the reserve may
well have been the salvation of some struggling National
League club owners, the game as a whole was little affected.

Early in November of '81 a group of promoters met in
Cincinnati, and proclaiming the slogan "Liberty for All," they
set about reviving competition in pro ball, in the form of a
new major league called the American Association. The organizers were a collection of former officials in the Inter-
tional League. They expected to make a good profit from their
policies of a 25-cent ticket, Sunday ball, and beer at the ball
park. The new association was known as "the beer-ball league,"
since there was beer or liquor money behind all six of its founding teams: Cincinnati, Pittsburgh, St. Louis, Baltimore, Louisville, and the Philadelphia Athletics. The club directors were
decidedly lower-middle-class. The Athletics were run by a
triumvirate including dive owner Charlie Mason, former
player and owner of a saloon and bookie establishment;
manager Billy Sharsig; and former player Lew Simmons, who
for many years had been a star performer in minstrel shows. It
was Simmons who obtained the financing for the Athletics in

the form of a $16,000 loan from Adam Forepaugh of Fore-
paugh's Circus. Louisville was run by a group of retail merchants and saloon keepers, a number of them Democratic
politicians. Cincinnati had the backing of some prominent
brewers, but the principal stockholder was soon to be the fish
merchant George Herancourt. The Association's president
was Denny McKnight, and publicity blurbs identified him as a
wealthy iron smelter; however, he had been only a bookkeeper
when he headed the officers' list of the Pittsburgh club in the
International Association, and by 1886 his iron business had
gone bankrupt and he was back at his former trade.

The leadership of the AA knew well that it had to move
cautiously in regard to the National League. The Association
refrained from going after any of the five players reserved for
each League club, but freely solicited the services of other
players in the League. No doubt the extension of the League's
reserve rule to cover full squads of players in 1883 was in
response to the Association's threat. The League accused the
Association of stealing players, and the Association made similar charges. One of the cases which ended up in the courts
resulted in the first of a number of instances in which local
jurists ruled that the reserve clause had no legal standing—
rulings which proved to be of no avail in the long run.

The Association was a sparkling success at the box office.
Apparently all its clubs turned a profit, while only Chicago
and Boston made money in the League. The Association had
launched the baseball boom, and there were those who reasoned: If there could be two major leagues, why not three?
The Union Association (which had beer money behind eight
of its twelve franchises) entered the fray for the 1884 season,
playing Sunday ball and charging a quarter for admission. The
Unions promised players more liberal working conditions, including contracts without a reserve clause. The American Association had also begun without the reserving of players, but
upon becoming a success the Association negotiated a truce
with the League and adopted the practice. The Union Association never reached that stage, lasting only one season.

The promoters were discovering there was a limit to the number of teams that could legitimately claim "big league" standing. But then there was the discovery of the untapped potential for pro ball in the Mudvilles, where brightly clad players performing in freshly painted new stadiums began to draw sizable crowds. The success of the American Association had encouraged promoters to create two minor leagues in 1883; each offered member clubs the option of scheduling Sunday games if they could get around blue laws and the pressure of the Sabbatarians. In 1884 there were seven "bush leagues," or Minors, in operation. By 1890 there were roughly 160 teams operating in back-country towns and small cities across the nation.

The stock company was the common form of organization —the membership club and cooperative forms having fallen into disuse. The team manager was often put in charge of keeping the books and making other financial arrangements, and representing the club at League meetings. The managers knew what was necessary to do in order to meet train schedules and keep hotel bills paid, since most of them were from the teams of a decade earlier, when players had taken a role in team financial affairs.

Itinerant sportswriters, ex-players, and other sporting types roamed the country testing local support for baseball in Paducah, Pueblo, Butte, and Waco. Few were as good at selling the game as was fast-talking Ted Sullivan. He had his start in 1879, when he handled a Dubuque, Iowa, team for the railroad company which funded it and employed him to run the concessions for the dining and smoking cars. During his quarter-century of small-town baseball promotion Sullivan acted variously as club manager, secretary, treasurer, and sometimes president. His business was creating teams; he rarely stayed in one place more than a year. Rumors as to where Sullivan was headed next added to the off-season gossip columns in *Sporting News* and *Sporting Life*. He did so much wheeling and dealing in railroad smoking cars that fellow promoter Ed Barrow tabbed the cars "Ted Sullivan specials." As a manager, Sullivan had a reputation for being tough with his players and for baiting the umpires.

Baseball histories have described the newfound popularity for the pro game almost exclusively in terms of the teams in the largest cities. Although the Leadville (Colorado) Blues and Birmingham Barons lacked the quality of the Chicago White Sox, those Mudvillian outfits deserve notice, for without the broad base at the bottom the show at the top would have been far less illustrious.

The professional game in the metropolis was ultimately reliant on a supply of talent that had to be trained and developed in the hinterlands. Through the territorial-rights provisions, pro sport in any metropolitan center was reserved to one team per league. To get the public to support the exclusive show, that one team had to be of special quality.

At a fundamental level baseball is a difficult sport to master —so difficult that an easier version of baseball called softball was invented. In the 1880s the difficulties were acknowledged by amateur athletic associations which allowed "amateur" teams to hire professional pitchers and catchers, because it was felt that without trained players in these positions the game could degenerate into endless bases on balls, wild pitches, and passed balls by the catcher.

At the start of the 1880s the number of players capable of performing up to twentieth-century major-league standards was minute. It had been only a decade since pitchers lobbed the ball to the plate in sandlot-softball style. During the 1880s the improvements in fielding among the professionals appear to have received more notice in the sports pages than did great hitting or pitching. In an era when all but the very best teams averaged around half a dozen errors a game, a shortstop who handled eleven chances without a muff made as much news as a pitcher who threw a no-hitter; a pitcher got almost as much favorable publicity for completing a game without giving up a walk as for not allowing any hits.

The minor leagues provided the training ground for the

improved players whose performances drew ever-larger crowds to major-league games. At the bottom of the professional ladder were organizations such as the Anthracite League of Pennsylvania. It was set up expressly to benefit local talent, and its constitution required that "the clubs must be composed of players from Schuylkill, Northumberland, and Carbon Counties, who have not played professionally this season and must have resided in the district at least three months." The Anthracite League was a decidedly low-paying organization. Its more capable players were subject to being pirated away by the better-paying Eastern League Scranton Miners or Wilkes-Barre Coal Barons. In turn, the major leagues raided the likes of the Coal Barons for talent, and did so rather regularly, even after an 1888 agreement through which minor leagues, for a fee of $250 to $1,000, could buy protection from major-league raids until the end of the playing season.

Until the season of 1888 the minor leagues did not have "the right of reservation," as Richter of *Sporting Life* explained. Up to that time the Majors refused to acknowledge attempts of the Minors to put their players under a reserve clause. The absence of the reserve clause in the Minors fostered instability, but it did allow the game to grow. To establish the Southern League, for instance, there had to be a means of getting players from northern clubs, since Southern League club owners were hard-pressed to find capable baseball talent in their own area. The South was still too rural for the urban game of baseball; and where there were cities, the bigoted club owners refused to consider the player prospects from the blacks in the population. *Sporting Life* noted that in the middle of the Southern League's third season it had hardly a single player from the South, and suggested that reports of poor play might have had something to do with "the northerners sick in the heat."

The so-called evil of the unreserved "revolving" ball players was essential to bring the professional game to Texas, to the Plains states, and to places like Leadville, Colorado, and

Butte, Montana. Many a skilled batsman and pitcher wandered out to California to enrich the professional game as it developed in the San Francisco Bay area. The California teams played the game on into December, and a number of major leaguers came out to San Francisco to get in a few more months of ball after the regular season back east had ended. Canadian professional teams, in Toronto, Montreal, Ottawa, Hamilton, London, and Guelph, mixed a surprising amount of local talent with "revolvers" from the States to make Canada an important part of the baseball world.

In boom towns the creation of a ball team was one quick way to provide the place with an identity; and becoming a rooter for the local nine helped newcomers from the farms condition themselves to the city. In the post-Reconstruction South there were very few locals with a sense of city ways, and when it came to organizing ball teams it was often the work of the carpetbagging players from the North, who doubled as managers and club officials and found financial support in the small Jewish communities. Jewish merchants helped to fund teams in New Orleans, Macon, Atlanta, Augusta, Mobile, Houston, and Birmingham. The Jewish contribution to southern baseball dated back before the Southern League. In New Orleans in the early 1880s, a league of black teams that played for gate receipts and prize money had been run by the Jewish leader and Republican politician W. L. Cohen. In other parts of the nation, there were many more Jewish backers of baseball.

The running of one of the new baseball leagues was a taxing and thankless task, and had it not been for the energy and leadership of many a hustler of sporting disposition the whole system of pro ball might never have gotten off the ground. Those lower-order journalists, the ones given the sports beat, made incalculable contributions to the organizing of the pro game. "Father" Chadwick of the *Clipper* set the style for newcomers, most notably the editors of the baseball magazines *Sporting News, Sporting Life,* and *Sporting Times*—editors who helped run minor circuits during the 1880s. The New

England League, one of the better-run minor organizations of the period, was organized by the former player and saloon keeper John P. Morrill, and run by a succession of three sportswriters and a Democratic politician from Lowell. The types who put together the Minors are reflected by the first presidents of the longest-lasting junior circuit in the game, the International League: 1884, Henry H. Diddlebock, Philadelphia sportswriter and city tax clerk, and W. C. Seddon, Richmond grocer and liquor dealer; 1885, Syracuse bartender George G. Campbell and Utica cigar box manufacturer Charles H. White; 1886, Sheriff Frank G. Gilbert of Buffalo.

The most important figures in the expansion of the game during the Golden Age had to have been the editors of the two leading baseball magazines, *Sporting Life* and *Sporting News*. Will and Al Spink of *Sporting News* devoted four columns of reporting on minor-league activity for every one column devoted to the Majors. Francis E. Richter of *Sporting Life* gave a similar emphasis to the happenings in those out-of-the-way places which today seem of no account in the world of sports. Richter had been the first to create a nationally circulated magazine devoted primarily to baseball, and when the Spink brothers came along three years later in 1886 they provided in one of the early issues of their *Sporting News* a biographical sketch of their editorial rival in Philadelphia, whose magazine they called "The Philadelphia Sewer."

Richter was described as a printer by trade, who had worked for a time as a shill for a theatrical troupe. Then he began writing "base ball squibs" for the *Sunday World*. "Being a shrewd calculating fellow, Richter saw that a base ball organ would pay. He made the acquaintance of Tom Dando, a printer, and the latter and his friends furnished the capital, about $900, with which the sheet was started. It has been a success and made money." The Spinks suggested that their rival had probably made most of the money to start *Sporting Life* in "poker rooms." For they had heard that "almost any day from about two in the afternoon until the wee small hours of the following morning this authority on the

National Game can be found raking in 'jack pots,' when he wins them over the green cloth. 'Jack Pot' Richter is his name among the sports now."

Will and Al Spink knew all about gambling. Their own journal appears to have been started with money from gambling houses in St. Louis, where *Sporting News* was published. During its first year the magazine carried regular reports of the goings-on among the wagerers of their city. Included were items with the appearance of payola plugs, such as: "At Wiseman's Pool Room you can bet on any odds from a quarter, fifty cents or one dollar up, the larger the bet the larger the win." The Spink brothers were former telegraph operators, and Will had been an officer of the Telegraphers Union and had played an important role in a telegraphers' strike. Judging by the election-time articles in their magazine, they appear to have been tied in with local Democratic politics. The Spinks were strong defenders of Sunday baseball, and of the right of club owners to sell beer at ball parks. Both *Sporting News* and *Sporting Life* supported the small-town teams in their fight to get protection from the player raids made by the major leagues.

The background of the Spinks brothers and Richter was typical of sportswriters, most of whom arose from the laboring classes, a good number being former ball players, umpires, concessionaires, and the like. They were a group whose guidance and insights were essential to the growth of the game. They often deserved the label "dandy," or "dude," as the Spinks brothers called Richter; but in this they were no different from the club owners of the day—such as San Francisco's J. J. Mone, "the snappy fellow with the whiskers," or Saginaw's imposing 250-pound J. J. Rusk, a man of fine clothes and good cigars, who, according to *Sporting Life*, "was far better looking than Mr. Nirdlinger or Mr. Morton," two other promoters in the Midwest. The sporting press seemed to find no end to club officials who were "energetic" or "hardworking." This they had to be. Running a ball team was a risky business. It was also a new type of enterprise, and those first into any venture are often destined to be brought to financial ruin by less creative but more methodical schemers. George W. Howe of Cleveland, who helped organize a club there for the American Association, certainly knew the unfortunate fall awaiting the innovators of the world. His uncle, Elias Howe, had been the inventor of the sewing machine and had had his patent to the machine stolen by Isaac M. Singer.

In the wild Golden Age of baseball, league officers had a special burden in handling seemingly endless complaints and problems. Managers sent in reports of opposing teams using cheap nonregulation baseballs; of fans being incited to violence against the visitors; of blacklisted or suspended players being used. The low-paid umpire often failed to show up, and substitutes were accused by the visiting clubs of being "homers." Hotel owners complained to league offices about visiting clubs leaving town without paying for their lodging. The manager of the Dayton club in the Ohio State League demanded that the League take action against the club's owners, who were alleged to have squandered the club's gate receipts in gambling. Arguments over scheduling were common, especially in regard to which teams got the best of it in terms of Sunday and holiday home games.

Among those who did the organizing for baseball there were bound to be a sizable number of fast-buck artists. Hustling the small towns was a thriving concern, not only for sportsmen but for circus troupes, theater companies, and traveling salesmen of all descriptions. Itinerant baseball promoters traveled from state to state making a living by juggling the books in ill-fated leagues over which they had set themselves up as president-treasurer-secretary. Among those who got caught in their schemes was Harry C. Smith, found taking kickbacks to grant franchises in his Indiana State League. Another con artist was manager James Jackson, who in 1888 organized a group of small towns along the Hudson River. By May 31 the Hudson River League was in dire financial trouble and about to fold. Jackson resolved he was not going to end up empty-handed. On that date his Albany team was to play in Newburgh, and Jackson arranged with the ticket taker to pocket the game's receipts. At the end of the game he told his players he had to go to the hotel, but instead he headed straight for the wharf; had the boat been on time, he and his accomplice might have made their getaway, but as it turned out they were almost lynched by angry bat-wielding players from both teams.

When the Southern League was launched in 1885, with Ted Sullivan's help, it sought to give itself stability by requiring each franchise to put up a "guarantee bond" to ensure that the club played the full season. Other leagues used these bonds, but their use in the Southern League was something special, a racket. The Southern League's bond was $1,500 to $2,000 per year, two to three times the usual fee. A few bigger cities (New Orleans, Memphis, Atlanta, and for a while Birmingham) could afford it, not only because of their size but also because they had Sunday ball. On the other hand, the smaller Bible Belt towns had too much Christian pressure to be allowed into the lucrative Sunday-game market. Small in size, and without Sunday ball, their franchises failed, thus contributing to the record of eleven League collapses in twelve tries, between 1885 and 1900. Despite the poor record the lure of pro ball was strong enough to continually draw suckers who put up big sums to get it in places like Macon and Augusta, Georgia, and Montgomery and Selma, Alabama. In 1887 the Southern League seemed to have run an auction granting franchises to the promoters in the towns paying the highest guarantees. In that season, as in others, the franchises in the Bible Belt towns would be out of business by July or August, at which point the Sunday-ball towns would divide up the guarantee bonds. Typically, at this point, the Sunday towns also called it a season, and waited till next year and another crop of suckers.

Cliques among club owners were common in many leagues.

In the International League those owners with clubs in the United States ganged up on the Canadian entries in 1885 to force the Canadians to grant visiting teams from the States a $100 guarantee per game; when the Canadian outfits visited the States they received only a $50-per-game guarantee. The Canadians had to accept this policy of economic colonialism in order to become part of organized pro ball.

Many a league meeting was conducted in an atmosphere of suspicion, with legal advisors at the ready to prepare suits and countersuits in case one group of club owners tried to freeze out another group. To get around constitutional restrictions on arbitrary expulsion of clubs, a clique in the International League in 1887 got a majority vote to dissolve the League entirely, and five minutes later the clique voted to create from among its own members a new entity called the Central League. Just as there were fights within leagues, there were stockholders' battles within clubs. The triumvirate which came to run the Boston club of the National League, for example, first had to overcome a court suit brought by minority stockholders.

Few stories of those who were run out of the game could match in seediness what happened to fish peddler George Herancourt, president of the Cincinnati Red Stockings in the American Association. In 1884 Herancourt ran up against the machinations of the power-hungry political boss John R. McLean, publisher of the Cincinnati *Enquirer*. McLean was then in a rather desperate situation politically; his ruthless rule of the city was about to come to an end as late in the year the citizens poured into the streets and rioted against him. What brought them to this extreme may be inferred from the way McLean treated Herancourt. The boss went after the fish merchant's franchise in 1883 by trying to get creditors to sue him and run him into bankruptcy. When the Union Association was created in 1884, McLean got a franchise in that league and put it in Cincinnati. As reported in *Sporting Life*, he then bought the lease on the ball park of the rival Red Stockings. When the Reds looked elsewhere, they were told the grounds were not available. McLean had leased every available park in the city, and his syndicate "openly boasted that they had the Cincinnati club frozen out of grounds." The Red Stockings were forced to build a new ball park in the suburbs.

At great loss, Herancourt's Reds survived in the suburbs—and McLean's Unions folded. But Herancourt's troubles were not over; he was stabbed in the back by a rival club owner in his own league. A good part of Herancourt's fish business consisted of selling oysters to saloons; he bought his oysters from S. B. Mallory in Baltimore, and the manager of the American Association's club in Baltimore talked Mallory into suing Herancourt for debts incurred during the difficult 1884 season. Herancourt managed to save his fish business by getting brewer John Hauck to pay the oyster debt in exchange for being given the Red Stockings' baseball franchise.

The manipulators in baseball were in a way no different from those in any other business—excepting, perhaps, that the dirty tactics of club officials were more often caused by their own dire economic necessity than by a hunt for greater profits. At least this was true in the minor-league circuits, where profits were hard to find for any club. These clubs were typically underfinanced, and were hard-pressed to sell enough stock to pay rent on the grounds and purchase uniforms and equipment; the funds for salaries were expected to come in through gate receipts. The cost involved in the smaller cities is suggested by the $2,600 loss in grounds and equipment suffered by the Johnstown, Pennsylvania, club in the great flood of 1889. Clubs in the Minors typically issued stocks in amounts of from $5,000 to $10,000. Apparently, few clubs managed to attract subscribers for the full amount. In 1896 the management of the Fall River, Massachusetts, club could sell less than $1,000 of the $1,500 in new stocks to be used to improve facilities for a team that was the perennial New England League pennant winner and had by far the best attendance record in the League.

Examples such as the foregoing led this writer to survey the background of the apparent skinflints who were the club officials. From various sources, occupations for 1,263 club officials and noted stockholders of nineteenth-century baseball were obtained. The blue- and white-collar workers, combined with the shopkeepers, tavern keepers, and the like, comprised the clear majority. Others had a more substantial social and economic role in their community, but only twenty-nine of the game's backers were noteworthy enough to be included in prestigious compendiums like the *Dictionary of American Biography*. About one in ten received mention in the city histories published in abundance around the turn of the century. These were voluminous, beautifully printed, and expensively bound testaments to an age of intense civic pride. They reveal that the molders of the national game rarely sat on the board of trade, but quite often served in the volunteer fire department or on the Fourth of July celebration committee.

Those engaged in selling the spectator sport of baseball were often the salesmen of new types of goods and services. Baseball had a sizable number of clothiers among its backers, and this at a time when Americans were shifting from handmade to ready-to-wear clothing. It was the formative period for the department store, and noted pioneers in this field also pioneered baseball in Chicago, Atlanta, Milwaukee, Columbus (Ohio), and other cities. An inordinate number of baseball people were in the streetcar business, a then highly speculative business: A city's many competing horse-trolley companies were made obsolete by cable trolleys, which were quickly made obsolete by electric streetcars.

The interplay of baseball and modern city life may be noted in the hypothetical case of Joe Fan, ardent follower of the Troy Haymakers. Mr. Fan might have had the following association with the various club officials of the Haymakers during the 1870s and 1880s. Mr. Fan arrives from a surrounding village the night before the game to attend a production at Haymakers promoter Griswold's theater. He spends the night in promoter Van Arum's hotel. Mr. Fan wants to look sharp for the game, so the next morning he puts on his new collar, shirt, and cuffs made at the factory of Haymakers promoter

Gardner Earl. He brushes his hair with the fruit of brushmaker McQuide's labor. He boards former club president
Fursman's trolley, pulled by McManus' horses, for a stopover
at Egolf's saloon and billard parlor, where he downs the brew
of local distiller William Holmes. Mr. Fan shoots a round of
pool while puffing on a Higgins cigar, bought at Draper's cigar
stand. Now it is time to ride F. N. Mann's new electric streetcar to the ball park; and during the ride he reads Sleicher's
newspaper, printed by promoter Hurley. At the park the
crowd is an unruly one, as usual, but Mr. Fan knows that
former Haymakers president Hotchkin, who is now sheriff, has
things under control. Troy loses. But for Joe Fan it could have
been worse. He might have made his usual stop to place a bet
at Congressman Morrissey's bookmaking establishment.

In an age of fervent prohibitionists and saloon smashers, the
national game had more backers from the beer and liquor
crowd than from any other branch of business—nearly one in
every five businessmen connected with the game. They were
salooon keepers for the most part, but there were some major
brewers, including the Busch family, present owners of the
Cardinals, who began their association with St. Louis baseball
in the mid-1880s.

Sporting-goods companies had a significant impact on the
pro game. Selling equipment was at first a highly competitive
business. The new leagues were able to pit one sporting-goods
company against another in bargaining for favorable equipment contracts. The contracts were good advertising for the
companies. Albert Spalding followed the selling of baseballs to
teams in the Midwest with the establishment of branch offices
for his sporting-goods company. One by one Spalding bought
out his rivals in the baseball-manufacturing business. Many of
them had had disastrous dealings with the pro teams; balls and
equipment had been mailed out only to see the team fold
before a payment had been made. When A. J. Reach sold out
to Spalding in 1892, the leading competitor had been eliminated, a competitor who had been burned repeatedly in deal-

ings with unstable minor leagues, including many years supplying the slipshod promoters of the Southern League.

Of the businesses which built baseball, trolley companies had perhaps the greatest financial impact. Fifteen percent of the businessmen in baseball had money in traction companies. At one time or another during the late nineteenth century, trolley companies were involved with baseball in seventy-eight cities. In the 1890s whole leagues were underwritten with traction money. One in 1899 was even officially titled the New England Trolley League.

Many a club with a saloon keeper or dry-goods merchant as president had a ball park built by one of the local trolley companies. Starting a trolley line was one of the great business crazes of the 1880s. The biggest cities had dozens of them, the medium-sized cities a dozen or more. At first trolleys were horse-drawn, with a sizable percentage of cable cars included. Then in the late 1880s there was a rush to put in electric streetcars. Building a baseball park out at the end of a new line was part of traction-company salesmanship, which included the inducement of the "first class" trolley car. As pictured in *Street Railway Journal* these cars offered the public cushioned easy chairs, reading lamps, a waiter serving refreshments. Here was one way for the well-dressed man-about-town who couldn't afford a carriage to ride out to the ball park in style.

The connection of baseball with politicians has something to do with trolley companies. Prominent city politicians typically bought into streetcars. Kickbacks to politicians in order to get a right-of-way for a new line was a substantial part of the business of politics. A check of city mayors against lists of traction-company directors suggests it was almost a civic duty for a new mayor to buy stock in local trolley companies.

The trolley and Brooklyn baseball have a special connection. In the 1890s the local National League entry was run by a consortium of traction magnates; and fittingly enough the team played at a ball park located at the junction of half a dozen different lines. The fans joked that going to see the Brooklyns was taking a grave risk of being run over in front of the stadium; and hence the team was named, in honor of its swift-footed fans, "the Trolley Dodgers." With the passage of time, the team became simply the Dodgers.

The streetcar lines extended the residential boundaries of the urban areas. New housing subdivisions went up, often with traction money behind the construction. A Boston *Globe* report noting a "West End Land Boom" added that "the street railway stock also advances." A ball park in the community at the new end of town added a touch of color, and if the Victorian prudes felt it was a negative addition, the traction companies, which lived off the patronage of the masses, felt otherwise. Quite often the ball field was part of the streetcar company's amusement park complex. In the mid-1890s there were nearly fifty streetcar-sponsored amusement parks, according to a lengthy piece on their profitability published in *Street Railway Journal*.

Competition in baseball and in the trolley business was occasionally intertwined. Competing traction companies backed the two major-league teams in Cleveland in 1890; and the two minor-league teams in Reading in 1892 were also backed by competitive streetcar companies. The two companies merged in '93 and Reading had only one team. The following season *Sporting Life* carried a report of Reading fans being angered over the traction company's refusal to continue its financial support of the local team.

The growth of the national game was intimately tied with the evolution of America into a modern, urbanized, consumer-oriented industrial state. Then again, modernization didn't just evolve—it was born of social and political conflict. Those who played, watched, and financed the game were caught up in those conflicts, which must be taken into account in any adequate explanation of the role of sports in society. The connection between the rise of sports and the declining power of organized religion was one case; and the role of sports in the battle between capital and labor was another, to which attention will be turned in the following chapter.

7

The Ball Players'
Rebellion: Mudville's
Last Stand

Between the triumphant 1869 tour of the Red Stockings and
the launching of the American League in 1901, the most
memorable baseball season had to be the campaign of 1890. It
was the year of the Players' League. Acting through their
trade union, the best ball players rounded up backers and
organized their own league, run as an economic cooperative.
There ensued a battle for control of baseball, an economic
war of extermination between the Players' and the National
League. Success for the Players' League, said its defenders,
would mean the end of the reserve clause and the buying or
selling of players from one team to another against their will.
Detractors said the Players' League was at one and the same
time a dangerously socialistic operation and a plot by players'
union officials to make themselves wealthy capitalists by
means of the profits of baseball.

In forming their league the players were, in effect, going
on strike against the existing club owners. There had been
many rumors during 1889 of an impending strike call by the
players' union. But instead of trying to stop the show with
picket lines, they produced a rival show. It took delicate
maneuvering to secure the necessary financing and not lose
control of their league, and in the end the players' backers

turned against them. In the interim, during the 1890 season, baseball became the focus of a raging national debate that mixed opinions on sports with class struggle. Politicians, businessmen, and labor leaders loudly proclaimed their views. In the process, public perceptions of ball players, and of the place of the game in daily life, were illuminated.

The players had yearned for a massive public response to their complaints about working conditions since they organized their trade union back in 1885. In that year the Philadelphia sportswriter William Voltz, who had helped launch minor-league ball in Pennsylvania, hit upon another idea for advancing the game: a professional players' benevolent association to provide health insurance, loans, and general care for needy athletes. He discussed his idea with players from numerous teams, and found little enthusiasm until he approached the New York Giants. Among the Giants' stars was shortstop John Montgomery Ward, who endorsed Voltz's plan and added the notion that the organization function as a trade union. On October 22, 1885, Ward and the other regulars of the Giants formed the first chapter of the Brotherhood of Professional Baseball Players, with Ward as president.

It was an organization dedicated to "protect and benefit the members collectively and individually," and in a short time it would demand collective bargaining with the club owners over players' working conditions. The union didn't catch on in the minor leagues, but Ward quickly spread the Brotherhood throughout the major leagues, with the help of fellow Giants Tim Keefe and Buck Ewing, and with Francis Richter of *Sporting Life* providing a national press outlet.

The Brotherhood leader was a rarity among ball players. He had a college degree from Penn State, and later became a lawyer by attending Columbia while playing for the Giants. Through his college education and his upbringing in the iron-mill town of Bellefonte, Pennsylvania, he had become familiar with the ideology of class struggle. This future member of baseball's Hall of Fame proved himself to be as capable a trade union leader as he was a player. He knew every facet of the game, since he had worked his way up from the Minors and had played both infield and outfield; and in 1880 he had pitched Providence to a second-place finish in the National League, winning 40 of his 63 decisions.

The workers in baseball needed an articulate and understanding spokesman, since a baseball trade union was in some respects an outlandish idea. At first glance, ball players didn't appear to be members of the exploited working class. The well-advertised stars of the major leagues made $1,000 to $4,000 or more a year, while industrial laborers made $100 to $300 a year, if they were fortunate enough to work for fifty-two weeks, which was not the case for a great many of them. Newspaper satires on "The Hard Lot of the Men Who Toss the Ball for a Living" were common. The Buffalo *Commercial* said in one piece, in 1885: "The baseball season has closed and about 200 professional ball tossers [have become] gentlemen of leisure for the next six months. The professional ballist has a hard time. He rises every morning at 10 o'clock, takes a snug breakfast in the cafe, reads the . . . newspapers, strolls out in the corridors and smokes a Reina Victoria, takes a nap before dining at 2 o'clock, and strolls out to the ball field about 3 o'clock, takes a little exercise for a couple of hours . . . and in the evening goes to the theatre."

The depictions of a ball player's easy life were misleading. Financially insecure teams were common in leagues big and small. "Stranded in Leadville" ran the *Sporting News* headline to a story of St. Joseph, Missouri, players left without a dime when the team's backers pulled out in midseason. John Ward drew upon his own experience to discuss the insecurity in pro ball. Writing in one of his two articles for *Lippincott's Magazine*, Ward noted that his compensation on his first team had consisted of his board and ten dollars a month. "I went [next] to Williamsport, Pennsylvania, on a promised increase of pay. I say 'promised,' for before pay-day came the manager had left town, but had neglected to leave his address. For a time I was particularly unfortunate in this respect. During my first ten weeks of professional play, including service with three clubs, I received only ten dollars."

Abysmal wages were common for the 1,800 or so players in the "bush leagues" of the 1880s. And although the wages for the few at the top levels looked impressive, they had to use a portion of their income to cover various incidental expenses. The cost of uniforms was often deducted from their salary. If they wanted their uniforms cleaned, they banged the dirt out against the locker room wall, or sent the uniforms to the laundry at their own expense.

The high salaries of the few notwithstanding, almost all professional players had to find other employment to tide them over the winter months. Almost every winter there was at least one sports-page account of a professional ball player losing his life in an industrial accident. "A Player's Horrible Death" was the headline of a *Sporting Life* account of how Charlie Schinstine was killed at a foundry when he fell into a molten-iron pit. A number of players lost their lives trying to hop freight trains.

The economic insecurity of one major league player was shown in a letter from Philly third baseman Joe Mulvey to club owner Al Reach in January 1884: "I being in very poor circumstances at the present, out of employment . . . am unable to pay my expenses as I am about three weeks behind in my board. Hoping you will oblige me by sending me $15.00 and I will promise you that it will be the last time I will bother you this season, not forgetting your past kindness." David Voigt surveyed the correspondence of Philly manager Harry Wright and found that much of the winter mail came from players pleading for a loan to tide them over till the next season.

Sporting News discussed how the Phillies planned to support themselves in the winter of '86. Bastian was going to work in a liquor store; Cusick as a plumber; McGuire as a molder; and Clements "will work in a mill." Fogarty "doesn't know what he will do," and Joe Mulvey appeared to be facing another winter of the same fate. The better players in the game tended to get white-collar jobs, but even some of these continued to labor during the winter in the trades—the Giants' Buck Ewing as a carpenter; John Kerins, star catcher for Louisville, as a boilermaker; and Jack Glasscock, one of the best shortstops of his time, as a shipwright. Members of the Cuban Giants, the best black American team of the period, worked winters in the South, as singing waiters in a hotel.

Professional sports is often thought to be an avenue of social mobility for the talented athlete. The New York *Clipper* assessed the ambitions of big-leaguers in 1887 and found a few with outside aspirations. There were a handful studying law or medicine, and there was Charlie Bassett, "a college man who writes." Some looked forward to buying a small business—a cigar store or the like. Many expected to be working in the trades, but the *Clipper* found most players expressing little hope of rising out of the proletariat. Having nowhere else to go when their playing days were over, many took jobs as umpires. It was a despised profession. Said one quipster of the period: "When a man sinks so low that he no longer has a friend on earth, the position of base ball umpire is all that is left him."

Players had a penchant for fancy clothes and rented carriages, but in other respects they were notoriously lacking in middle-class decorum in their off-the-field behavior. It was not uncommon to read in the sporting papers stories of players in trouble with the law, for robbery or worse. At least half a dozen professionals were charged with murder, including pitcher-outfielder Frank Sweeney, who killed a policeman in a saloon fight. Syracuse catcher Fleet Walker, one of the rare black Americans in organized ball, won an even rarer court decision when an all-white jury found that the death of a white man killed in a street fight with Walker was justifiable homicide. Sometimes it was the player who was murdered. Pittsburgh pitcher Florence Sullivan died "from a pistol wound received in a political dispute." Catcher Bradley of Dallas in the Texas League was shot down in the street by gunmen hired by a wealthy cattle rancher who felt the player was stealing his mistress. Reportedly the woman, Dolly Lare, "manifested the utmost grief at Bradley's death and went immediately after the killing to where the corpse lay and wept." Working conditions in the Texas League were menacing. *Sporting News* carried a report on "depraved" Dennison, where "hoodlums rule the roost," where visiting teams don't want to win, because "win a game from them and you would get sandbagged and run out of town."

The last years of a great playing career were often tragic ones. Alcoholism, suicide, and other destructive behavior seemed to reflect an intense pressure in the struggle to stay in the game, and a corresponding psychologically depressed state when that struggle was lost. Among those drinking themselves into an early grave was the great Mike "King" Kelly, batter and base stealer extraordinary. There were a surprising number of suicides, including Hall of Famer Ed Delahanty. On July 13, 1896, "Big Ed" had become the first major-leaguer to hit four home runs in a single game. On July 2, 1903, he jumped to his death off the International Bridge at Buffalo, New York. When Ed Larkin left the big leagues in 1884 he took to the bottle, and in one drunken fit tried to kill his wife. A year later he got in an argument with a bartender, went home and got two guns, and returned to the bar. He challenged the bartender to a duel; the police intervened; and Larkin explained plaintively that all he wanted was a fair fight, perhaps thinking of the competitive battles in which he had once made a living.

During the 1880s the social standing of ball players actually declined while the game became more popular. In the 1870s players had frequently been stockholders in teams; they had served as club officials, and as league officials in the National Association and International Association. Into the early 1880s there were still a few player-run cooperative nines. In the acting profession the manager who took care of a theater's business affairs was usually either an actor or a former actor. But baseball was developing a rigid separation between management and labor. An acting troupe could secure financing for a new theater and still retain a share of control over the production; but the financiers who were building new and bigger baseball stadiums were forcing the performers in the game to accept membership in the proletariat.

From the formation of the players' trade union to the showdown struggle of 1890, tensions mounted between labor and management. In the growing conflict the issue was not so much the low salaries themselves as the degrading policies employed by club owners to keep them that way. When the showdown came, the players' decision to go into business for themselves was in part a response to claims by baseball management that the workers were too shiftless to be deserving of either good salaries or responsibilities in the affairs of the front office.

Great strides were made during the 1880s in the practices of treating professional athletes like infants—the bed checks, dress codes, and the like. Voigt's baseball history relates stories of players getting in trouble with managers for such improprieties as eating with a knife, using spoons to eat pie, drinking the contents of fingerbowls, and piling food scraps in soup bowls. Gentlemen and ladies of this Victorian period tended to equate workers with drunks. Heavy drinking among ball players helped management stereotype them as members of a shiftless working class. Said Spalding in his 1884 *Official Base Ball Guide*: "The number of League and [American] Association matches that were lost last season by dissipation of players would surprise the fraternity were they enumerated in full." He proposed as a solution "the rule which insists upon total abstinence during the entire championship season."

Efforts to control players' behavior increased, significantly enough, at a time when leading clubs were becoming profitable and players were receiving an ever-smaller percentage of the gross income. The control of wages seemed to go hand in hand with fining players for drinking, wearing dirty uniforms, missing practice, showing poor table manners, and talking back to the manager. Under the guise of controlling drunkenness, club owners in the major leagues began in the 1880s the practice of hiring private detectives to follow the players from town to town. In one of the first such cases, a detective for Spalding's White Sox reported on seven players who had taken drinks, and the guilty were called before club owner Spalding and told to determine their own punishment. They decided to fine themselves $25 each, which covered the $175 fee the detective service charged Spalding. *Sporting News* of August 23, 1886, said of this incident: "If there is any one particular thing calculated to make a man red hot it is the thought that he is being shadowed constantly by a hired man." *Sporting News* suggested that the anger of the players was affecting their performance on the field; and a White Sox fan was quoted as saying: "Do you know why the Chicagos are losing games . . . and why they are going to forfeit the championship this season? I will tell you. It is because detectives have been put on the track to shadow them and to report every thing they do to President Spalding."

It seemed fitting to the club owners that if their business was to be run like an industry, the popular use of the "blacklist" for industrial troublemakers should be applied as well to baseball. Spalding declared in his *Guide* for 1882: "No piece of legislative work has been accomplished by the League, since their expulsion of convicted knaves guilty of crooked play, that is so well calculated to lead to good results [as] the establishment of the 'black list.' " It was declared a cure for "gross acts of intemperance or insubordination," or acts "subversive of discipline and good order in League ranks." Historian Seymour noted that the vague wording of the blacklist rule meant "anything a particular owner wanted it to mean at any particular time." The owners found reason to put from two to three dozen players a year on the blacklist. Players were allowed to appeal their sentence at the winter meeting of the League; but then, they had to have the train fare to get to the meeting. A number of blacklisted players of 1885 formed their own barnstorming team, named "the Blacklisted." It drew quite well, and made money.

The notion that players were easily tempted to wrongdoing became central to management's argument in defense of the reserve clause, the clause which became the single biggest bone of contention between the players' Brotherhood and the National League. According to Spalding, players had little appreciation of the difficulty in creating financial stability in the baseball business. Writing in his 1884 *Guide*, he declared the players were too easily dazzled by some fly-by-night operator's promises of a fat salary. They showed little appreciation of the way the National League had attained stability through control of player movement, as a result of which it could now offer a player a secure job, "a permanent position so long as he does faithful service in his position." As to the complaints that the reserve reduced the player's bargaining power, and consequently his salary, Spalding retorted: "Here is a ball player, who, as a street car driver or conductor, a brakesman, a porter, or an assistant at some ordinary trade . . . can only demand ten dollars a week for his services, and to earn that he has to work laboriously from ten to fifteen hours each day; and yet this self-same individual" is led to believe he is hardly treated fairly "if he is not readily given $2,000 as salary for six months' services as a ball player, in which his work is comparatively a pleasant recreation, requiring but two or three hours of each work day."

The position of the Brotherhood of Professional Baseball Players was presented at length by John Ward in a discussion of the reserve in *Lippincott's Magazine* of August 1887. He argued that players as well as management had a stake in maintaining baseball's financial stability, and that the players were willing to work with management in devising policies which were fair to both sides. The unionized players were willing to compromise on the reserve, and have "contracts . . . made for periods of more than one season." But not for life. Ward argued, in effect, for the situation in baseball today, wherein players may obtain freedom from the reserve after a set number of seasons, the number being open to negotiation with the club owners.

Ward conceded that the reserve had initially helped "to make the business of base-ball more permanent." He acknowledged in regard to the effect of the reserve in reducing salaries that in the first years of the reserve profits were rare and some salaries "exorbitant." But he believed there had been "a complete departure" from the original intent of the reserve. He found that although the game had eventually proven lucrative, the top clubs continued to reduce salaries, or hold them to modest gains, while profits skyrocketed. If sacrifices were necessary for the good of the game, Ward wanted to know, where were the sacrifices of the owners? At every turn, the application of the reserve seemed to be made at the players' expense.

The reserve, Ward declared,

> inaugurated a species of serfdom which gave one set of men a life-estate in the labor of another, and withheld from the latter any corresponding claim. No attempt has ever been made to defend it on the grounds of abstract right. Its justification, if any, lay only in its expedience. . . . I scarcely believe there will be any one found to justify it in the purposes to which it has been recently applied. . . . Instead of a measure of protection, it has been used as a handle for the manipulation of a traffic in players, a sort of speculation in livestock, by which they are bought, sold, and transferred like so many sheep.

Ward found the buying and selling of players the ultimate insult in the reserve clause. The selling of players' contracts for a profit was first instituted in 1884 by Columbus and Toledo of the American Association. At the time Henry Chadwick had noted "considerable indignation over the action." Of all the complaints of Ward and the Brotherhood, those concerning the inequity of the buying and selling practices of the owners received the widest public support. Forcing a worker either to toil for one owner or find another profession was

odious enough to trade unionists of the day without adding
insult to injury by allowing players to be traded against their
will. Both practices ran against the factory owner's argument
that workers in free America always had the opportunity to
try to improve their condition by changing bosses.

The practice of selling players' contracts fostered a type of
owner who seemed to care little about baseball but saw profit
potential in shuffling his human property. Ward explained
that in sales of players "a fictitious value was always given,
because the buying club bought not only the player's services
for the unexpired term of his contract, but the right to reserve
or sell him again. . . . The rule is, therefore, being used not as
a means of *retaining* the services of a player, but for increasing
his value for the purpose of sale." To Ward, the use of reserve
power to arrange the buying and selling of players was "a clear
perversion of the original intent of the rule. The assertion of
any such claim at the time of its adoption would have killed it
then and there."

The Brotherhood of Professional Baseball Players had to
undergo an incubation period before it could strike against its
enemy. It gathered 107 members in its first year, and by the
fall of 1886 had established chapters in each National League
city. But as a spokesman for the union explained in 1887:
"The players as yet are not sufficiently organized to fight the
National League. It will take time to get them in a position
in which they can insist upon their rights."

Sporting Life coverage of Brotherhood meetings and pronouncements revealed concern for improvement of the game
on and off the field. The Brotherhood seemed eager to display
players as contributors to the game's growth. There were suggestions for improving umpiring and winning fan support.
Brotherhood official Fred Pfeffer of the White Sox wrote a
book entitled *Scientific Baseball*, in which brain power was
rated over brawn in playing a winning game. Mike "King"

Kelly headed the Brotherhood's chapter in Boston. Although he had a drinking habit that fit him for A. G. Spalding's stereotype of players as irresponsible, Kelly invented most of the modern base-stealing techniques, along with an assortment of defensive strategies, and some gimmicks that forced rule changes. A rule had to be put in prohibiting a change of players in mid-play after Kelly pulled the stunt of leaping from the dugout and yelling "Kelly now catching for Boston!" as he grabbed a foul fly.

Concurrent with the Brotherhood's growth in numbers and respect among the players, management was also gaining new strength. Increasing profits added to club stability. Then in 1888 the reserve clause was extended to minor-league players. Up to this point, the baseball business in the small towns had been sufficiently chaotic for renegades from the Majors to find occasional employment there, if they were willing to work for a pittance. Now the sanctity of the reserve clause contract was spread throughout the system. The national game was now controlled from the top to the bottom, as Rome in the days of the Empire had controlled the provinces. The only escape was to play among the barbarians on outlaw teams in outlaw towns like Butte, Montana; Cairo, Illinois; and Tucson, Arizona.

Drunk with power, the National League club owners took one further step in the degradation of their workers—the classification plan. It was the proposal of Indianapolis club president John T. Brush, a stickler for propriety in the game and an inventor of elaborate player-behavior codes. His idea was to set players' salaries by a five-step classification. The idea would have created outcry enough had he made the distinctions in terms of batting averages and pitchers' won–lost records; but the opposition was going to be louder still because his standards for pay would be "habits, earnestness, and special qualifications" as displayed during the previous season. Personal conduct—which no doubt meant kissing up to the manager and owner—was to be the consideration in granting

the athletes one of the following salaries (two classifications of
which were below the existing minimum for National League
players):

class	salary
A	$2,500
B	2,250
C	2,000
D	1,750
E	1,500

Variations in the classification idea had been discussed earlier in the National League and never acted upon. The John
T. Brush version was voted through at the winter meeting of
1888, despite some pungent arguing against it. A. G. Mills
opposed it on the grounds that when added to the reserve it
amounted to "overloading the business end of the game." In
his estimation, the manager who "can't handle salary with the
powerful reserve rule at his command ought to have a wet-
nurse."

While the National League was voting in the classification
rule, John Ward and many of his top lieutenants in the Brotherhood were out of the country. They were playing for Spalding's touring All-Americans, who were introducing baseball to
four continents of the world. The classification scheme would
prove to be the straw that broke the camel's back, so far as the
resentful players were concerned; in this regard it was somewhat symbolic that the Brotherhood leaders should learn of
the plan while they were in Egypt. They read a scant report of
it in an American newspaper, and in their off-time, between
visits to the pyramids and the sphinx, they discussed retalia-
tory measures, including the idea of forming their own professional league.

When the all-stars reached Germany, Ward asked to be
released from his contract, and he abandoned the tour to return home. "I am called home upon matters of a purely pri-

vate nature," he told a reporter from the New York *Herald*; one bit of gossip had it that he came back to settle a domestic squabble with his wife, a noted Broadway actress. But editor Richter of *Sporting Life* reported having heard players in the States excitedly discussing "the true cause of Ward's departure." Said one: "Had it not been for the action of the National League clubs in undertaking to put a new yoke upon the necks of the ball players Ward would not be going home at present, in my opinion."

"To what do you refer?" Richter had asked, and the player replied: "The classification scheme."

Through the spring and summer of 1889 there were rumors of an impending strike of the ball players. The hints came out in offhand ways, as when one Giants player blurted out the threat of a strike during an argument with manager Mutrie. The threat was implied in Ward's demand for a meeting between the Brotherhood and the League to discuss the classification plan. From a closed-door meeting of the Brotherhood in July 1889 word leaked out that many rank-and-file members had expressed a willingness, then and there, to man the picket lines in a strike. Ward was reported to have argued against it in the interest of making one last attempt to negotiate the classification rule with the League's magnates. This was a publicity ploy. Ward didn't want a meeting, and was relieved when the National League's office suggested the Brotherhood bring up the request at the end of the season. By September the League's magnates appeared to have a conciliatory posture toward the union, and it was their turn to offer a meeting, and be politely refused by Ward, who claimed he would regrettably be unable to round up a negotiating committee at that time.

The idea of a Players' League, hatched in Egypt, was secretly and cautiously being carried to fruition. The plan was for an economic cooperative of teams to be jointly run by players and financial investors. It was, on the one hand, a popular tactic for labor groups in those days to organize cooperative businesses, which then relied on the union label as a selling point in the coop's competition with capitalist companies. The powerful Knights of Labor organized cooperatives numbering in the thousands. But on the other hand, while the forming of cooperatives was a popular activity of organized labor, its coops were rarely launched on the financial scale which would be necessary to start a new major league of baseball players. To compete with the National League, the players would need stadiums of comparable size, and this meant building new ones—a costly proposition. To attract capital to a project of a trade union wasn't going to be all that easy, especially capital in the range of $25,000 per club, the figure Ward and his aides set as required for any of the new league's franchises. Then there was the question of the strings the capitalists might attach to their money. Could they accept the idea of sharing profits with the workers, or sharing equally in all financial decisions with a group that hadn't put up a tenth of the investment?

To Ward, the relationship between players and capitalists in the new baseball cooperative was not nearly as questionable as it might first appear. He saw the player as a very special brand of laborer. He was convinced that capitalists could be found who would acknowledge this special quality, and because of it grant the players a just share of the profits and control in the enterprise. He presented his case in *Sporting Life*. In his opinion, the time had come to dispense with the "favorite argument" of the National League "that $2,000 was a big salary for a ball player who in any other calling would be unable to earn more than $10 a week." The owners

> seem to forget that the players not only earn their salaries, but actually draw the money which represents the profits. The players certainly deserve a fair share of what they actually earn. The magnates' argument could be as well used in the case of Adelina Patti. Why pay her $5,000 for singing a few selections? She doesn't actually earn it. No, but she draws more than that into the treasury, will be the reply. This is exactly the case

with base ball players. While they may not actually earn large amounts of money, they certainly induce the public to put large amounts into the base ball treasury, and consequently should at least be entitled to a fair portion of these sums.

Above and beyond the issues of player remuneration, the Brotherhood plan entailed rule changes and experiments for the purposes of bettering the game for all concerned, including the fans. Ward, Keefe, Ewing, Mike Kelly, and other leaders of the Brotherhood were attempting much more than do today's Reggie Jacksons and Catfish Hunters, who claim the right to become rich while displaying little commitment on their part to restructuring and improving the game.

The newfound profitability of baseball in the late 1880s had raised questions as to the existing organizational structure, in which there continued to be financially unstable clubs. Ward found it quite irrational that the National League could clear $200,000 to $300,000 a year and still have franchises on the verge of collapse. The leader of the Brotherhood was not the only one to question the structure of the game. Editor Francis Richter of *Sporting Life* was pushing his hotly debated "Millennium Plan." Condemning the financial inequality between wealthy and poor clubs, Richter made an assortment of proposals. He wanted each league to grant only one player reservation per team, all the other players going into a pool, to be distributed annually by a lottery. The luck of the draw would equalize the strength of teams. The Millennium Plan was Richter's offer to those in the baseball fraternity who didn't like the way the reserve clause created dynasties by holding talent in one club year after year. In the view of these critics the reserve clause created a boring situation for the fans. As one sportswriter explained: "Everybody knows about what the clubs are capable of . . . before the championship season opens. . . . No theatre could live without a change of plays, no person without a change of diet, neither can base ball clubs go on, year after year, without a change of players except, perhaps, the team at the top of the heap. Constant change is the order of the universe. Motion is life; stagnation, death."

In planning for the Players' League, the Brotherhood took into account the public interest in baseball reform. Those who bought stock in Players' League clubs were going to share in more than just a new financial relationship between player and backer. There was a provision for equalizing the financial potential of all clubs. To equalize the teams financially, the visiting clubs were to get 50 percent of the gate, instead of the 25 percent in the National League. Profits of each club, up to $20,000, were to be divided fifty-fifty between the players and the backers. Club profits exceeding $20,000 were to go into a League fund to be divided on a pro-rata basis between the first seven clubs in the final standings—with equal shares to the players and backers. This provision provided an incentive to good hard play for clubs in the lower division of the standings. As Players' League backer Al Johnson of Cleveland explained: "There will be, even to the end of the season, something more than empty honor, as at present, to play for." To uplift the quality of the game, there were two umpires instead of one, a reform often discussed but never utilized by the older leagues.

Each franchise was run by a board of directors, composed of four players and four backers. A League board of directors was composed of one player and one backer from each club. The reserve clause was abolished, and in its place there was an absolute one-year contract, with a two-year option to renew—in effect, a three-year hold after which the player became a free agent. Trading of players without their consent was prohibited. Releasing a player during the season required a vote of the team's board of directors. Among the lesser innovations of the Players' League there was a new lively baseball, which was advertised as an aid to the batters, adopted in honor of the fans, who liked to see plenty of hits.

For a time during the summer of 1889 it must have appeared to Ward that the Players' League was going to die stillborn before the public ever got wind of it. Financing was harder to find than had been expected. A breakthrough came when Larry Twitchell, Brotherhood leader for the Cleveland National League club, notified Ward of an interested prospect. When shortstop Ward's team, the New York Giants, got to Cleveland, Twitchell put Ward in touch with Albert Johnson, and the Players' League had its first, and most important, backer. Johnson agreed to use his influence in business circles to drum up support in other cities. He also agreed to meet with delegations of players—in effect, to be inspected as a living example of a capitalist willing to join in partnership with labor.

Late in October 1889 banner headlines in sports pages announced the beginning of "The Great Rebellion." The players had formed their own league, which was to include almost every star player in the game. The festering resentment over years of abuse had come to a head. Seymour explained: "As far back as 1880 the New York *Mercury* recommended that the players 'rise up in their manhood and rebel,' and the Cincinnati *Enquirer* predicted that one day they would." Some form of action by the Brotherhood had been expected, but the announcement of a Players' League caught the sportswriters and the public by surprise. Excitement over the event made the press in England. The London *Sporting Life* magazine devoted nearly a column to comments on what it called "The Great Strike of the American Professional Base Ball Players." The London magazine declared: "No event in the American sporting world has caused so much excitement . . . as the revolt or strike of the professional ball players. . . . Rumors of impending trouble have been carried all through the season just closed. . . . The strike has come, and the men are 'out.' "

The Players' League was officially proclaimed at a November 4 meeting in New York, attended by well over a hundred players and numerous prospective financial backers. In the lobbies of the meeting hall clusters of sportswriters, lawyers, and minor-league managers discussed the prospects of the new league. From the meeting came the Brotherhood's "Manifesto," which some called the players' "Declaration of Independence." The statement singled out the National League:

> There was a time when the league stood for integrity and fair dealing; today its eyes are upon the turnstile. Men have come into the business from no other motive than to exploit it for every dollar in sight. . . . [The] owners gave the managers unlimited power, and they have not hesitated to use this in the most arbitrary and incendiary way, and players have been bought, sold, and exchanged as though they were sheep instead of American citizens! . . . We believe that it is possible to conduct our national game upon lines which will not infringe upon individual and natural rights. We ask to be judged solely by our work, and believing that the game can be played more fairly and its business conducted more intelligently under a plan which excludes everything arbitrary and un-American we look forward with confidence to the support of the public and the future of the national game.

The opposition had been caught off-guard by the Brotherhood; and the players were able to cash in on the novelty of their new league, and on public resentment of the baseball monopolists, to build substantial support during the winter of 1889–90. The Players' League lined up on its side powerful organs of the press. *Sporting Life* and *Sporting News* were favorable from the beginning, and by December the National League was considering the *Clipper* a Brotherhood organ as well. To obtain a nationally distributed journal for its side, the National League had to buy Erastus Wiman's *Sporting Times*. Among the newspapers, circulation leaders like the Boston *Globe*, New York *World*, Philadelphia *Inquirer*, Pittsburgh *Dispatch*, and Chicago *Tribune* were strongholds of Brotherhood views; and historian Voigt could find only four well-known sportswriters siding with the National League.

The support of the press for the Players' League was, however, relegated to the most knowledgeable of the sportswriters, who were generally those employed on papers that had publishers willing to spice their columns with a dash of schmaltz in the form of sympathy for new causes which caught the public fancy. These were not the majority of newspapers. The majority were skeptical of, or hostile to, the Players' League from the start. Part of the National League's counterattack against the Brotherhood involved attempts to appeal to the conservative streak in publishers of the lively big-circulation papers which initially supported the players—attempts to convince them to instruct their sportswriters that support for trade-union baseball was wrong. In the long run, these efforts had much success.

John Ward was said to have put little stock in the role of the press. In the past he had experienced too many instances of newspapers refusing to publish news about the Brotherhood. As a player he had developed a distaste for the locker-room groupies he called "hare-brained reporters." Rather than rely upon the press, Ward had the players take their case directly to the people. The leaders of the Brotherhood spent the winter on tour, speaking in saloons where the fans hung out, at meetings of labor groups and Elks clubs, and even at church socials. Mike Kelly took the Brotherhood's argument out to San Francisco. En route he stopped off in Chicago, where he was induced by a vaudeville promoter to take, for one night, a role as a policemen in a popular comedy routine. He took the occasion to pause on the stage and produce a Brotherhood contract, which he signed with a great flourish in full view of the audience. "The cranks in the gallery well nigh went wild," reported *Sporting Life.*

The players could hardly have asked for more public support than what was bestowed upon them in the immediate aftermath of announcing the formation of their own league. The Massachusetts state legislature voted almost unanimously for a resolution endorsing the Players' League over its big-league rivals, the National League and American Association. Baseball preference polls run in newspapers in Boston, New

York, and Philadelphia were overwhelmingly in favor of the players. A New York *World* poll ran 1,201 to 209 in favor of the Brotherhood. Among the arguments made in letters accompanying the *World's* mail-in poll were the following: "Cast my vote for the Players' League; because players should not be sold like cattle." "As a trade unionist I must array myself on the side of the men who make the money, rather than on the side of the men who pocket it." "Baseball players should not be treated like race-horses and sold from one syndicate to another for magnates' speculation." "I thought that when Abraham Lincoln issued his Emancipation Proclamation . . . slavery would never again be tolerated in our country. Hurrah for the Brotherhood." Among the letter writers was a suffragette who noted that while she was not allowed to vote at the political ballot box she could see no impropriety in voting in the poll for the Players' League, since she felt she was as great a ball fan "as some men."

The immediate outpouring of sympathy for the Brotherhood from organized labor was remarkable. The trade-union baseball fanatics had come out of the closet. The Players' League opened an opportunity for union spokesmen who had long been out of the baseball picture, despite their knowledge that workers and fans were almost synonymous. Open support for professional baseball had been difficult for trade unionists when the game was identified with gambling, liquor, the likes of Boss Tweed, and quick-buck artists. Now it appeared that labor had its chance to speak up for the national game.

At the American Federation of Labor convention in December of '89 resolutions were passed endorsing the Players' League and condemning "iron-clad" contracts in baseball or any other industry. A resolution from the Committee on Boycotts signaled to union members of the nation just where they were expected to spend their baseball dollars during the coming season. At the close of the convention a delegate from Detroit raised a toast to the "Labor Cranks" who now had a cause of their own. Samuel Gompers led a delegation from the

AFL which met with Brotherhood leaders in Philadelphia, where measures of support were discussed. The heads of the carpenters' union and Amalgamated Steel issued calls for all good ball fans to support the Players' League. A press report told of a flood of endorsements coming into the Brotherhood's office from local branches of the Knights of Labor. A midwestern leader of the Knights explained:

> The latest subject of discussion among organized laboring men is the baseball war now on. It may appear a little singular to outsiders, but a peculiar interest is being manifested in the trade-union element favoring this Baseball Brotherhood movement. The way we look at this matter in its present shape is that the Brotherhood is a legitimate organization of skilled workmen. . . . The men are hired on salaries, and, outside of the oppressive restrictions under which they are placed, they are to be as fully recognized as are the skilled workmen of the printing craft, the moulder or the carpenter.

For the trade unionists, their support for the Players' League put union issues in the public eye, in much the same way as their fight for union labor in construction at the World's Fairs of the period publicized the movement. Along these lines, the Clothing Cutters Assembly No. 2853 of Jersey City added to an endorsement of the Players' League a vote to impose a fine on such members "as attend non-union picnics, parks or baseball grounds."

The new organization needed all the help it could get. The 1890 season was to be "a war of extermination," said the New York *Tribune*. The National League magnates had stockpiled a quarter-million-dollar "war chest" from the profits of previous years. The Players' League had to throw what funds it could get into the purchase of equipment and the building of ball fields. The construction task was a race against time, and many of the parks were barely ready by the opening of the season. The backers had been forced to pay exorbitant prices to building contractors; and when the backers sought bank loans to cover the cost, the banks were reluctant to come through for what appeared to be a very high risk.

One advantage for the Players' League was its array of talented performers, including the top spectator draws in the game—with the exception of a handful of "scabs," and some capable players who remained in the American Association. The Association tried to remain neutral during this baseball war. As for the Players' League rival, Paul Hoch noted: "The National League was decimated. Even by paying huge salaries, it could hold so few of its players that it had to fill almost every position with rookies. It became known as the sand-lot league." Actually, between the renegades from the Brotherhood and players taken from the American Association, some National clubs had talent, but there were others, like Pittsburgh, whose players were termed by one sportswriter "a crowd of stiffs."

However, the National League had its war chest and it used it most creatively. One application kept the minor leagues in line. In the small-town clubs many a manager and club official had been openly supportive of the Players' League; and it first appeared that many a minor-league association was going to join sides with the players. Had they done so the war might have ended differently. But with the coaxing of Spalding the situation was changed, and the Minors accepted a two-part deal whereby the Nationals promised, first, to strengthen the power of the reserve in the Minors, and second, to pay high prices for players the Minor clubs were willing to sell. The Players' League didn't allow for buying and selling of ball players; besides, it had all the talent it needed. The National League's need for players was fulfilled through the Minors, where the game really did degenerate in 1890 to the level of the sandlots.

From the war chest came funds to buy press support. The funds were also used to pay detectives to spy on the players and their backers, and to pay agents who were "at work constantly, trying to induce our men to sign with them," as one

Brotherhood player noted, adding, "but they don't seem to get them." The bribes offered to the stars in the Brotherhood to desert and become "scabs" were twice the sums ever paid players for a year's salary. One of the few to take an offer and get on the *Player's Guide* scab list was pitcher John Clarkson, who received $10,000 from the Boston Nationals. Spalding admitted having offered Mike Kelly a blank check, which the player refused, saying: "My mother and father would never look at me again if I could prove a traitor to the boys." Utilizing a common strike-breaking ploy, the agents of the National League pigeonholed players individually to tell them their teammates were ready to abandon the Brotherhood, and it would be better to be among the first rather than the last to come back into the fold. To quash one such rumor, Danny Richardson had a facsimile of his handwritten statement of Brotherhood loyalty published in *Sporting Life*. In one bit of propaganda from the Brotherhood, John Ward offered bets at ten-to-one odds that there wouldn't be twenty deserters when the season opened. He would have won the bets.

When the National League magnates met to decide strategy for the war, one of the initial resolutions was to bring suit against every contract jumper. The reserve clause would be tested in the courts; and if the League lost it could still gain by having tied up Players' League money in court cases. Suits were initiated against a score of players. After courts in New York and Pennsylvania ruled that the reserve clause had no legal standing, the remaining suits were dropped.

The prospects for the Brotherhood league looked good going into the 1890 exhibition season. The problems of a shortage of financial backing, reported off and on during the winter months, seemed to have been rectified. Franchises were ready to go in New York, Brooklyn, Boston, Buffalo, Philadelphia, Pittsburgh, Cleveland, and Chicago. Support from fans was being tested and found to be at a fever pitch. In city after city Players' League exhibition games were setting attendance records. A total of 15,000 fans turned out for a game in St. Louis. When two Players' League teams came to

Holyoke, Massachusetts, for an exhibition game, the athletes
were mobbed outside the stadium by thousands of overjoyed
well-wishers. According to the New York *World*, the players
feared they would be trampled to death, and they armed themselves with bats and beat their way into the ball park. The
same two teams had to fight their way past a mob of fans to
get into the Boston ball park for an exhibition game. In the
public eye John Montgomery Ward was now a celebrity with a
stature far beyond what he had achieved for Hall of Fame–
quality ball playing. He was known as "the poor country boy"
from Centre County, Pennsylvania, who had the ambition to
go to college. He was being called a great orator. The Pittsburgh *Commercial-Gazette* said of him: "His arguments are
always convincing, and . . . if Mr. Ward could have talked
personally with every man who was against the Brotherhood
movement the League would not to-day have a supporter
aside from those financially interested."

"The Brotherhood Captures all the Good Umpires" had been
the heading for one optimistic *Sporting News* report; another
announced the attempt to launch a second Players' League in
the Midwest, which didn't materialize. In the opinion of a
Brotherhood spokesman in Chicago: "The newspapers generally favor us. Half of the journals, which last fall viewed our
great project as utopian and weak in its foundations, have
changed their tone, and now admit that the ball players in our
organization have shown enough business ability to manage
their own affairs." By the opening of the season the Players'
League had grown from a vague hope into a formidable
organization.

In the struggle ahead, the advocates of cooperative baseball
organization were destined to lose. But most of the baseball
magnates who opposed them also lost. In the end, the emer-
gent winners turned out to be the financial backers of the
Players' League, who, when the chips were down, disowned
the Brotherhood, bought into the National League, and soon
became its controlling force. The baseball war of 1890 was

officially fought out in the stadiums, with the head counts of attendance measuring the success of daily battles for patronage. But behind the scenes, the struggle had from the beginning hinged upon the manipulations of finance.

A. G. Spalding, the premier strategist for the National League hierarchy, had realized the central issue quite early in the struggle. *Sporting News* reported that the announcement that the players had formed their own league sent Spalding into "conniption fits." A week later, however, a reporter for the New York *Herald* told how Spalding "laughed heartily when I spoke to him on the subject, and said he was anxious to see the first capitalist put up one dollar to back the Brotherhood." Spalding, a man of the business world, was as convinced on his side as socialist Eugene V. Debs was on the other that there could be no real common ground between capital and labor.

The Brotherhood obtained capital more readily than Spalding might have expected, but it was given at the price of compromises with the cooperative ideals of Ward and the other players. In a sense, the Players' League capitalists seemed from the very beginning intent upon using the players' trade union to get a foothold in the game and then usurp control of the union's league. For example, the press got word of the Players' League a week before its official founding meeting; then, when the players and backers came together to sign their agreement, the latter threatened to pull out and leave the former on a limb unless compromises were made in the blueprint for the new league. Ward had planned to have the players in the majority of decision-making positions. He had to agree to equal power with the backers. Ward expected the new league to pool all profits, and divide them evenly among all franchises. Instead, he got the division of only a share of the profits, and that by the pro-rata system; and he obtained the fifty-fifty split of the gate, which still meant that clubs with the bigger stadiums could earn more than those with smaller ones. In the opinion of the New York *Herald*, "by abolishing the

idea of pooling the profits the Players' League has knocked
from under itself one of its strongest props. It was done, however, at the demand of the capitalists, and the players were
compelled to obey." In January the new league met to elect
officers and another concession was made: the backers took
the presidency, vice-presidency, and positions of secretary and
treasurer.

The backers of the Players' League included politicians,
streetcar magnates, and the like in the same proportion as
found elsewhere in the pro game. The PL's club in Boston, for
instance, had behind it the Democratic machine, which would
rival the National League's club, one of whose owners was a
GOP committeeman. The president of the new Boston club
owned a suburban commuter railway line, and was installing a
new station just where the PL's club was building its new ball
park. In Brooklyn, the PL's club had a consortium of traction
magnates behind it, including one Republican soon to be
elected to the state legislature. The rival Brooklyns of the National League had a future state assemblyman of their own,
Democrat Charlie Ebbets.

In the bringing together of capital and labor for the Brotherhood, a special role was played by Cleveland traction mag-
nate Albert Johnson. In addition to being the first in line, he
was the one capitalist in the bunch who could most easily
tolerate the trade-union spirit of the players. With Johnson the
players felt a genuine sense of camaraderie. Albert was the
brother of one of the era's most noted political reformers,
Tom Johnson, who was elected in the fall of 1890 to Congress
and a few years later became mayor of Cleveland. Tom
owned a few shares of Brotherhood stock. Tom and Al were
liberals of the country club set, having substantial wealth, including controlling stock in traction companies in at least four
cities. In helping the players they helped themselves. Their
Cleveland Players' League club was competing with the local
Nationals owned by the rival traction magnates, the Robison
brothers. And there was political competition here too. Tom
Johnson was on his way to becoming the most influential

Democrat in Ohio; and the most prominent Republican in the state, Senator Mark Hanna, owned a substantial portion of the Robisons' trolley stock, and was himself a longtime financial supporter of Cleveland baseball.

The Players' League capitalists were siding with a group of workers who in National League propaganda were being ridiculed as ignoramuses strutting around like businessmen, and were also being viciously red-baited. The Brotherhood was branded by Spalding as "an oath-bound secret organization of strikers." Ward and his followers were called "hot-headed anarchists," "socialists," and "ultra-radicals"; and Ward was singled out as "the chief conspirator," who was employing "terrorism peculiar to revolutionary movements." The latter accusation came from *Spalding's Official Base Ball Guide* for 1890. For evidence, the *Guide* pointed out that the Central Labor Union of New York City had supported the players.

Under these attacks the Brotherhood seemed to develop an obsessive desire for respectability. In selecting a president, the PL chose the head of the New York State Republican Committee, Col. Edwin McAlpin. The PL opted for the NL's prestigious 50-cent admission price, instead of the plebeian American Association's two-bit fare. The sale of beer was prohibited at PL ball parks. After much debate, the players decided against Sunday games. Without Sunday ball they would be cut off from the typical six-day-a-week, twelve-hour-a-day schedule of the proletariat. As noted sarcastically in the National League organ *Sporting Times*, "the sentimental Brotherhood Labor-Unionists" would now get little help from their "falsely founded sympathy for the Brotherhood among factory hands, mill hands and laborers."

In later years, Spalding would write about baseball's "fight to the death" in 1890, and how "in place of powder and shell, printers' ink and bluff formed the ammunition used by both sides." He declared: "No general ever planned a campaign or conserved his forces with more painstaking care than did the commanders of the League and Brotherhood warriors." The making of a financial profit was going to be difficult for all teams concerned, since the Players' League had put seven of its eight franchises in National League cities. In the first strategy of bluff, the Nationals waited until the Players had announced their season schedule and then published theirs, showing conflicting home dates on almost every occasion possible. Spalding's supporters in the press spread the rumor that a panicked Brotherhood was hastily rearranging its dates; instead, the Players' League called the bluff and retained its schedule. The American Association teams in Brooklyn and Philadelphia frequently had the same home dates as the other teams of these cities, a situation creating a three-way battle of the turnstiles. By one combination or another, the season began with one group of ten cities sporting twenty-two baseball franchises. The baseball scene was not only more crowded than ever—it was bigger than ever, by the addition of the Brotherhood's league, and by four more minor-league circuits than in any previous season.

"The fans will decide the conflict," said spokesmen from both camps. When the season began, the Players' League press devoted much space to comparisons of attendance figures, which were going in the players' favor. There were charges of fraudulent counts leveled against both sides in the struggle, but it appeared to be the National League which did the most inflating of the figures. The NL papers claimed interest in baseball was being killed off by the distasteful intrusion of labor issues into sports. The PL press tried to prove the opposite.

Brotherhood newspapers, like the New York *World*, compiled tables showing not only how the respective teams were doing in 1890, but how overall attendance on given dates was significantly higher in 1890 than the year before. There was, for example, the comparison for Memorial Day attendance— a day when all teams played doubleheaders, a morning game being followed by a late-afternoon contest with a new crowd of spectators. The announced totals for the games of the three major leagues were as follows:

Players' League	39,080
National League	28,166
American Association	20,546

The *World* noted that on Memorial Day of 1889 the National League had drawn 41,497 spectators for four doubleheaders; and the combined total for eight doubleheaders in the Players' and National leagues was 67,246.

In games played through the first three months of the 1890 season the Players' League held a 24 percent lead in attendance over the National, a per-game average of 2,027 spectators to 1,535. But in the final two months the lead was only 7 percent—a change brought about by a drop in PL attendance to an average of 1,638 spectators against 1,526 for the NL. The change was effected by a drop in PL support in two areas, the press and organized labor.

Special efforts were made by the NL to win back the sporting press. The leading sporting goods companies advertised in the daily newspapers and in the sporting weeklies, and these companies were tied through holdings of stock to National League clubs. Prominent dry-goods merchants and other businessmen also had long-standing connections with the old league. The influential Al Spalding combined red-baiting arguments with appeals to old friendships to get a substantial part of the business community to threaten to withdraw advertising from the papers that continued to support the Players' League. Many a newspaper caved in quickly to this threat. Richter of *Sporting Life* stood the test and remained loyal to the Brotherhood. The Spink brothers of *Sporting News* bravely declared that they preferred the friendship of the players to the paid advertising of Spalding; but by July they had been forced to give in to the enemy, after being subjected to a barrage of postcard hate notices and threats from other advertisers.

As the press support diminished, so too did the coverage of Players' League games, it being the policy of National League papers to treat the players' organization like an insignificant

minor league. The players needed a sizable press for responses
to National League propaganda claiming the Brotherhood
was wrecking baseball—responses such as the one given in the
loyal Players' League paper, *Taggert's Times* of Philadelphia:

> Pray, what have the Players done to wreck the game? . . .
> Has anybody heard them squeal about the attendance
> or observed them doing anything to bring scandal upon
> them or the good name of base ball? On the other hand,
> what have the magnates done? Did they not offend
> self-respecting men all last winter in going around the
> country bribing players? Did they not sour people by
> bringing uncalled for lawsuits against players to harass,
> annoy and bluff them and then go into open court and
> wash dirty base ball linen in public? Have they not since
> then endeavored to create apathy among the people by
> openly asserting in public print that base ball is dead?

Early season Players' League optimism was based heavily
on expectations of strong support from the trade-union movement. At the season's opening there had been a unity meeting
between Philadelphia Players' League officials and AFL leaders, including Samuel Gompers. An enthusiastic statement
was issued by stockholder J. M. Vanderslice, a local police
court judge. He applauded the AFL and said: "These gentlemen represent over 600,000 skilled workingmen . . . who
want to see the players succeed in freeing themselves from
League slavery." Vanderslice added his concurrence with the
labor leader at the meeting who said: "Base ball would have
died out long ago but for the liberal support given it by the
laboring men. Four-fifths of the spectators at any game on any
day are men who do manual labor for a living, and it is to this
class base ball clubs must cater if they expect to be in existence
for any length of time."

The players squandered their trade-union support. They
turned down an offer to join the AFL. Their decision not to
play on Sunday was regrettable. The attendance lost in this

decision can be estimated from attendance on Saturdays, the second easiest day for laboring people to attend a game. The Players' League outdrew the National League on Saturday by almost two to one. The players let their financial backers take charge of economic arrangements, with some embarrassing results. In Chicago and in Boston, construction of the PL's ball parks was begun with nonunion labor. At the time, the AFL was capitalizing on the Players' League struggle to demand complete unionization of sporting-goods companies and anything else connected with the national game. And in the midst of this drive a strike had to be instituted in Chicago to get unionized construction crews at the PL ball park. In Boston a brief work stoppage was halted by intervention of Players' League officials forcing the contractor to hire union carpenters. However, the action was not taken quickly enough to stop some very damaging national publicity about the incident. The New York *Herald* reported a Boston carpenters' union delegate complaining that the sympathy of the Brotherhood for the cause of labor "exists only on paper." He said he had made "every effort . . . to induce the Brotherhood to give their work to a union contractor, but in vain."

Spalding and company red-baited the ball players on the one hand, and on the other, depicted them as incipient capitalists who were using moralistic slogans for the purpose of making themselves the monopolists of baseball. There was probably some truth to the latter charge; the Players' League did include the famous twentieth-century club owners Charlie Comiskey and Connie Mack.

Control of the Players' League slipped bit by bit from the Brotherhood to the financial backers. The season wasn't long under way before the League office was declaring: "The Players' League is above all things a business organization"—not exactly the kind of statement to keep trade-union support at a fever pitch. Class-struggle oratory could hardly be expected from the office of the New York Players' League club, run by the head of the state GOP and a Wall Street stockbroker; nor could much be expected from the directors of the Pittsburgh

Players' club, an assortment of hack politicians of Boss Magee's GOP machine. Pittsburgh trade unionists conducted a highly successful boycott of the local National League team, which was forced for lack of fans to play many of its "home games" in other cities. And all the while, the head of the Brotherhood chapter in Pittsburgh was buttering up the Republicans in the club's front office. This erstwhile labor leader, John K. Tener, later became a Republican governor of Pennsylvania.

In the end, the overall major-league baseball attendance for 1890 was substantially above that of 1889, but it was spread too thinly for there to be much in the way of profits. In addition, there had been much papering of the house; free tickets were handed out in cigar stores and saloons, and at the gates of the ball park. In overall attendance the Players' League had surpassed the National by nearly 20 percent and had outdrawn the American Association by nearly 50 percent.

The really critical measurement of the conflict was the amount of financial loss for the leagues. A New York judge close to the baseball scene estimated the National League deficit at $300,000. Discounting $70,000 in bonus payments to lure scab players, the NL's loss in normal operating expenses came to $230,000. The PL's loss in operating the clubs was $125,000; but on top of this there was an outlay of $215,000 in ball-park construction.

As the season wound down through September it became apparent that the real test of who would win the war was going to be who would avoid bankruptcy. All eight Players' League franchises came through solvent. In the American Association four teams were virtually bankrupt. Pittsburgh's National League club did go into receivership, in part due to the effective trade-union boycott against the team. National League franchises in Boston, New York, and Cleveland had been barely saved from bankruptcy by infusions of money from the National League's war chest. Shortly after the close of the season the Cincinnati Nationals were sold to the Players' League. The directors of the American Association now figured that the National League was finished, and they made an offer to merge with the Players' League. The offer was rejected. In haughty tones, PL secretary Brunell declared there was no need for a merger, since "every club in the Players' League is now on a solid footing," and "no Association city could keep the pace with our clubs either in paying salaries or in playing ball. . . . They have nothing to offer us and we certainly can get along without consolidating or compromising with the National League."

The players who had won the battle of 1890 could not know, as they listened to the pronouncements of Secretary Brunell, that they were soon to lose the war. Behind the scenes the Players' League backers were having second thoughts. They were, after all, "long-chance capitalists whose only possible interest" in the game was "the amount of money they hope to realize out of it." This had been Albert Spalding's assessment of them early in the year. During the last months of the season Spalding and others of his league met individually, in secret, with one after another of the PL's backers. No doubt one of the points impressed upon them was that in the Players' League they would be forced to share the profits of the business with the workers.

Early in October word was leaked that Col. McAlpin and Wall Street broker E. B. Talcott of the New York Players' League club were trying to buy into the New York Giants. The PL's backers in Pittsburgh were reportedly dickering for a National League franchise. Accusations of treachery were thrown about at the annual meeting of the Players' League—at the close of which newly elected president Charles A. Prince of Boston issued a statement declaring that his league would hold together, and that "relying on the loyal players to fill their part, we have confidence in the generous support of the public as in the past." It was the loyalty of the backers which was in question. Among them, Prince was going to stick with the players and the public, since he hadn't yet found a way to

desert without losing the $45,000 investment he had made in
construction of his Boston club's ball park, and the adjacent
new station for his rail line.

The season had hardly ended when the National League
announced it was willing to attend a peace conference bringing together its representatives with those of the American
Association, and with "a committee representing the Players' League capitalists." The Brotherhood was not invited.

A conference was arranged for late October by the "White-
Winged Angel of Peace," Allen W. Thurman of the American
Association, son of a recent Democratic vice-presidential
candidate. Three representatives of each league walked into
the meeting room, and so, too, did three spokesmen of the
Brotherhood. The National League representatives flatly refused to take their seats until John Ward and his group left the
room. Al Johnson threatened in turn to pull out the Players'
League representatives if the Brotherhood wasn't allowed.
Thurman spoke of important work of conciliation to be accomplished, and after others had argued back and forth John
Ward had his turn. In an emotional speech he declared that
the bylaws of the Players' League required representation
from the players. To the argument that capitalists should sit
only with capitalists he replied that the players were stockholders in their league, and that he had invested "every dollar
he had." He reminded his listeners that each of the committees
contained a former ball player. "Do these gentlemen," he
asked, "wish to go on record as saying that the occupation of a
ball player bars him from business association with respectable
men?" Turning directly to Spalding, Ward challenged: "Are
you willing to place such a stamp of infamy upon the profession of which you were for years a member and to which you
owe your start in life?"

All through the long season Ward and the Brotherhood had
been throwing barbed insults at Spalding, the former player
who had turned his back on his own kind, hired Pinkertons to
spy on them, and among other things, derided them for contract jumping although back in 1875 Spalding himself had

been a notorious contract jumper. Now Ward stood face-to-face with Spalding trying to prick his conscience and provoke a shouting match. But the Brotherhood leader was up against a man whom Henry Chadwick had tabbed as the craftiest and most deceptive pitcher of all time, and Ward was about to be delivered quite a curve ball. Spalding avoided a direct reply, choosing instead to address the gathering as a whole with a statement that couldn't but impugn Ward's good sense in trusting the Players' League capitalists. Spalding said calmly: "Before the National League consented to any negotiations whatever, it was mutually decided that the question of a compromise should be settled between the moneyed men of both organizations on a purely business basis." The Brotherhood delegation was formally asked to leave the room, and their sheepish backers uttered no further protest. The players went outside to wait in the corridors.

However, the capitalists couldn't legally divide the spoils of war at that meeting without Brotherhood representation, and it was quickly adjourned. Emerging from the room, the Players' League backers assured John Ward that no deals had been made; but in the aftermath of the meeting it became clear that the backers were going to be seeking ways to get around their commitment to the players' trade union. The New York *Sun* reported a group of Players' League capitalists issuing a public apology for the way the National Leaguers "had been treated relative to the action of the Brotherhood of Base Ball Players in refusing to allow them to keep their agreement as explicitly made with the National League that no player would be allowed on the committee." In turn, a spokesman for the National League said his group "extends its sympathy to the gentlemen who have been led into this tangle by the Brotherhood players."

Continuing the war meant the ruin of all concerned, said the businessmen to the press. One way out of the tangle was to compromise with the Brotherhood on issues of working conditions in return for consent for mergers and other deals among the backers. The classification plan was dropped. The reserve clause was modified and given loopholes. All 1890 Players' League rookies were to be free agents in 1891. Some player stockholders accepted payoffs to drop out of the business end of the game, and the Brotherhood split into factions.

By mid-January of '91 the various deals had been accomplished. The Pittsburgh National League franchise was given to the local Players' League backers. Charles Prince and his associates received an American Association Boston franchise for their club. Philadelphia PL backers got the Athletics' franchise in the Association. A substantial block of New York Giants stock went to the PL's erstwhile backers, and a year later they took controlling interest in the club. The Brooklyn PL and NL clubs were merged in an agreement which had the team playing in the Players' League ball park, located at the crossroads of trolley lines owned by the former PL backers. Al Johnson had a Cincinnati American Association franchise, but his claim was being contested in the courts by John Brush, who was eager to get back into the game. PL backers in Buffalo got a franchise in the International League. The Chicago PL stockholders were bought out for $18,000, with additional cash going to local players to keep them from bringing suit to block the sale. In total, seven of eight sets of backers of the Brotherhood's league remained in the baseball business —although Johnson was soon to lose in the courts to Brush. The National League had maneuvered on many fronts to put Al Johnson in a position where he could be eased out of the game. He had been all too friendly with the player rebels.

The Brotherhood held a wake for the fallen league at Nick Engels' saloon in New York, attended by players, Francis Richter, and other loyal friends. In a sardonic mood, Ward raised a toast: "Pass the wine around, the League is dead, long live the League." Richter replied: "Base ball will live on forever. Here's to the game and its glorious future." The Brotherhood's last gasp before it went out of existence was the winning of assurances that all its members would be allowed back in the fold without reprisals. *Spalding's Official Base Ball Guide* for 1891 satirized the players' return:

Backward, turn backward, O Time in thy rush,
Make me a slave again, well-dressed and flush!
Bondage come back from the echoless shore,
And bring me my shackles I formerly wore.

The players had improved working conditions, which lasted only one year. In 1892 the National League achieved a true monopoly in big-league ball and began acting against the players as would be expected of a monopolistic nonunion industry. The American Association had folded, with four of its clubs joining the NL to form one twelve-club league. In the next few years the reserve clause was reinstated as before; the trading and selling of players increased; and the blacklist lengthened as strict behavior codes were invoked. Historian Voigt found salaries "slashed to the bone." Where there had earlier been a $2,000 minimum, the Phillies in 1894 had a $1,800 maximum salary. Around the League, rookies were getting $600 to $700. The old penny-pinching tactic of releasing an entire team before the expiration of contracts was revived. Powerless to resist, bench warmers were forced into double duty as ticket takers, ushers, and grounds keepers. The changes in the game were disheartening to the former members of the Brotherhood. In 1893 only 54 of the 128 players in the Players' League of 1890 remained active.

The players acted out the frustrations of their jobs in displays of violence. A new style of roughhouse baseball came into vogue, epitomized by John McGraw's scrappy Baltimore Orioles—experts at spiking, tripping, and grabbing the pants of base runners when the umpire wasn't looking. In the Majors and in the Minors, press reports of fights among the players, between players and fans, and between players and managers became far more common than in the past. One story told of a fistfight between a player and the manager of a club in Harrisburg. The manager ended up in the hospital, but since it had been a fair fight no action was taken against the player. In the National League, action was taken against the rowdies, their behavior providing the excuse for instituting stiff fines for assorted breaches of proper decorum. John T. Brush had the League accept a behavior code with twenty-one different clauses, dealing with violence, inebriation, swearing, and acts of insubordination to authority.

Although the players' trade union lost in 1890, the union movement did gain something. The argument that labor connected with the workers' sport of baseball should be union labor was heard again and again during the 1890s. It was invoked during a strike at a baseball-manufacturing plant in Reading. In another case, a labor boycott was called against a team in Minneapolis that was wearing uniforms that did not carry a union label. A Worcester team was boycotted until it got rid of a player who the previous winter had worked during a strike as a scab. When the Baltimore Orioles hired some nonunion carpenters in 1895 the AFL threatened to put a boycott on the Orioles, not only in Baltimore but extending to their games in every other city.

At the time of the Players' League struggle, baseball was already undergoing a small but significant change in ownership. A handful of industrialists and bankers, and the wealthier streetcar-company owners, represented a new type. They were gentlemen of the upper classes, which hadn't been noticed in baseball since the decline of the Knickerbocker Club; and in part, they were the descendants of the "Old Fogies," who had been too stuffy for even the Knickerbockers. In their absence the running of the national game had been identified with the "sporting men" who socialized at the pool hall and the tavern, where the fans gathered. The preponderance among baseball backers of saloon keepers, sportswriters, cigar-store proprietors, and the like had given the game the appearance of a production of the people and by the people.

As the game became more of a business and management was separated from the game on the field, it began to draw investors from the classy side of town. They had long despised the people, but now they were willing to produce sports for

them. In time the wealthy assumed a leading role in professional sports, as evidenced in the spate of recent books with
such titles as *The Rich Who Own Sport*. The wealthy had a
gradual ascendancy, however. There were Victorian prejudices against mass sports, and initially the rich needed special
incentives to become involved. The first industrialists to get
into the national game were new entries in the long procession
of groups using investment in baseball for ulterior motives.
The wealthy industrialist was hardly as interested in baseball
games as in his golf, yachting parties, and polo ponies. Nor
was the rate of financial return in baseball much of an incentive to successful capitalists. What investment in baseball
could do, it was hoped, was buy peace with labor. The trade-
union struggles of the 1880s and 1890s rivaled in intensity the
battles of the 1930s Depression era. Funding baseball provided the capitalists a common ground with labor and supported the contention that class divisiveness was irrelevant in
the United States. As Boss Tweed had earlier sponsored baseball to win votes, and the beer barons had done so to sell beer,
the capitalists became involved to sell their philosophy,
through pro teams and through industrial-league sports for
factory workers.

Garret A. Hobart, U.S. vice president under McKinley, ex-
emplifies the factors attracting the industrialists to baseball.
Hobart practically owned the city of Paterson, New Jersey,
where he ran silk mills, trolley lines, railroad yards, and other
industries. Early in 1896 Paterson was swept with a wave of
labor turmoil. Placard-carrying strikers identified the town
boss as the town enemy. In the midst of the trouble the roving
baseball promoter Edward Grant Barrow came to Paterson
with a new franchise for a team in the Atlantic League. But
Barrow didn't have the funds for a team. He approached
sporting people in town and got nowhere. Then he was di-
rected to Hobart. "Hobart thought a ball club was a good
thing for Paterson," Barrow later related, because "at that
time the silk mills were on strike and the Rogers Locomotive
Works were shut down."

During the last years of the nineteenth century a strike in the factory seemed the inspiration for the owner to discover the need to fund professional baseball in a number of instances. A loose check for such correlations uncovers cases in Pittsburgh, Birmingham, Joliet (Illinois), Saginaw (Michigan), Newark, Haverhill, and Brockton (Massachusetts), and Lebanon, Braddock, and Homestead (Pennsylvania). During an 1897 strike in the anthracite fields of eastern Pennsylvania a whole minor league was organized and funded by Alvin Markle, one of the prominent mine owners, and the head of the owners' committee for negotiations with the union.

Among the leading industrialists Andrew Carnegie showed the most impressive commitment to policies designed to buy labor peace. Until the bloody strike at his Homestead steel mills in 1892 he had been a notorious skinflint with labor. The many dead and wounded in the 1892 conflict changed his attitude. He put a baseball team in Homestead in 1893 and was soon pioneering in worker-welfare programs, accident and burial insurance, cheap home loans, and profit-sharing plans. At the turn of the century he underwrote the nation's first professional football league.

Another pioneer in the development of social programs for workers was the Colorado Fuel and Iron Company. After many years of fighting the militant Western Miners Federation with aggressive tactics, including the use of the state militia, the company opted for the soft sell. In the wake of a protracted strike in 1896 the company hired industrial-relations experts to run a "Sociological Department," which organized programs for the workers in the company's mining camps of Colorado, New Mexico, and Utah. An attractive magazine for the workers was published under the title *Camp and Plant*. The magazine applauded the efforts of the company in funding local libraries, daycare centers, playgrounds, and baseball teams. There was more space devoted to company baseball in *Camp and Plant* than to any other subject except hospital reports. The latter were column upon column of notices on the recuperative progress of workers maimed and mangled in the apparently very unsafe mines and mills of the Colorado Fuel and Iron Company.

The largesse of companies like Colorado Fuel and Iron in giving workers participatory sports they might not otherwise have had is rather admirable—but this doesn't carry over when the funding is for professional spectator sports. The drama of pro sports is diluted when the funding comes from aloof individuals who take little or no part in the affairs of the team. The fans and the sportswriters, ever eager for lively copy, prefer the involved, swashbuckling type of club owner. In his absence our leading teams might as well be run by bureaucrats from a federal department of sports.

BASKETBALL

CHAPTER

8

The Liberal's Game

Basketball is the liberal's game. In recent years it has been a popular subject for writers sympathetic to life in those tough neighborhoods nobody wants to walk through at night. We have Axthelm's book *City Game*, Telander's *Heaven Is a Playground*, Wolf's *Foul*, and assorted other books and articles tying basketball to sociology and urban problems. Basketball was invented in 1891 to meet the needs of the YMCA, which required a nonviolent game that could be played in the gyms that were becoming fixtures in the crowded city slums. Basketball is the only sport which has had a big-league professional franchise totally owned by a trade union—the 1943 Chicago Studebakers of the United Auto Workers. Thirty years ago Herbert Ribalow claimed basketball was a Jewish game. Writing in *The Jew in American Sport*, Ribalow was exaggerating a bit. More to the point, basketball was the game of Franklin Roosevelt's New Deal urban coalition of Jews, Catholics, and blacks.

During the 1976 presidential primaries *Sport* magazine ran an article called "The Jock of Your Choice." There was Ford the footballer, Wallace the boxer, and among others Morris Udall, the ultra-liberal of the bunch, whose claim to fame was a year with basketball's Denver Nuggets. Significantly enough, this team of the 1948–49 season was no ordinary pro outfit; it was socialistic, a worker's cooperative, owned and run by the players themselves.

Basketball is a fitting sport for the less affluent half of society on numerous counts. Equipment costs are minimal. Space for a half-court game can be obtained in even the most crowded inner-city neighborhood. A pickup contest of three or four to a side can be conveniently played on a floor half the size of a tennis court. The fundamentals are easy to master; and a bricklayer with a ten-hour workday can play once a week and become expert enough to make a mark at the local playground.

The working classes move often from city to city and neighborhood to neighborhood. Basketball affords the opportunity to play a team sport without having to know anybody; just show up at the playground, and if you are not picked to play, announce "I have winners," and you'll be in the next game. Then there is shooting baskets alone, an adventure into the realm of individual sport, and without the expense of a back-yard swimming pool, lift tickets at a ski resort, or membership fees for a gymnastics club.

Basketball has traditionally brought sports glory to groups that couldn't afford it elsewhere. In the years before World War I, when basketball was in its infancy, it provided sporting fame for YMCA and settlement house teams, and such outfits as the Cornells of Chicago's Armour Playground, the team which won the AAU National tournaments of 1913 and 1914. College basketball has a long history of outstanding teams from small or minuscule colleges. In the Midwest at the turn of the century there were varsity basketball teams at fifty institutions like Illinois Normal, Rose Polytech, and Eastern Michigan at a time when football-crazed University of Illinois, University of Michigan, and Northwestern University didn't bother to field basketball teams. From the 1930s into the 1950s a procession of Catholic colleges dropped expensive intercollegiate football and shifted emphasis to basketball. In the process the college game came to be dominated by teams from St. John's, DePaul, Marquette, Duquesne, University of San Francisco, and the like.

Competitive team sports tend to be surrogates for the challenges of warfare—clearly so in football and rugby, suggestively so in the brave baseball batter facing a fast-balling side-arm pitcher. The attraction to sports for militarists and other lovers of violence would appear to have a counterpart in an aversion to sports on the part of pacifists, which dates back to their go-limp routine when they were thrown into the gladiatorial pits of the Romans. But then there is basketball—the game specifically devised to appeal to the polite Christians of the YMCA; the game which makes a pallid slap on the wrist a foul; one of the most widely followed games on the planet.

Basketball's birth in 1891 at the Springfield training school for YMCA personnel was a new departure for the Y, a sign of the organization's involvement in the "social gospel" movement to uplift the slums. Not too many years earlier the YMCA had condemned almost all sports, along with dancing, card playing, and vaudeville shows, on the grounds that these activities were "distinctly worldly in their associations, and unspiritual in their influence," and therefore "utterly inconsistent with our professions as disciples of Christ." But a new breed of Christian armed with the social gospel was changing the YMCA. Special efforts were being made to bring the Y's program into those troubled neighborhoods where church attendance was low and crime and social disorder rampant. The new effort required compromise, a willingness to meet the masses partway in activities not quite pure by ideal Christian standards.

The Springfield school had a new program for training YMCA gym teachers. When the program was proposed at the 1889 YMCA convention, old-line Protestants argued that the concept of a Christian gymnasium teacher was a contradiction in terms, and that it would be impossible to find any. "Well, then we'll make them," retorted twenty-four-year-old Dr.

Luther Gulick, proposer of the program, who was soon to be director of physical education at Springfield. Gulick has been voted a spot in basketball's Hall of Fame for his work at Springfield, his leadership role in the movement for sports in the public schools, and his crusade in behalf of basketball's nurturing ground, the public playground.

Gulick gathered an impressive phys-ed staff at Springfield, including two other future members of basketball's Hall of Fame. One was James Naismith, a recent graduate from Presbyterian College in Montreal, the game's inventor; the other was Amos Alonzo Stagg, who was to become the noted coach for basketball and football at the University of Chicago. It was a staff with a social conscience; Stagg, for instance, was politically active and was a presidential elector for the Progressive party in 1912.

Gulick had been given carte blanche to develop an athletic program at Springfield, but his work was being watched suspiciously by the orthodox Protestants in the Y, who remained unconvinced that sports and Christianity were compatible. At Springfield the detractors were found among the students training to be branch secretaries. Gulick insisted that he had not come to Springfield merely to train gym teachers, and that the future branch secretaries, too, should know something about athletics. Gulick believed that if he could devise a sports program that would win the interest of the secretarial types, the cause of sport in the Y would be secure.

An experimental gym class for secretarial trainees was added to the program. It was probably the most analyzed and doted-over gym class in history. The students were given military drills, and the German, Swedish, and French forms of gymnastics. The students were thoroughly bored. Two instructors gave up, telling Gulick the class was impossible. The director then enlisted James Naismith. In discussions over the troublesome class Naismith had told Gulick: "The trouble is not with the men but with the system that we are using. The kind of work for this particular class should be of a recreative nature, something that would appeal to their play instincts."

Naismith suggested that perhaps "we can invent a new game that will meet our needs."

In assigning the new instructor Gulick said: "Naismith, now would be a good time for you to work on that new game that you said could be invented." As the inventor of basketball explained in his memoirs, he hadn't really had in mind a totally new game, but rather an indoor adaptation of existing outdoor games. A variety of adaptations were tried and all failed, either out of boredom on the part of the secretarial students or, as in the case of indoor soccer, because hard kicks knocked out the windows of the gym.

Naismith felt he was about to become the third faculty casualty of the frustrating class. But he had said a new game could be invented; and he decided he would have to make a systematic attempt to analyze games as a whole and devise from scratch a game that would be both interesting and appealing to those Christians turned off by the rough and violent aspects of sports. He had intimate acquaintance with rough sports, having been a professional lacrosse player. He had also been a member of his college track team.

Naismith later described how he invented basketball. His guiding concern was to create an indoor game that was both interesting and safe. He first concluded that a ball game would be the most interesting. The next question: Was the ball to be a big one or a small one? He concluded that a big ball was preferable, since less potential violence would come from an effort of an opposing player to steal the ball away. What shape should the ball be? A round ball was better for throwing, while the shape of the American football was better for carrying under the arm. To carry the ball meant there would be running with it. Runners would get tackled, which meant that players would get hurt. Naismith decided players could not run with a big, round ball. Perhaps they should hit at it with a stick or netted implement? No, because in a small indoor playing area this could be potentially dangerous. The game needed an objective, a "goal" in which the players would try to place the ball. It would have to be rather small or success would be too easy; but a small goal could be blocked off by a line of defenders and the result would be violent pushing and shoving. Therefore, the goal would have to be elevated above the players' heads. The unique twist of having the goal parallel to the ground, so that the player had to lob the ball up into it instead of throwing it straight on, was inspired in part by a makeshift kids' game of lobbing rocks which Naismith had played in his Canadian hometown and in part by a desire to keep shots at the goal from coming with bullet speed.

The horizontal goal was supposed to be a box. Naismith asked the janitor for a couple of suitable boxes, and the janitor said he had none of the desired size, but he did have a couple of round peach baskets in the storeroom. The baskets were tacked to the walls of the gym, and before the first encounter Naismith put a typed page of the rules on a bulletin board. The sheet was titled simply "A New Game." Since there were eighteen men in the class, the first game was played with nine to a side. The game was an immediate success. Before a week was out, it was drawing spectators. When one of the players asked Naismith the name of the new game, he replied that there was no name. The player responded: "Why not call it basketball?" The inventor answered: "We have a basket and a ball, and it seems to me that would be a good name for it."

The secretarial students met daily at 11:30. Coach Naismith, like the coaches of a million succeeding troublesome gym classes, simply issued the ball and let the students play what was to become one of the world's most popular games. Students and teachers from a nearby women's school took to spending their lunch hour watching the play. Within a few weeks the watchers were playing it themselves at the women's school; and basketball had been adopted by the first of the long line of "minority groups" to take the game to heart. Maude Sherman, one of the players on the first women's team, later married James Naismith.

Dr. Gulick's original phys-ed staff did not remain long at Springfield, but instead took their new gospel to YMCAs throughout the country. Stagg went to Chicago in 1892. In 1895 Naismith went to Denver, where he helped develop a basketball program in the YMCA and in the public schools. In 1898 he was hired by the University of Kansas and introduced varsity basketball at that institution. Among the many students of Springfield who spread the game there was Henry F. Kallenberg. He left the YMCA's school in 1892 and enrolled as an undergraduate at the University of Iowa, where he interested other students in forming a team. Kallenberg traveled widely through Iowa and surrounding states promoting basketball. He introduced the game at a conference of Sioux Indians at Big Stone Lake, South Dakota, in 1892; and after attending the Sioux conference the following year Kallenberg wrote enthusiastically to Naismith that the Sioux had made basketball "their chosen form of recreation."

Copies of the rules sent in response to inquiries in the mail did as much to spread the game as the physical presence of disciples from Springfield. Spreading the game via the mail produced a memorable misinterpretation. A confusing diagram in a set of instructions sent to Clara Baer of Newcomb College in New Orleans in 1893 led to a distinctive women's basketball rule relegating certain players to nonshooting guard positions. The diagram had lines dividing parts of the court and depicted players stationed in the different sections. It was intended to show relative positioning, but Ms. Baer interpreted the lines as actual restraining areas. She developed a noted team, and began getting inquiries from women wanting to know how to play the game. She mailed them rules which relegated guards to a midcourt area. Her rules found national acceptance on the grounds that they made for a less strenuous game than the men's.

The men prominent in basketball's growth took an active interest in the women's game—an interest rarely seen in the generally macho world of sport. But then, basketball is the liberal's game. Luther Gulick wrote in the 1901 *Basketball Guide for Women* that their enthusiasm for the game was a positive sign of their changing social role at "a time of great unrest in regard to the status of women." Naismith devoted a chapter of his memoirs to women's basketball. He noted with pride his wife's lifelong involvement with the game, and found another family connection in the active interest in women's basketball on the part of Amos Alonzo Stagg's sister.

Naismith had done his job in creating a "game that would be interesting, easy to learn, and easy to play in the winter and by artificial light." But basketball as played in its first two to three decades was not today's game.

It was floor play rather than scoring which gave the early game its popularity. In the 1890s scores of 8–6 or 10–3 were common; and two decades later a 20–16 score was quite normal. The size of the basketballs made scoring difficult. The initial use of a soccer ball was discarded in 1894 when the Overman Company produced what would be the standard-sized basketball for the next forty years. It was nearly three inches larger in diameter than are the present spheres.

Scoring was difficult when there were no backboards, and this was the case in many locales until World War I. There was simply a basket attached to a pole. Where there were backboards they were of little value for bank shots, because the inner rim of the basket was twenty inches away from the board, instead of today's five inches.

One quality of basketball has been present from its inception to the present day. The sport puts a premium on creative players whose brainstorms force rule changes. No running with the ball was allowed, according to Naismith's rules. So players took to juggling the ball over their heads to keep it to themselves as they ran down the court. When this was outlawed, they invented the dribble.

The initial out-of-bounds rule gave the ball to the team whose player went off the court and retrieved it. What changed this rule was an incident in a game played in a gym with a second-tier balcony. As described by Naismith, a loose ball bounced into the balcony, and the players of one team made a mad rush for the stairs. The opposition had a better strategy. They hoisted one of their players on their shoulders, and he grabbed the lower part of the balcony, swung himself up, and retrieved the ball.

Continuous action is part of basketball's appeal. Out-of-bounds plays stop the action. One solution, which retained widespread use in professional basketball on into the 1920s, was to surround the court with a wire cage ten to eleven feet high (hence the term "the cage game"). Where wire cages were unavailable, strong ropes were used to keep the players from flying into the first rows of spectators when chasing loose balls.

"We bounced off the heavy cord netting like pugilists in a boxing ring," wrote Nat Holman, star of New York's Original Celtics in a description of the pro game some sixty years ago. "We were geared for a rough game," Holman noted. "We wore hip pads, knee guards and an aluminum cup. A cut eyebrow or a loosened tooth were common injuries." He vividly remembered an arena in Providence. It had a wire cage for basketball that was drawn very tightly. When the Celtics played there they were subjected to hard body checks into the wire, in the manner of the body checks into the boards that occur in hockey.

A sizable volume could probably be written on the changes in basketball rules pertaining to fouls. For many years the foul rules differed from one part of the country to another, between the pros and the amateurs, between different professional leagues, and between the colleges and the AAU. Players then and now have declared that while basketball may be a noncollision sport it is definitely not a no-contact sport. Initially, players could get away with much more than they can today. Well into the 1920s some professional leagues had a "covering players" rule which stated, "Both arms around a player shall constitute an offense." As for one-armed mayhem, anything went that was not obviously intentional "striking" or "slugging." Allowances for body contact included the pros' three-man held-ball rule. As Holman explained: "The ref did not call for a held ball until the second opponent slammed or wracked his man up." The amateurs were barely less physical than the pros. Around 1905 there was a campaign to abolish college football because of its violence, and the president of Harvard insisted basketball be included in the ban, since, in his opinion, the two sports were equally vicious.

The lack of uniformity in rules mirrored a lack of formal structure in the competition. Amateurs played pros; colleges played high schools; and there were few organized leagues at any level. This confused period in basketball's first two decades was something of a blessing in disguise. It established a crowd-pleasing David vs. Goliath tradition, which is retained today in college basketball, enabling institutions like the University of North Carolina at Charlotte and Long Beach State to have a shot at the national title—a chance only a handful of schools have in the far less democratic game of college football.

A shortage of indoor gyms with a big enough playing floor and a high enough ceiling contributed to basketball's openness. Teams of all levels had to rent National Guard armories and dance halls for games, and playing in the same places they came to play each other. Sports in the public high schools were too new for many of the schools to have a gym of their own. Facilities of adequate size were also rare in the YMCAs and the colleges. Where big enough gyms existed they tended to have pillars in the middle of the court and other drawbacks. Ralph Morgan, later athletic director at the University of Pennsylvania, has described an 1899 contest between his high school and Temple University, played at the Temple gym. It was "a dark, irregularly proportioned room, and we, the schoolboys, won by the score of 4 to 2. . . . We played around corners and among apparatus, and . . . with a fine disregard of rules."

Some of the toughest competition of basketball's early years was on the courts of city playgrounds, those neighborhood gathering places which were beginning to dot the urban landscape around the turn of the century. The dribble appears to have been first refined into an offensive weapon on the playground courts in Philadelphia, where players from the University of Pennsylvania learned it, subsequently spreading its use throughout eastern colleges. In those years pro basketball was not particularly lucrative, and a number of the best players worked on the side as playground directors, including Ed Wachter, the game's first great center; Edgar Bredbenner, leader of the Reading Olivets; and Richard P. Williams of New London, who had that memorable record as a sprinter to go with a solid reputation in pro basketball.

Basketball lacked a formal, compartmentalized structure in part because a great many of the builders of the game had more pressing goals. Finding activities to keep young people out of trouble was one objective. Basketball came in as child labor went out, and the nurturing ground of quality basketball became the tenement districts which housed the youngsters who had formerly toiled long hours in sweatshops and mills. Working with youths in tough neighborhoods became the self-appointed task of reformers in the settlement houses, who had an even more influential role in these neighborhoods than the YMCA. The settlements provided child care, and for the teenagers offered social and athletic activities. Basketball was the number-one game offered.

The settlement houses initiated athletic programs in the 1890s, and their success paved the way for a movement to put organized athletics in the public schools. Chicago, for instance, launched public school sports in 1899, and New York City in 1903. The most notable contribution to basketball by the settlements was the famous New York Celtics pro team, a collection of all-stars from houses on the East Side. Many other professionals received their basketball training on settlement teams.

The people running settlements were hardly the kind one would expect to encourage the highly competitive play that spawned pro basketball. The settlements were run by idealists, people who believed in a cooperative society rather than a competitive one. For example, the New York settlement with the best team was the University House on the Lower East

Side, run by the highly intellectual socialist William E. Wall-
ing, with the help of volunteers, including Eleanor Roosevelt.
In Chicago the settlement team to beat represented Hull
House, run by socialist Jane Addams. One Chicago newspaper
lamented the "cruel fate which guides the ignorant immigrant
into the socialist precincts of Hull House," and another paper
called Chicago settlement houses, in general, "schools expressly established . . . for teaching anarchy."

The senior team in the extensive basketball program at Hull
House became good enough to take on college competition
and the top athletic clubs of the area. Hull House even took on
Notre Dame, unsuccessfully, since the Irish, then as now, had
one of the nation's best college teams. Hull House was supposed to be a model of the new cooperative society. It was a
place where all cooks and other employees in a unionized
trade had to have a union card, a place where orators waxed
eloquent on the evils of economic competition. And yet Hull
House had a highly competitive basketball program. James
Naismith had a simple enough explanation for Hull House
basketball; he noted that the workers there found "basketball
was a material help in keeping some of the boys off the street."
Keeping youngsters of the tenement districts out of jail was a
large part of settlement work. The key issue, as Jane Addams
saw it, was that "every city in the United States spends a
hundred-fold more money for juvenile reform [policing] than
is spent in providing a means for public recreation, and none
of us, as yet, sees the folly and shame of such a procedure."

The settlement houses and the first playground courts were
located in neighborhoods where entire families often lived in
one-room apartments. Photographs of the early playgrounds
depict a swarm of youngsters. James Naismith found a surpris-
ingly large number of young basketball players when he vis-
ited a Brooklyn settlement, and consequently he decided to
look into the settlement game nationwide. He was impressed
with the way the program got so many individuals involved
rather than with the by-product of quality play, and he credited the settlements with the attention "given to the develop-

ment of the boys rather than to the winning of the games."
The emphasis on mass participation carried over into the
movement for public school sports. When New York City
schools began athletics this spirit was manifested in the practice of awarding all competitors a ribbon or button, win
or lose.

Getting city hall to fund young people's sports was a hard
and frustrating task. Jane Addams fought for years to get
Chicago city officials to fund public playgrounds. Officialdom
was loath to listen to Addams, even though she had a fine
working example in a playground her workers built in 1893.
She had acquired the site for the playground by talking the
owner of two firetrap tenements into tearing them down and
clearing away the rubble.

The New York City Council had voted authorization of
playground funds in 1887. But twelve years later not a dime
had been appropriated. In 1899 New York settlement workers
cleared the land for what was to become the large Seward
Park playground. But when they asked the city to supply
sandboxes, basketball courts, and play equipment the parks
board balked. The board argued that they had better uses for
public money than children's games, and suggested Seward
Park be landscaped with grass and trees to make it a pleasant spot for adults of the neighborhood. Seward Park got its
athletic equipment in 1903, and later developed a memorable
basketball team, good enough in 1913 to go on a nationwide
tour.

Sports in the public schools were born amid controversy.
Conservatives who viewed schools strictly in terms of the three
Rs saw no more justification for public expenditures for athletic coaches than they saw for drama teachers or band leaders. But a part of the Progressive movement of the period was
a fight for Progressive education, which initially was a fight for
such "frills" as athletics, drama, and music. Reminiscing about
his role in creating the New York Public School Athletic
League, Luther Gulick noted that in the year in which the
initial appropriation was voted through city hall "practically

all the papers expressed a constant desire to discuss matters relating to public school athletics."

The cause of public sport attained a cover of respectability in 1905 with the creation of the Playground Association of America (now known as the National Recreation Association). Its leadership included Teddy Roosevelt, military brass, noted liberals like John Dewey and Jacob Riis, and YMCA workers including Dr. Gulick. The sizable executive committee also contained Jane Addams, other socialists, and the noted left-wing philanthropist J. G. Phelps Stokes. The Association put out a monthly journal, *The Playground*, which carried discussions of how to get funds from city hall, how to get volunteer workers, and how to develop appealing programs. Among the many propaganda items was the following, from the May 1910 issue:

Boys Sent to Playgrounds Instead of to Reform School

There was a gang of Polish boys in East Buffalo, N. Y. For months they had made of themselves a public nuisance by finding their recreation and amusement in throwing of stones at the windows of passing railroad coaches. Several of the boys were arrested, but the mischief did not abate. . . . Then the Broadway playground was opened in East Buffalo, and the members of the gang came to the playground. They did not stop throwing; they only changed their missiles from stones to basket balls, and their targets from passenger car windows to goals; by this transition they themselves were changed from anarchists into law-abiding citizens.

Naismith created a new game, but it took years to develop the game into a sport. Basketball became more than a game—more than dodgeball, capture the flag, or stickball—when it attained distinct levels of competition between teams representing specific collections of fans. In the evolution of the game into a sport there was a sifting-out process in which it was learned which class was attracted to basketball. It was discovered that basketball was not going to become one more sport for society people, as intended by the organizers of short-lived teams in posh athletic clubs.

The first significant effort in giving structure to basketball was made by the Amateur Athletic Union. During the 1890s the AAU became the ruling body for most amateur sports. Under its supervision were the sports of athletic clubs, YMCAs, National Guard groups, and even the colleges, since the colleges had not yet founded the National Collegiate Athletic Association (NCAA) or any other major regulatory body, aside from their track and field federation.

AAU control was maintained through registration of athletes. Athletes were told that registration in the AAU gave them the social standing of the gentleman sportsman. Domination of AAU sports by prestigious athletic clubs lent credence to this claim. The leaders of the Athletic Union were confident that order and regulation in the new game of basketball would be attained as easily as in gymnastics and track and field. In 1899 in New York a "National Basketball Tournament" was sponsored by the AAU, with competing teams representing well-known athletic clubs. The Knickerbocker Club was the winner, and won again in the 1900 tournament. But the tournaments failed to draw enough fans to turn a profit. Perhaps the fans were aware that far better teams than the Knickerbockers had not been invited to the tourneys.

Basketball was mushrooming in popularity, and the vast majority of new teams failed to sign up with either the AAU or its aligned YMCA Athletic Association. As of 1901 only 3,000 players of the nation's YMCAs, colleges, athletic clubs, and other institutions which provided sports had registered with either organization. The AAU fee of 25 cents per player was modest enough, but rules and red tape associated with membership were discouraging.

In 1900 a major AAU campaign to register basketball

teams was launched. It was a failure, partly because it was an effort made in behalf of "all those interested in the perpetuation of the game for gentlemen," in the words of AAU basketball director George Hepbron. Basketball's following was not among gentlemen, but among those who would have been turned away at the door if they had tried to enter the premises of the Knickerbocker Club. The best basketball players were of the same class of people who had driven the Knickerbockers out of baseball three decades earlier.

The registration drive was doomed also because teams that failed to register were categorized as professionals or collections of cheats. Hepbron equated his cause with the salvation of amateurism, and wrote in the AAU's 1899–1900 *Basketball Guide* that the failure of the registration drive would see basketball "degenerate into a game where men would be welcomed who play for money, enter under assumed names, and make a business of the game." A writer in the 1900–1901 *Guide* declared: "The men who set up a howl against paying 25 cents a year to register are not only 'cheap sports,' but are a class termed 'fault finders.' . . . Sometimes these men risk more of their loose change than 25 cents, but not when they're anxious to bet on a game, for the game is generally 'fixed' when these men put up money." The writer declared that basketball players who didn't have an AAU card were easily recognized, because "they always act as if they're being followed by a detective."

The unregistered teams were declared "outlaws." By 1905 the "outlaws" included half the colleges of the Northeast, the nation's basketball stronghold. Any registered team playing an outlaw was booted out of the AAU and became an outlaw itself. George Hepbron defended the AAU's position on the grounds that basketball, like any other sport, needed order and structure, and "the practical way to accomplish this is to affiliate your team with this organization and play only such other teams as will do the same, leaving the irresponsible teams to play among themselves without any order or regulation."

There were, however, hidden costs in joining the AAU. Indoor facilities for a full-court game were mostly armories or dance halls, which had to be rented, with the rental recouped through admission charges. The superior teams were outside the AAU, and it was these "outlaws" who were capable of drawing a sufficient gate to break even financially. A team joining the AAU ran the risk of committing financial suicide.

The financial pinch hit not only the teams in the tenement districts but those in the colleges as well. Basketball historian Bill Mokray has noted that "in almost every instance" the introduction of basketball in a college was the effort "of one or two individuals," who acted without help from the administration and "scheduled games with nearby high schools, YMCAs, colleges, travelling professionals, or local town teams whose guarantees helped meet the team's expenses."

Ralph Morgan has described how his University of Pennsylvania team, lacking faculty sponsorship, had to rent an armory with the players' own cash; and they had to show up early and stay late to set up and then put away the folding chairs for the spectators. After the game he took the proceeds home and placed them "under my pillow, safe from robbers." Game profits paid train fare for road games.

The casual approach to team financing that had money going under a pillow instead of into a bank account contributed to AAU suspicions that players on many teams were skimming off the top. Further suspicions were aroused when "outlaw" teams claiming to be amateur competed against teams that admitted dividing gate receipts among players. (There were only a dozen or two openly professional outfits operating in 1900.) Hepbron found other evidence of creeping professionalism, including "the practice of some teams requiring a much larger guarantee than their actual expenses. A notable example of which was the team of one of our largest colleges in the East."

Even the informal games at the public playgrounds came under AAU attack. All sorts of players frequented the playgrounds, including outlaws; and as one AAU report noted, outlaws "do their utmost to keep novice teams from registering." To purify the playground the Amateur Union adopted a policy that, if followed today, would strip a teenager of amateur standing for participating in a pickup game with one of those National Basketball Association pros who make occasional appearances on the local courts. Warning of the "professional ball menace" in Philadelphia, the AAU's *Guide* for 1902–1903 declared: "Boys were playing with professionals one day and with amateurs the next, seemingly totally ignorant of the fact that by so doing they were surrendering their amateur standing and jeopardizing their whole future in athletics in their school or college."

A Philadelphia *Ledger* sportswriter couldn't believe the AAU's stand. He wrote the Basketball Committee asking if he was correct in assuming the Athletic Union would take away a youngster's amateur standing for an informal game against an outlaw, "whether any money was exchanged or not." The Committee replied: "That is correct," and suggested the young people organize "a purely amateur league."

The Amateur Athletic Union's attempt to regulate basketball had one significant effect: it forced the opposition to organize. Instead of stamping out professionalism, the AAU policies seemed to contribute to the sizable expansion of pro basketball. Attempts to regulate the colleges drove the colleges to bolt in 1905 and set up their own basketball association, aligned with the high schools. Then in 1907 a substantial block of National Guard, settlement house, and other amateur teams deserted the AAU to create their own Protective Basketball Association. It lasted only a few years, but it established liberalized relationships with the pros; and when the AAU reemerged as a prominent organization for basketball during the 1920s, it accepted the new relationships. Pros and amateurs were free to fraternize at the playgrounds. And special dispensations were allowed for such contests as the annual game between the South Philadelphia Hebrew Association's youth team and the Association's professional team, the famous SPHAS, the South Philadelphia Hebrew All-Stars, one of the nation's best during the 1920s and 1930s.

Philadelphia was the site of many important developments in basketball. The first, in 1901, was the decision of the Philadelphia YMCA council, which followed the AAU, to drop basketball on the grounds that games at the Y were becoming too rough. YMCA sports in Philadelphia dated back twenty years, much longer than in most cities. The Y's track meets and then its basketball games became important spectator attractions for city sports fans. Fierce competition led to rough basketball, specifically the use of the dribble, then outlawed by the AAU, and consequently by its ally the YMCA.

The dribble, which was sort of a dividing line between the gentleman's game and the playground game, was the subject of one of the major controversies of basketball's early period. The AAU Basketball Committee was of the opinion that a dribbler was inviting physical attack. Putting the ball on the floor was "making of necessity a rough game," said George Hepbron, adding: "This might be 'hand polo,' but it is not basket ball. Keep the ball off the ground and play standing on two feet instead of on all fours. Disorder is the result of ground plays."

It was in Philadelphia, as we have noted, that the art of the offensive dribble, driving in for a lay-up, was first refined. At this time the dribble, where allowed, included two-handed as well as one-handed bouncing. Discontinuous dribbling—stopping and starting again—was also allowed. The proponents of this style of dribbling, who kept it alive in the professional ranks until the late 1920s, felt it made for a more exciting game.

After the stars of the Philadelphia YMCAs were kicked out for dribbling and other uncouth styles of play, they continued playing by turning pro, renting halls, and dividing profits among themselves. The local Catholic archdiocese also had an extensive basketball program, with plenty of dribblers. In

1901 a whole professional league of Catholic teams was launched, called the Philadelphia League. Between this organization and the teams of former Y players and others, Philadelphia now had more pro teams than all the other cities in the nation combined.

The Philadelphia League, which later included the SPHAS, had been organized by Philadelphia *Press* sportswriter William J. Scheffer. He gave pro basketball a touch of class in 1902 when he produced the first annual *Reach, Basketball Guide*, which was to be the guide for pro basketball's rules and records for a quarter of a century. Scheffer's annual was a sounding board for criticism of the AAU. In one article he said of the dribble: "This spectacular play is a feature of every game, and why the A.A.U. rules do not permit it seems strange." Scheffer conjectured: "The rules were formed by men that took little interest in the game."

The ban on the dribble became a pretext for the colleges to leave the AAU behind and create their own rules, in their own basketball association. It was a student-run association, founded in 1905, a year before college administrators got together to form the NCAA. In his article "Reminiscences of Basketball Government" Ralph Morgan of Pennsylvania described how the college basketball organization was born at a post-game drinking party of Penn and Yale players at the New Haven House Rathskeller. The "outlaw" status of the two teams came under discussion. Neither team had bothered to register with the AAU, and AAU secretary James E. Sullivan had recently sent letters to unregistered colleges informing team managers that their teams would be "disqualified" if they played unregistered opponents. Sullivan had informed Penn manager Morgan that his team was going to be disqualified if it played Yale, already disqualified for playing another unregistered team. The students at the Rathskeller, no doubt full of beer, found it amusing that James Sullivan was dictating schedules to teams that hadn't yet joined his organization. The captain of the Yale team suggested that the players and team managers form their own college association.

Two months later, at the meeting to officially launch the new group, the assembled representatives of thirty-five colleges were in a more serious mood. They decided all effort should be made to keep their association on peaceful terms with the gentlemen of the AAU. It was agreed that their actions that April day were not being taken in anger over the outlaw issue, but were being dictated out of need for new playing rules, including the legalization of the one-handed dribble. They titled their organization the Collegiate Basketball Rules Committee. In July Morgan and other leaders met in a New York hotel room for a session of rule writing that lasted until 4:00 A.M.

The following day Morgan, accompanied by Columbia player-coach Harry Fisher, paid a visit to the AAU's James Sullivan. The two young men hoped to show their good will toward the AAU by asking Sullivan to have his sports publishing company publish the new college rules. Of the meeting, Morgan writes: "When we stated our errand I thought he would have apoplexy. He stormed at us; then he pleaded with us to forget the separate body and join the A.A.U. Committee, and upon our refusal he then began to laugh." Sullivan gave in and agreed to publish the rules; and Morgan left feeling that Sullivan deserved credit "for being thoroughly sporting."

The following season found many new college teams in operation, and a new league in the Midwest that comprised most of today's Big Ten schools. Scheffer attributed much of the expansion to the new college rules, especially the legalizing of the dribble. Morgan's Rules Committee allowed colleges to take on professional teams, a policy maintained until the 1916 season, the first season under a new, unified set of college and AAU rules. While the open competition lasted, a number of colleges took a shot at the greatest of pre–World War I pro teams, the Buffalo Germans, formerly the Buffalo YMCA. The available and regrettably incomplete records show the Germans with eleven wins, including two over Notre Dame, and one loss, to Niagara University in 1914.

Control of college teams gradually passed from students to

faculty. Coaches were hired and assorted leagues were formed. But the scarcity of large gyms and a lack of inter-sectional games minimized the prestige of the college game until the mid-1930s. High school basketball was probably a bigger show. It had the fierce loyalty of fans in small towns; and beginning in the 1920s there were national tournaments for both Catholic and public high schools.

During the 1920s and 1930s basketball attained a peculiar spot in the nation's sports hierarchy. It had more players than either baseball or football, but the same could be said for volleyball. Unlike volleyball, basketball was a sport with spec-tators, more than baseball or football had. For all its popu-larity, however, basketball was a second-rate sport, at least by the usual measurements of such standings. It was without a class connection of the kind associated with country club sport; it didn't have a secure major-league professional level until the late 1940s; and the college game didn't come into its own until the launching of the National Invitational Tourna-ment in 1938 and the NCAA tournament in 1939.

Before the coming of the college tourneys and the profes-sional NBA, basketball had much in common with bowling. It was a community activity. Basketball coverage in the daily papers consisted of dozens of minuscule game reports on YMCA, ethnic club, industrial, college, and pro contests—much as the sports pages then ran long columns of bowlers' scores. When it came to pre-game promotional articles, the game touted in the small-town papers was likely to be a high school or even junior high school contest. The big-city papers took more interest in college promos, but hardly more than was given to the better teams of community centers, ethnic clubs, and the like.

In the neighborhoods of the settlement houses immigrant groups created a bewildering assortment of teams and leagues. By the 1930s there were tournaments for the titles of Lithu-anian National championship; Jewish Recreational Council Tri-State championship; National B'nai Brith championship; Polish Roman Catholic championship; Serbian championship;

and National Federation of Russian Orthodox Clubs championship. In Chicago one of the big games of the year pitted the CYO (Catholic Youth Organization) All-Stars, against the B'nai Brith All-Stars. Chicago-area tournaments of ethnic organizations developed enough interest to draw crowds in excess of 10,000 spectators for the championship games.

In addition to ethnic clubs, community basketball was widely sponsored by lodges such as the Elks, Moose, and Foresters, as well as by the YMCAs and the settlement houses. The *Spalding Official Basketball Guide* reported the "exceedingly well patronized" community tournament in Pittsburgh in 1931. The 121 teams entered represented five divisions, with a "Midget Class" at the bottom, and at the top a "First Class," which had teams "composed of ex-college and independent stars of wide repute." The entries were the better teams of assorted leagues for boys, teens, and adults who played in the Allegheny Mountain Basketball Association. Team sponsors included YMCA branches, various lodges and fraternal orders, the American Legion, church organizations, ethnic clubs, factories, and retail businesses; and some of the adult teams were run by, and named after, their star player or coach.

Professional basketball was essentially an activity put on by community groups and for community groups, rather than a promotion of individual entrepreneurs. Pro basketball, it may be remembered, began when opportunities for a full-court game were at a premium. The first pros were players who hired themselves out to groups interested in embellishing a social affair with a ball game. Historians generally agree with the assessment in the *Encyclopedia of Pro Basketball* that "these first professionals . . . turned pro not to make money, but simply to keep on playing their game."

The "cage game" of the pros developed a connection with dance halls and armories that was retained for decades. Most games were played as part of a twin attraction advertised as "Basketball Game and Dance." Sometimes the evening started with a game, followed by a dance, and on other occasions the game was played between sets of the dance band. Nat Holman recollected how the pros of his era were in constant search of a shoe that provided adequate traction on a polished dance floor. He found it helped to fill the suction cups of his sneakers with Vaseline.

Professional ball was largely an ethnic sport. The heroes of the cage game had names like Borgmann, Husta, Friedman, Dehnert, and Chizmadia. The popularity of playing in a cage may in part have been an extension of the tenement-district playground rule that a ball bouncing off the fence was still in play. The dance-and-game format was one the minority groups used for amateur as well as pro contests. Harlem's Manhattan Casino, home court for many black professional teams, had a heavy schedule of amateur basketball over the Christmas season of 1910. Advertisements in the black weekly the New York *Age* announced the "Biggest Basketball Game and Dance," the "Greatest of Them All! Basketball Game and Dance," and a "Matinee Basketball and Dance."

The ethnic connection for pro basketball was established in a period of great effort among minority groups to build a community solidarity to alleviate the conditions described in Thomas and Znaniecki's 1920 study, *The Polish Peasant in America*. These conditions included rampant alcoholism, "the disorganization of the marriage-group among Polish immigrants," "vagabondage and delinquency of boys," and "sexual immorality of girls." Sponsoring a pro basketball team like the all-Polish Detroit Pulaskis was a means of rallying the group. Similarly, the SPHAS hired only Jewish players; and the Brooklyn Visitations hired only Irish. Then there was the first great black American team, the Harlem Renaissance Five, founded in 1922 at the height of the cultural movement known as the Harlem Renaissance. The fever of group loyalty is seen in the prizefight boom of the 1920s, when it was said in New York that the riot squad had to be on call whenever a promoter presented a mixed fight card of Irish and Jewish pugilists.

"The SPHAS often shopped in my store," comments a retired South Philadelphia storekeeper proudly. But this team
contributed more than community pride; it brought the community together physically. One Philadelphian says his fondest
memory of the Hebrew All-Stars regular Saturday night "Basketball Game and Dance" at the Broadwood Hotel is that "a
great many married people of my generation first met at the
Broadwood on basketball night."

The preference of pro basketball fans for local heroes of
their own group made it difficult to create a major league.
Such leagues are marketed according to the notion that their
teams represent superior talent first, with any homegrown
aspect being merely a coincidental plus. Major-league players
are considered *real* professionals—that is, in it strictly for the
money. But William Scheffer, whose *Reach Guide* was the
bible of pro basketball, saw the sport in a different light. The
1915–1916 *Guide*, for example, described the professional
team of the Newark Turnverein Society with the comment
"Though defeated many times, they always played good clean
ball during the season. Manager Charriat's aim has always
been to promote the game as a sport rather than a money
proposition, and the followers of his team are well pleased
with their record." In 1924 Scheffer editorialized about professional basketball leagues, declaring: "The fans do not care a
continental about how strong a team is unless there is a team
equally as strong to meet them. Take two teams equally
matched but of mediocre calibre, fighting for the championship, and the halls will be jammed to see them play."

The first professional league was launched in 1899 with
teams in the Philadelphia and south New Jersey areas. For the
next forty years, with one exception, leagues were collections
of teams in mining and mill towns, or in the neighborhoods or
suburbs of big cities. The exception was the American
League, which started in 1926 with six of eight franchises in
major-league baseball cities but was forced to take in more
franchises in places like Paterson and Ft. Wayne in order to
survive five shaky seasons.

There were far more independent teams than league teams. The Newark Turnverein club was one of a dozen independent professional outfits operating in northern New Jersey in 1916. Independents and leaguers alike were almost all in the Northeast during this period. The best independents were barnstorming outfits of full-time pros, like the Buffalo Germans and New York Celtics. Their opponents were often teams of part-time pros. One of the better of these was the Pittsburgh black team, Leondi's Big Five. This club "was composed of rugged men who toss steel ingots and mailsacks as a daily toil," noted a sportswriter in 1920. William Betts, a star for the team from 1917 through the 1920s, recollected that "We used to get $25 a game when we played little teams. But when we played the big teams, like Coffey and the Original Celtics, we got as high as $75 a game."

When the barnstorming Celtics toured the South and the outer regions of the Midwest, they played opponents unfamiliar with professional rules. Consequently, half of a game was played under amateur rules, and half under professional rules. The famous Celtics became showmen; offering more than a game, they pioneered in the fancy ball-handling routines of the kind later associated with the Globetrotters. Celtic star Nat Holman, who was coach at City College in New York at the same time, was an innovator in slick-passing teamwork offense. The showboating of the Celtics was only an extension of basically sound basketball principles which the team helped introduce to the country. Scheffer's *Guide* says of a Celtics southern tour in 1926 that at Jacksonville, Florida, every school and college in that section of the South had representatives present to witness the play, and it is safe to say that glimpses of the Celtic style will be visible when the schools of the South open in the fall."

The better barnstorming basketball teams, like barnstormers in other sports, made a practice of going easy on mediocre opponents in order to entice them into a return game with increased guarantees and wagering. Amazing comebacks to

University Settlement House, the New York City AAU Champions, 1907.

Playground basketball, Newark, 1914.

Basketball's evolution from cage to court included a period using wire netting, as shown here at the University of Michigan in 1929.

In the 1940s the annual game between the top pro team and the college all-stars drew such crowds as the 23,912 in Chicago stadium in 1945.

Roughness in early pro basketball seen in the 1945 game between Ft. Wayne and the college all-stars. Bob McDermott (24 of Ft. Wayne) mangles Bruce Hale of the all-stars, in order to steal the ball. Hale has his fingers twisted and is thrown to the hardwoods. There was no foul called on this play.

The Miami Army Air Force team beat the Navy teams so often the Admirals had to rush in all-American reinforcements.

World War II sport was often connected with USO, the program most remembered for Bob Hope's shows for the troops. This photo shows Lucille Ball on the bench with her team, the Wright Field "Air Techs," at a 1945 game in Los Angeles.

The 1940 Harlem Globetrotter team that won the professional world championship tournament. A reminder that the Trotters were then more than a show team.

The CCNY "Cinderella" team of 1950, winners of both the NIT and NCAA tournaments. Many of its stars were implicated in the fixing scandal of 1951.

LIU players hounded by the press as they leave court hearing on fixing scandal: Sherman White on left, LeRoy Smith on right, shading his eyes, and Adolph Bigos in center with hat.

The old American Basketball League folded in 1952 rather than start the new season with game fixers. Alex Groza, Ralph Beard of Kentucky U, and Sherm White of LIU had all been hired by the Jersey City team.

Anita Ortega of the Pioneers drives on Donna Geis of the New Jersey Gems in the Women's Basketball League, 1979–80 season.

The nearly empty house at a home game of the now defunct Los Angeles Dreams. Pat Mayo (13 of Pioneers), battling with Michelle McKenzie (26 of Dreams).

A crowd of 8,000 watched as the 1978 gay softball league champs, Oil Can Harry's Oilers, beat the San Francisco Police Department in the annual "Peaches vs. Fuzz" playoff. The Oilers' cheerleaders were also named best in the league that year.

Mudville's Revenge is in part a tribute to hang-loose fans. A contemporary bunch of baseball fans shown here at Chicago's Comiskey Park.

snatch victory from defeat were part of the Celtics' legend. A report on their 1925 season noted two memorable comebacks in which the New Yorkers were down by a point with just seconds remaining and the other team was in possession of the ball. In the first contest, Holman stole the ball and let fly with a long shot that swished through the net as time ran out; and in the second instance, Johnny Beckman turned the same trick.

The Celtics added drama to their tours by advertising every game as a contest for the World Championship, no matter how mediocre the opposition. The Celtics did get beaten once in a while, which was to be expected in their grueling season of more than 150 games. In the 1923 season they went 193–11. The teams that took away the Celts' World Championship rarely held it long, since the Celtics invariably won the re-match; and they claimed in 1927 to have never lost a season's series to any team.

A team that beat the Celtics was in a position to launch its own barnstorming tour. Good play against the Celtics in 1926 launched the SPHAS and Harlem Renaissance clubs into the national basketball picture. The Rens broke even in a six-game series with the Celtics. The SPHAS took one out of three with the Celts, but then swept a two-game series with the Renaissance Five. The Celtics disbanded in 1928, were re-organized late in the 1929 season, and played off and on during the decade of the Depression. The SPHAS and Rens became the dominant teams of the 1930s. In 1933 the barnstorming Rens won an incredible 88 straight games in 86 days. Then they met the Celtics and lost 39–32, a defeat the Rens' fans could attribute to exhausted players who had spent the past three months sleeping in the team bus.

In their heyday the Celtics were known as "the Original Celtics," because a previous owner of the club back in the 1910 era refused to relinquish the name "New York Celtics." As Holman, Beckman, Joe Lapchick, Dutch Dehnert, and other Celtic stars of the 1920s retired, there sprang up during the 1930s a number of clubs claiming to be "the Original

Celtics." It appears that the true carriers of the name made
their last tour in 1943, with a team that included Davey
Banks, who had first starred for the Celtics back in 1926.

Pro basketball in the era of the Celtics had a working-class
following and was a rather theatrical production, of the kind
the same sort of fans appreciated in roller derby and professional wrestling. Basketball promoters were of the upwardly
mobile working class. Jim Furey, who owned and managed
the Celtics in their prime, was a cashier in a clothing store;
and Celtics tours were financed, in part, with the $187,000 he
embezzled from his employer. After his conviction and jail
sentence in 1926 the players took control and ran the team as
an economic cooperative. The SPHAS were originally run by
the Hebrew Association. Eddie Gottlieb became the owner in
the late 1920s after serving as team manager. He was a
product of a local high school and first joined the SPHAS as a
player. The West Indian immigrant Bobby Douglas, who
came to own the Renaissance club, had previously been a
player and manager of various Harlem teams.

There were promoters in other sports who took notice of
the basketball crowds in dance halls and armories and envi-
sioned sizable profits in a basketball league organized like
leagues in pro baseball and football. Charles Power, a Pittsburgh sportswriter with years of organizational experience in
minor-league baseball, made an attempt in 1908. Scheffer applauded Power's new professional basketball Central League
as a new departure in the game. It had teams representing
towns rather than a group, and it offered good salaries to top
talent. The League lasted one season, and two reorganization
attempts were failures.

When the American League was organized for the 1926
season, its sponsors claimed a new departure for pro basketball. The league was going to use college rules, thereby en-
couraging well-known collegians to turn pro. At the time few
college players went on to pro basketball. The American

League had able leadership in Joe Carr, commissioner of football's NFL. The league had money from NFL owners behind two of its franchises, and another was bankrolled by baseball star Harry Heilmann. For the first time a basketball league was more than a regional operation. Franchises stretched from Boston to Chicago, and six of the nine teams were in major-league baseball cities.

The new league began without basketball's three best teams —the Renaissance, Celtics, and SPHAS. Race prejudice kept black teams like the Rens out of the organized leagues, while the Celtics and SPHAS felt there was more profit in barnstorming. The Celtics and SPHAS did join the league in its second season, and, with the Celtics obtaining Madison Square Garden for their home court, the prospects for the American League looked excellent. But the Celtics failed to draw good gates at the Garden. It was not for lack of victories —they slaughtered the opposition. They went 32–5 their first season; and in their second and last year with the American League they went 40–9. Yet the Celtics' crowds at the Garden were hardly more than the capacity house of 3,000 they could get in an exhibition game against the non-League Rens up in Harlem's Manhattan Casino, or against the non-League Visitations in Brooklyn.

American League promoters expected that a big-league image would entice through the turnstiles segments of the public that were unfamiliar with pro basketball. But for the big-league mystique to work there has to be a semblance of competitive balance among the teams. The Celtics destroyed this. The League had to rely on the already initiated fans. But the faithful fans considered pro basketball more than a game. It was also a social affair, a dance party, a regular gathering of friends. Long after the American League had folded, the SPHAS were still packing the Broadwood Hotel ballroom for the Saturday night "Basketball Game and Dance."

By 1930 professional teams no longer played in a cage, nor did they use the two-handed dribble. But on into the World Was II years the pros retained their ethnic and community followings, and still played in ballrooms and armories. The rather charmingly communal world of professional basketball did have its drawbacks. The crowds were too small for players to make a decent living at their game, unless they were on one of the handful of overworked barnstorming outfits. Black players couldn't jump to white teams, and this reduced their power to bargain for good salaries from the owners of the black teams. Playing before small crowds, with little press coverage, the best players in the game failed to get the public recognition for athletic excellence that their counterparts of more recent decades have received.

Changes in American life during the 1930s and 1940s led to a transformation in basketball, first at the lower levels, and then among the professionals. We may now turn to the story of basketball's flowering in this period.

9

A New Deal for College Basketball

In 1930 basketball played to crowds in the hundreds, or to a couple of thousand spectators at important contests. College basketball teams were often stocked with football players keeping in shape for the really important gridiron game. Newspapers considered January and February dead months for sport and shortened their sports sections accordingly, until March and the approach of baseball season.

The country was slipping into an economic depression, and one could hardly imagine in 1930 the immense growth that awaited basketball in the decade ahead. The Depression caused a number of baseball's minor leagues to fold, and attendance declined sharply in the major leagues during the worst years of the slump. In college football "the sale of big-game tickets declined just as severely as that of any other market commodity," noted Foster Dulles in his history of recreation.

While the reigning spectator sports were having their problems, basketball was a different story. John L. Griffith, editor of the coaches' magazine *Athletic Journal*, surveyed the sports scene in 1936 and found basketball a special case. He found that the hard times were having little adverse effect upon the game, and "in fact, basketball has arrived." It had more players and more fans than ever before. "We salute basketball on its ascendency to the ranks of the elect," Griffith said enthusiastically.

College basketball in the 1930s featured an ever-increasing number of inter-sectional games. The elevation in the stature of the college game was climaxed by the inauguration of the National Invitational Tournament in 1938, and the NCAA tournament in 1939. Industrial teams began drawing large crowds. Sponsoring businesses recruited talented players, and in the Southwest and on the Pacific coast the best of the industrial outfits took on the leading colleges of the area. In the Midwest, factory teams joined the swelling ranks of professional basketball. The itinerary of a barnstorming professional outfit touring the Midwest in the mid-1930s might be mistaken for a stock-market report; there were the rubber teams in Akron, Goodyear and Firestone; there were steel teams, Cleveland Midland, Youngstown Sheet & Tube, Wheeling Corrugated; and there were the electronics pros, Pittsburgh Westinghouse, Ft. Wayne General Electric, and Erie G.E. In 1938 industrial teams formed the backbone of the professional National Basketball League, forerunner of today's National Basketball Association. High school basketball attained new heights during the 1930s. The *Athletic Journal* chronicled a startling attendance rise at state basketball tournaments of the high schools.

The spark that set off the basketball explosion was provided by Franklin D. Roosevelt's public works program. The work crews of the WPA, PWA, and various state agencies doubled the nation's available seating capacity for basketball games. The New Deal constructed new civic auditoriums, college field houses, and innumerable high school gyms. As of 1937 the WPA had allotted some $500 million, about 10 percent of its total expenditures, for new recreation facilities and parks. Before the New Deal was through with its work it had constructed thousands of new playgrounds. Increasing the number of neighborhood basketball courts added participants and overall interest in the game. In much the same manner the

8,000 public tennis courts constructed by the New Deal work crews helped double the number of tennis players in America between 1930 and 1960, and in the process created a body of tennis fans who would provide greatly increased gate receipts at professional tennis matches.

New Deal expenditures on sports facilities were viewed with some concern by editor Griffith of *Athletic Journal*. He suggested in June 1937 that it might be wise to keep in mind maintenance and running costs before rushing ahead with an expensive new athletic plant for a high school or college. In addition, Griffith saw an alarming acceptance of "the totalitarian idea"—a reliance on government to provide the good things that would lead the people to believe in "an omnipotent and providential state."

From the other end of the political spectrum, it could be said of the New Deal's contribution to basketball that it was only fitting and proper that the game nurtured by the immigrants of turn-of-the-century tenement districts was being pushed into maturity by the downtrodden masses who wielded picks and shovels for the WPA, PWA, CCC, and other agencies. The economically disadvantaged might even be credited with launching the Madison Square Garden college doubleheaders, which by 1940 were basketball's biggest spectator attraction. The initial college doubleheader in the Garden, actually a tripleheader, was a benefit in December 1931 for New York mayor Jimmy Walker's Unemployment Relief Fund. It filled the Garden, as did two subsequent doubleheader shows for the employment fund. These financial successes paved the way for promoter Ned Irish's commercial college doubleheaders.

The Works Projects Administration was ridiculed by conservatives as an agency that hired loafers to soak the public till while producing little of value. Not so with the new basketball plants. The latest architectural techniques were used to make the new arenas and gyms some of the first in the nation to provide ample seating without any view obstructed by support pillars. Scoreboards were installed which, while not having all the gadgetry of today's boards, were impressive enough for their day. The *Athletic Journal* noted that the University of Nebraska Coliseum provided spectators a clear view of "Nebraska's electric clock. . . . This is an important feature in holding the interest of the fans."

To make sure that the seats were filled at basketball games the playing rules were altered to create a more exciting game, one with more action and far more scoring. So many aspects were changed so fast that a coach wrote to the editor of the *Basketball Guide* in 1936 asking if it was not about time to call a halt to the tinkering and let some of the effects sink in. The coach went on to suggest a dozen changes of his own which he felt were essential. Then, realizing that his attitude was illogical, he proposed that the ban on revisions be put into effect after his changes had been adopted.

When the rules makers began their transformation of basketball, a "point-a-minute team," one scoring 40 points a game, was considered a group of prolific scorers. By the time the rule changing subsided in the 1940s the prolific scorers were aiming for 80 or more points a game. The modifications included: the advent of the rule requiring a team to get to the midcourt line in 10 seconds; the establishment of a 3-second lane, which opened up play underneath the basket; increases in the allowable number of time-outs, personal fouls, and substitutions; reduction in the size of the basketball, cutting 2.5 inches from the circumference; and reduction of the ball's weight by 2 ounces. Legalization of the more easily handled laceless ball, in 1938, also increased scoring potential.

The most talked about revision was the elimination of the center jump after each basket, in favor of giving the ball in the backcourt to the team just scored upon. If one had to pick a date for the onset of modern high-scoring basketball, it would be March 1937, when the tip-off after each basket was discarded.

The center jump had to go. Big new stadiums awaited big crowds, and slick coaches and players were using the center jump to make the game a bore. The way they used it fans didn't have to watch until the last two minutes (a problem which for other reasons plagues the NBA today). With a jump ball after each basket, a team with a tall center and good musclemen to grab the tip could score repeated baskets without the opposition ever getting a chance at a shot. This made for some exciting comebacks, but it also allowed teams to coast and save hustle for a last flurry of baskets. Eliminating the center jump, noted one coach, forced both teams to hustle the entire game, since "a team that is lagging five or six points in a game without the tip-off can no longer sit back . . . and play a waiting game."

The increase in action was measured scientifically. Researchers for the *Athletic Journal* put pedometers on a group of college players in 1938 to see how much ground was covered in a game without the tip-off play. The players averaged just under 4 miles a game. When a pedometer test had been conducted in 1931, while the center jump was in use, players had averaged from 2½ to 2¾ miles a game.

Longer playing-courts altered the game as significantly as did the many rule changes. The extra touches of class the designers incorporated into the new basketball plants included "regulation size" playing floors of 94 by 50 feet, or close to this. Older gyms, especially in the high schools, were often anything but regulation. "I estimate 90 percent of our basketball coaches are working on courts of 60 by 30 feet," declared an Indiana high school coach in the March 1934 *Athletic Journal*. On the longer court a fast-break offense was a potent weapon for wearing a team out. The fast break first received notice as a successful strategy through the Purdue University teams captained by Johnny Wooden and coached by Ward "Piggy" Lambert in the early 1930s.

It was not until the late 1930s, however, that a substantial number of teams began using this high-scoring offense. Piggy Lambert argued at length that the fast break won games; but coach W. H. Browne of Nebraska made a perhaps more important selling point. He wrote in *Athletic Journal* of November 1936: "The fast-break-type offense, even though not always on the winning side of the ledger, assured basketball fans of plenty of action and thrills. It has been a great factor in increasing the crowds at the University of Nebraska Coliseum. Last year, in spite of sub-zero weather, all of the Cornhusker home games were played before near-capacity crowds."

The college teams that flouted tradition and employed the fast break and other run-and-shoot offensive systems tended to be schools needing to bolster attendance. The cause of this need could be a poor won–lost record, or it could be that there were now a great many more seats to be filled than before. Nebraska needed exciting basketball on both counts; it had a new coliseum, and in the three years before coach Browne adopted the fast break his teams had a 16–36 won–lost record.

The "home teams" in Madison Square Garden doubleheaders had 18,000 seats to fill. As these doubleheaders became regular features in the late 1930s, such home clubs as Long Island University, New York University, Manhattan College, and St. John's University produced scores far above the national average.

Small out-of-the-way colleges looking to enter the big time and get an invite to Madison Square Garden often appeared to throw defense out the window in an effort to become headline-grabbing scoring machines. West Texas State College, from the town of Canyon near Amarillo, had been relegated to playing such unknowns as Chihuahua State, Panhandle Agricultural & Mechanical, and New Mexico Normal before coach Al Baggett turned the Buffaloes into a high-scoring outfit with a startling 62-points-a-game average in 1941. The next season the Buffaloes averaged an amazing 72 points a game, played in twelve different states, and got invited to the Garden. Little Rhode Island State was the talk of basketball in the 1945 season. Coach Frank Keaney's "race horses" averaged an unbelievable 81 points a game. By way of comparison: As of 1945 six of the eight Ivy League colleges had never had a basketball team score 81 points in a single game in all their many years of college basketball, much less average 81 for a season.

A substantial increase in basketball press coverage was due in part to the lively copy provided in debates over the merits of different playing styles. Was the fast break superior to the traditional patterned game with its tightly diagrammed set plays? Was the coach at Valparaiso conducting basketball or a circus with his 1944 team of giants? A tall front line seemed sensible, but could his 6'4" and 6'5" guards get the ball up-court against the ball-hawking 5'8" or 5'10" guards then common in the game? Valparaiso went 18–7 in the won–lost column that year.

A half-dozen successful coaches published books on the same subject as the opus titled *Winning Basketball*; there were, among others, *Better Basketball* and *Practical Basketball*. Post-season coaching schools and seminars grew in number in the late 1930s. The instructors were a mix of well-known college mentors and successful high school coaches. The game was changing too fast for the sponsors of a clinic to worry over an instructor's rank. Good ideas were wherever you could find them. Brilliant basketball minds in the high schools, like the clinic instructors Everett Case, Cliff Wells, and Glen Curtis, would later move up to distinguished coaching careers at higher levels of the game.

Revolutionary one-handed shooting styles excited fans, baffled many coaches, and had the sportswriters skimming their thesauruses for hyperboles. Traditionally, the only shots taken with one hand were lay-ups and an occasional hook from close in. Anything tossed up from far out was attempted in the common style of foul shooting, with the ball held in both hands and with both feet firmly on the ground. Coaches had devised elaborate weaves intended to free a player for a two-handed set from behind a double, or triple, pick. The set shooter appeared like a football quarterback protected by linemen. It was a dramatic moment in the game; regrettably, the two-handed-set-shot artists rarely averaged more than 25 percent of their shots. Rule changes had provided a slightly smaller ball, more running, and more one-on-one opportunities. Some players began shooting one-handed push shots on the run. As they developed "a touch" for one-handers, they began shooting set shots that way too.

Stanford University's Hank Luisetti was the right man in the right place for popularizing one-handed distance shooting. On December 30, 1936, Stanford, featuring Luisetti and his one-handed push shot and set, met Long Island University in Madison Square Garden. LIU had a 43-game winning streak on the line. Stanford won 45–31. Luisetti scored 15 points, but he hadn't shot that often, choosing to pass to the open man when possible. When he did shoot he was accurate, and appeared almost impossible to defense.

He hadn't convinced everyone. "That's not basketball," sneered CCNY coach Nat Holman, who declared: "If my boys ever shot one-handed I'd quit coaching." Other coaches made similar threats; none were known to have carried them out. The anger of Nat Holman was understandable. A running one-hander was instant offense. It threatened to destroy a type of basketball of which Holman was probably the foremost coaching exponent—a carefully patterned passing game. In describing his early years with the Celtics, Holman noted that when he started in basketball it was a game played with little continuity. He developed an effective continuity game: set plays, crisp passing, and players positioned in designated spots. The one-hander threatened to bring back the free-form one-on-one play Holman had struggled to eliminate.

One-handed shooting was called "Wild West style." While Luisetti was the only practitioner capable of throwing in 50 points in a game (which he did against Duquesne), he had many West Coast contemporaries who were almost as good. Washington University push-shot artist Ed Loverich actually preceded Luisetti into Madison Square Garden, and scored 20 points there against DePaul in the 1936 Olympic trials. George Barsi, who coached at Santa Clara University from 1936 to 1943, explains: "My teams practically all shot one-handed. The only two-handed player we had was from New Jersey. One-handed shooting in this area started in the high schools, and Luisetti had a lot to do with that."

Luisetti starred for Galileo High in San Francisco in the early 1930s, a time when high school basketball received wide exposure. San Francisco city championships filled Kezar Pavilion with 9,600 fans. Newspapers played up high school sports, and Luisetti was known all over northern California for his play at Galileo. By the time he joined the Stanford frosh team for the 1934–1935 season, the one-hander was the rage in local colleges. Ben Neff, coach of San Francisco's Lowell High, graduated more than his share of one-handed stars in area colleges. Neff credits Luisetti with starting the craze in San Francisco schools, and with forcing him to rethink the patterned game he had been coaching. "I could see the one-handed shot was almost beyond defense. I began to wonder about the value of continuity plays where you can make mistakes with too much passing." On a national scale the revolution wasn't accomplished overnight. An ample contrast in teams' playing styles was a crowd-pleasing feature of the college game on through the 1940s, as when a run-and-shoot outfit went up against a team employing a four- or five-man weave and the old double pick for a two-handed set.

A substantial increase in the number of college teams added to the opportunities for innovative players and coaches. The cost of maintaining expensive football programs in a time of economic depression drove many colleges to switch to basketball, while others upgraded basketball programs while downgrading football. Then too, the New Deal poured money into state college systems. Increased enrollment seemed to warrant upgraded sports teams, and basketball was the cheapest avenue to sports recognition for institutions like Northwest Missouri State or Murray State in Kentucky. "Jumpin'" Joe Fulks, a graduate of Murray State in 1943, went on to become the first great one-handed shooter in the NBA. The increase in noteworthy basketball teams can be traced in Bill Mokray's massive compilation of college records. In Mokray's compendium there were forty-seven colleges added to his lists in the seasons of 1930–1934, and thirty more during the late 1930s, compared with twenty-two additions in the seasons of 1925–1929. The very worst months of the Great Depression coincided with the basketball season beginning in December 1932 and ending in March 1933. It was a time when the banks were closed, mobs fought sheriffs over evictions, and National Guard units were on alert for possible insurrection; it was also the season of the largest increase in the number of college basketball teams since the pre–World War I period.

Conditions were ripe for an enterprising promoter when Ned Irish organized his first college doubleheader at Madison Square garden in 1934. A standing-room-only crowd watched Westminster best St. John's and NYU top Notre Dame in the second and feature contest. Irish had an arrangement with Garden officials to put on six doubleheaders during that 1934–1935 season, but with the success of the initial show two more twin bills were arranged. By the end of the season the twenty-nine-year-old Ned Irish was being hailed as "the Boy Promoter." He went on to become the most powerful individual in the game, a man to be listened to when he said of basketball: "It's going to be the greatest sport in this country or any other."

Irish came into the promotion business by way of writing sports for newspapers, starting as a stringer for five papers while he was in high school. He worked his way through the University of Pennsylvania with a job at the Philadelphia *Record*. In 1929 he got a sportswriting position with the New York *World*, a paper with flaming liberal columnists like Heywood Broun, and an offbeat sports section that gave an unusual amount of space to local college basketball. While writing for the *World*, soon to become the *World-Telegram*, Irish had a personal experience that helped convince him that local college basketball could draw in a large arena. At that time the teams were playing on home courts seating approximately 1,000 spectators, or, in the case of Manhattan College, 500. Irish had been assigned to cover a game at the tiny Manhattan College gym. He arrived late and found such a crush of people inside that the only way he could enter was to crawl through a window, and in doing so he tore his pants. After this experience he determined to free college ball from tiny gyms, or so the story goes. There are those who believe that the torn-pants episode was an invention of the publicity-hungry Ned Irish.

The potential for college basketball in the Garden had been shown in the benefit games for Mayor Walker's Unemployment Relief Fund, three gala affairs which Ned Irish had helped organize in 1931, and again in the following two seasons. These games, with their lineup of local teams, established an important precedent. They were promoted for reasons other than the play and viewing pleasure of college students. In its fully developed form the Madison Square Garden college doubleheader was a sports-business promotion aimed at selling courtside seats to fashionable socialites, while the rooting section for the local college students was banished to the third-tier balcony up behind the basket—the very worst seats in the old Garden.

Playing in the Garden wasn't exactly campus sport, but then, the campuses of the colleges hosting the Garden shows were mostly collections of office buildings turned into classrooms. The students arrived via the subway rather than from a nearby dorm. For these colleges the doubleheaders provided broad exposure to fans, better press coverage, and competition against major universities around the country. One could not expect the University of Texas to come to New York to take on Manhattan in a 500-seat gym, but Texas did come to play Manhattan in the Garden. Ned Irish made a point of making the doubleheaders inter-sectional matches. In his first three seasons of twin bills the lineup included Kentucky, Purdue, North Carolina University, California, Rice, Stanford, Tennessee, West Virginia, and Pittsburgh, as well as Notre Dame.

Taking a long trip to play in the Garden was made more

attractive when Philadelphia Convention Hall began double-headers, providing a second stop for teams on tour. Irish had gone to Philadelphia to help launch the Convention Hall productions. By 1938 he had also lined up the Memorial Auditorium in Buffalo, creating a three-city doubleheader circuit. When the University of Oregon came east on a tour of "the Ned Irish circuit" in December 1941, it played twin bills at Chicago, Detroit, Buffalo, New York, Philadelphia, and Pittsburgh. By 1946 Boston, Washington, Cleveland, and St. Louis had been added to the system.

The doubleheaders put many minuscule colleges on the sporting map. Garden "home teams" in 1938 included LIU (student body 1,006) and Manhattan College (1,238 students). Convention Hall hosts in Philadelphia included St. Joseph (424), Muhlenberg College (436), and La Salle College (350). Teams touring through Buffalo were hosted by Canisius College (670), and Niagara University (870). Then there were the host teams of schools with several thousand students but without the resources to make a mark in the expensive game of football, e.g., CCNY, NYU, and St. John's.

Playing doubleheaders in the Garden did not enrich the schools financially. "Colleges get crumbs in comparison to the Garden's 'take' in basketball," wrote Brooklyn *Eagle* sportswriter Lou Niss in 1945. He noted that "when basketball first came to the Garden as little as $100 or $200 brought an attraction to the big arena." By 1945 lesser attractions received a flat fee of approximately $1,000, while bigger schools received a cut of the gate, taking in about $3,000. The cut for Irish and Madison Square Garden came to $12,000 to $14,000 per doubleheader in 1945.

Inter-sectional competitions added stature to a college's basketball program; and Ned Irish tapped into this desire, and provided a means at a time of growing emphasis on basketball in the colleges. George Barsi explained how his Santa Clara team got involved, and toured the circuit in the 1939, 1940, and 1941 seasons. He had coached Santa Clara for two years and created a team that would be called by eastern scribes "the magicians of the maplewood." But before he could get his team east, Barsi had to threaten school officials with his resignation, declaring: "If we are only going to play in the San Francisco area I will quit." He had previously coached at a small Minnesota college and didn't like to think he had come to California to be relegated to another small-time operation.

The Santa Clara administrators told Barsi that if he could earn at least three-fourths of the travel expenses he could take a tour east, providing the players missed no more than four days of class. The doubleheader circuit didn't pay much, but guarantees and arrangements for a cut of the gate did ensure payment of travel expenses. He set the tour for the Christmas vacation period, a heavy time of year on the circuit, since many schools found this time optimal for trips without much missed class time for players.

Barsi got Ned Irish interested in Santa Clara through New York Yankee scout Joe Devine—who had friends at Santa Clara, knew of the Broncos' ability, and worked with Irish, who did some PR for the Yankees. Getting into the Garden "was quite a break," Barsi explained. "It was the apple of everybody's eye. We got a lot of publicity playing there." Two wins over CCNY in successive seasons helped. Being scheduled into the Garden, Santa Clara was made part of the circuit, and Barsi was informed he was playing in Philadelphia against La Salle. Catholic Santa Clara played other Catholic schools on the circuit, and scheduled still others to fill out the three eastern tours under Coach Barsi. Catholic schools frequently helped each other attain the elevated stature of a college that played inter-sectional basketball.

There were aspects of the doubleheader craze that caused concern from the very beginning. Less than a month after Irish launched Garden twin bills, the New York *Tribune* was editorializing about a disturbing gambling interest in college games and noting: "Fifty thousand dollars, the peak of the betting to date, changed hands on the recent Temple–NYU game at the Garden." When basketball came to Chicago Stadium the gamblers established a regular bookmaking

operation in the south end of the mezzanine, according to a
report in the Chicago *Sun-Times*. When George Barsi brought
Santa Clara to the Garden he found a sizable and intense-
looking crowd viewing the team's morning practice session.
Barsi asked Irish about the viewers and was told: "They are
just here to look you over." Irish couldn't bring himself to say
they were gamblers. At a Santa Clara practice session in the
NYU gym Barsi noticed faces pressed to the windows. NYU
coach Howard Cann candidly explained: "They are gamblers
sizing you up, looking for a sign on how to bet." In *Scandals
of '51—How the Gamblers Almost Killed College Basketball*,
author Charles Rosen quotes numerous unnamed sources to
the effect that fixed games were frequent from the very earliest
years of the doubleheaders.

When the games were taken out of college gyms they became shows for "the sporting crowd." Once in the doubleheader system there was little a college administrator or coach
could do about the gambling problem, short of preachy press
releases about honesty and integrity. The subway colleges of
Garden games were in no position to handle the gamblers in
the manner suggested by an official at Duke University in
North Carolina: "Run them out of town." That might work in
Durham, but not in New York. When the New York schools
played their games in their own gyms they had some measure
of supervision, but by the early 1940s the Garden was featuring sixteen to eighteen twin bills a year. The games left for the
cozy college gyms were now the inconsequential matches
against patsies—games the gamblers bypassed.

The colleges that were the backbone of the doubleheader
circuit were enticed to play home games in the big arenas
when asked, and they also had their road-game schedule dictated to them by the promoters. To get on the Ned Irish circuit
a college had to sign a contract. It stipulated that a team
would make only one appearance that season in a city where it
was the visiting team in a doubleheader game. If Niagara
played St. John's in a Garden twin bill, that was it for Niagara
so far as New York–area games were concerned. This prac-

tice enabled promoters to advertise "the only appearance this year" for this or that team. It also forced teams to travel more. Niagara would play once in New York, and after a double-header at Philadelphia's Convention Hall there were no more Niagara games allowed in that city either. A school like Niagara had to fill out its road schedule by hitting all the stops on the circuit—an ever-expanding circuit through ever more cities where a team could be billed as making "the only appearance this year."

Commercialization of college basketball attained its highest form in games in which neither competing team was playing in its home city. Cheerleaders, a school band, and other trappings of college spirit were unnecessary when Kentucky took on the University of Wyoming at Buffalo, or when LIU took on Bowling Green from Ohio at Boston. When cities were first entering the doubleheader business, many of them didn't have more than a couple of local teams able, or willing, to be "home teams" for doubleheaders. Buffalo, Boston, Detroit, and Cleveland had this problem. To fill out the twin bills in these cities it was frequently necessary to match two out-of-town teams in one of the games.

Fans were enticed into watching teams from distant places in many ways. There was the gambling interest; the big bettors cared more about the odds than the school colors. Then there was the promotional hoopla about exceptionally tall players—so much of it that Ned Irish was accused of raiding the circuses for their sideshow freaks. Sports photographers had a field day with 7-foot Oklahoma A & M center Bob Kurland, and 6'10" DePaul center George Mikan. They were shown in promotional pictures holding a ball over their heads while small teammates reached for the ball in vain. One photo had a shapely female standing on a stepladder trying to get the ball that Mikan held at arm's length.

Promoters created a category called "the tallest team in the nation," the one with the starting five that had the most total inches in height. In the early 1940s West Texas State took the honors. The Texans looked quite tall in their promotional

photos showing them in cowboy hats. Valparaiso was the next
to claim the "tallest team" title. This 800-student college near
Gary, Indiana, had been struggling to get recognition and a
higher caliber of competition than other tiny colleges and the
nearby brass-foundry team. A starting five averaging 6'7" got
Valparaiso on the doubleheader circuit.

Individual scoring stars were grist for the PR writer's mill.
Good shooters were not as numerous as in later years. A
coach who had one had teammates feed "the gunner" the ball
as often as possible. By the early 1940s a handful of prolific
gunners were averaging over 20 points a game. When a team
with one of these players came to town to make its "only
appearance this year" there was little need to promote the
whole team, or talk of traditional rivalries and the like. Fans
were told to expect the star to put on a show worth watching,
as when Hank Luisetti scored 50 points against Duquesne on
"the neutral court" of the Cleveland Arena.

The attraction of games with teams outside the home region
was commented upon by sportswriter George Carens in an
official program sold at a 1945 Boston Garden doubleheader.
"In a sense it is astonishing that college doubleheaders without
a New England angle can thrive in Boston, but I suppose there
are enough customers with a burning desire to contrast the
playing qualities of stars of proven ability." Carens predicted a
big Boston Garden turnout for an upcoming University of
Akron vs. Brooklyn College game, because Akron scoring
star Fritz Nagy was on a hot streak and might well break the
Boston Garden scoring record of 27 points.

Fritz Nagy's chances at a Boston Garden individual record
were even better than sportswriter Carens suspected. Five
Brooklyn College players were planning to lie down and let
Akron roll up the score. The five had each received $1,000
from gamblers, with a promise of another $2,000 if Brooklyn
threw the game. But the plot was uncovered and the game was
canceled. The Boston Garden promo piece had talked of the
appeal of stars, but an angry Brooklyn fan declared that it
should have been obvious to schedule makers "that a Brook-

lyn College–Akron game could have no appeal in Boston except as a medium for gambling."

In the wake of the Brooklyn College scandal, coaches in the hinterlands threatened to withdraw from competition in commercial doubleheaders, but none appear to have taken action on their threats. There was ample evidence to warrant a full-scale investigation of college basketball. At the time of the scandal, rumors abounded concerning players with flashy new cars and girl friends in fur coats. A number of former New York–area collegians came forward to tell of past incidents when they had been approached by gamblers and had turned down offers to fix games. There was no major investigation. But at Mayor Fiorello LaGuardia's insistence the Garden promised to give colleges a bigger cut of the doubleheader gate; and lawyers got to work on stiffer laws, since the existing statutes failed to stipulate a penalty for tampering with amateur sports. The Brooklyn players were punished with expulsion from school, whereas the players caught fixing in 1951 were whisked off to jail.

The promoters and the gamblers weathered the Brooklyn scandal of 1945, and in 1946 attendance for doubleheaders in Madison Square Garden, and in most other arenas, set all-time records. The records were broken again in '47, '48, '49, and '50. In the 1950 season the New York Garden featured 28 twin bills; and the combined attendance for 169 doubleheaders in thirteen cities was 1,314,933.

During the rise of the doubleheader business the majority of the best attractions in college basketball were teams representing schools tied to managers and promoters of big-city arenas. The schools tied to promoters had many of the most influential coaches, as well. NCAA basketball policies were thereby indirectly determined by commercial promoters. For a time it was this relationship between colleges and commercial interests which helped the game grow. And consequently there were complaints but little action against abuses in the system.

Gambling interest, similarly, had a functional role in building the college game. Gamblers helped get the general public interested. They bolstered attendance. They were animated fans, the kind who add to the excitement of the show. Of course, what excited the gamblers was not necessarily what thrilled the uninitiated. When the Chicago *Sun-Times* reported on the gamblers' section in the Chicago Stadium mezzanine, it was by way of explaining the gamblers' passion. They had been noticed going crazy over a last-second basket that cut the final margin of a game from 8 points to 6. As the newspaper explained, that basket might have been meaningless to the winning and losing teams, but it put the score under the game's 7-point spread, and made all the difference in the world to the wheeler-dealers in the mezzanine.

The spread is an odds-making technique. Instead of quoting a team at 3–1 or 5–2, as in horse racing, the relative merits of a team are expressed in how many points it can be expected to be ahead or behind at the end of a specific game. A fan may say: "I expect the home team to win this game by about half a dozen points." The point-spread maker calls this a 6-point spread. To collect on a wager on the home team in this game, the team has to win by more than 6 points. An even 6 will be considered a tie game and all bets will be canceled.

Evaluating teams by point differentials wasn't originally a gamblers' operation, at least not as obviously so as in recent decades, when a syndicate-connected clearinghouse in Minneapolis has established the spread for the nation's teams. The first point-rating system was developed by Dayton sportswriter Dick Dunkel in 1929, according to an article in *Pic* magazine in 1943. Dunkel established a mail-order business selling ratings sheets to football coaches in 1929, and shortly thereafter he added basketball ratings to his service. His weekly ratings for basketball became quite popular. By the early 1940s Dunkel was claiming that his method predicted basketball winners with a 79.2 percent accuracy rate. The Converse shoe company had begun distributing his weekly ratings sheet. Converse claimed that the Dunkel "ratings and forecasts have been enthusiastically received by coaches and players from coast to coast." It didn't seem a particularly nefarious enterprise. Other ratings sheets were distributed by the Pabst beer company and by Sears Roebuck.

In the Dunkel system the projected point differential was arrived at by study of comparative game scores. The importance of a victory of team A over team B was determined by team B's record against C, D, and E, etc. To be accurate, just about every team playing college basketball had to be evaluated; and industrial teams too, if they played college competition. An office was established in New York, with a two-man, three-woman staff that collected scores from newspapers mailed in from all parts of the country.

The Dunkel ratings proved extremely valuable to small colleges in out-of-the-way towns. There was so little information available on many of these colleges that the National Association of Intercollegiate Basketball underwrote the Dunkel service. As the writer for *Pic* explained: "This tie-up was brought about by Dunkel's love for the smaller college basketball teams. He gets a kick out of the lesser-known schools that get booted around by the sportswriters. Through the forecast he has brought a few of these so-called jerk-water college quintets to the attention of the basketball world."

A high rating by Dunkel could earn a team a better schedule the following year, and it could help a little-known school receive a post-season tournament bid. In 1941, for example, Dunkel had Ohio University listed as the nation's number one team at the end of the regular season. Ohio U., led by future baseball star Frankie Baumholtz, was invited to the NIT and went to the finals before losing to LIU. The next season Dunkel had Western Kentucky rated number two. Some fans might have questioned such a high rating for a team that fattened its record with wins over schools like Southwestern Louisiana State, and couldn't beat Tennessee Tech. But Dunkel said the Hilltoppers were number two—and they went to the NIT and got to the finals, where they lost by a mere field goal.

Team ratings became a serious item in the battle for sports prestige, serious enough to warrant parody. Little Hanover

College could claim number one honors in 1941, by reason of beating Cincinnati, which in turn beat Ohio U. Dunkel was more scientific. In his system each point scored was considered in establishing a numerical figure for a team. A quintet rated 45.9 was set as a 3.8-point favorite against a 42.1 team. However, there were 4 points added to a team's rating when it played at home. So when the 42.1 team played the 45.9 quintet at home, the former was expected to win by .2 points.

The gamblers and their point spread contributed to basketball's rise at a time when the college game needed help to become more than just another lesser sport on the campus. But by the time of the basketball scandals in 1951 the bookies and their customers were no longer useful. The game had all the popularity it needed.

Moreover, the gambling influence had gotten out of hand. Rumors of fixed games became ever more frequent during the late 1940s. There were so many weird scores in 1948 that losing bettors pressured bookies into lowering their wagering fees, according to a report in the New Orleans *Times-Picayune*. It was estimated that $10 million a week was being wagered on college basketball. The game was becoming a profitable business for all but the workers in the trade. Charles Rosen showed in his study how one or two players went eagerly after their share of the profits, while others were coaxed into fixing games for money with the argument "Everybody else is doing it." A story carried in papers across the country in 1948 seemed to suggest that fixing was easily done. A New York gambler eager to secure the desired result in a Butler University–Ohio University game in Indianapolis didn't bother to come to the Midwest to wine and dine prospective cooperating players. He wrote Butler scoring ace Charlie Maas a letter suggesting a "business proposition." When Maas failed to reply, the gambler put in a long-distance phone call and offered Maas $500 to see that Butler won by less than 9 points. Maas told his coach, who told the story to the press.

The angry Indianapolis mayor then phoned the New York City district attorney and demanded "an immediate investigation." An effort to locate the gambler at the address on his letter failed and that was the end of it.

Butler didn't play the circuit. Coach Tony Hinkle could afford to go public with the offer to Maas. It was not so easy for a coach of a school locked into the doubleheader system. In 1945 Nat Holman had been told by one of his players of a bribe offer tendered by a teammate who admitted to dumping CCNY games. Holman's response was to have the fixer quietly removed from the basketball squad on account of poor academic grades. Brooklyn College had just been caught in its fixing scandal, and the administration had withdrawn Brooklyn from doubleheader play. Had Holman gone public CCNY might have been similarly forced to deemphasize its basketball program.

For the players who took the money, their working conditions deteriorated as the number of fixed games mounted. Their employers became more brazen and requested that players go under the spread when it was only 2 or 3 points. This was not easily managed without losing the game entirely. Rumors of dumping created tension throughout college basketball. After a close loss for Duquesne in Pittsburgh a spectator yelled: "You threw the game!" Duquesne's John Barry, who had played with an injured elbow, leaped into the stands and began punching the heckler.

Strange upsets in the spread had gamblers and bookies at each other's throat. Players on the fix were told to make a special effort to appear on the up-and-up and avoid contributing to growing suspicions. One syndicate accused another of messing around with college basketball. One group of bookies stopped accepting wagering on the University of Kentucky, believing its games were fixed. They were. LIU and CCNY games were avoided by the smart money for the same reason, and with equal justification. The sleaziness of it all got to LIU All-American Sherman White. Faking it for the socialites in the Garden was one thing, but White's hardworking father was his greatest fan. Being forced to cover up the fixing with a lie to his father hit Sherman White hard. He had never before lied to his father.

The cracks in the system became all too visible at the December 28, 1950, Madison Square Garden doubleheader featuring CCNY vs. Arizona University in the opener, and LIU against Western Kentucky in the nightcap. CCNY had four players being paid by gambler Salvatore Sollazzo to go under the announced 6-point spread. Arizona turned out to have a bad case of the Garden jitters. The Arizona players passed the ball out of bounds instead of to each other, and they could hardly hit the backboard when attempting a shot. To reward Sollazzo CCNY had to play just as poorly. Nobody could do anything right. The fans began to boo. CCNY wound up losing 41–38.

In the second game LIU was deemed an 11-point favorite. In this game Sollazzo was betting on the home team. The Blackbird players working for him were expected to win by more than 11 points. But the four Blackbirds on the take doublecrossed Sollazzo, and they did it blatantly. Perhaps they were sick of it all. Things looked good for Sollazzo with two minutes to go in the game. LIU led by 20 points. The team then went into a bizarre routine. After a Western Kentucky field goal LIU's Adolph Bigos took the ball out of bounds and threw a long pass to the nearest LIU player, who was standing on the midcourt line. Western Kentucky intercepted and went for a lay-up which Bigos was unable to stop. Over and over LIU took the ball out of bounds and lobbed it up in the air toward midcourt. When the gun sounded LIU's 20-point lead had dwindled to 7. The CCNY game was a stinker, but this was an atrocity. Gamblers and innocent fans alike left the garden furious. Out-of-bounds plays after an opponent has scored are supposed to travel about two feet, but the nearest LIU player was at midcourt. On January 4 LIU was back in the Garden decimating another 20-point lead in the final minutes. Sollazzo requested the Blackbirds to go under the spread in this game; however, he could not appreciate the way they once again made it obvious. "What's the points tonight, huh—ya bum?" yelled one angry fan at Blackbird Leroy Smith.

Ten days later Manhattan College center Junius Kellogg was offered $1,000 by former Manhattan star Hank Poppe in return for throwing the upcoming DePaul game. Like many of the players offered a bribe, Kellogg could have used the money. He was one of eleven children of a poor black family in Portsmouth, Virginia. Like many of the fixers, he was a World War II vet working his way through college on the GI Bill of Rights. Kellogg refused the offer. He informed his coach, Kenny Norton, just as others had told other coaches of a bribe offer. Some years earlier a coach in Norton's position might have congratulated the young man on his honesty and told him to avoid bad company. But now a scandal was all but in the open. Reporters were writing exposés on which players were seen with which underworld figures in which night spots.

Norton informed the college administrators, who called a meeting, at which the school president decided to call in the police. New York District Attorney Frank Hogan launched an energetic investigation, one matching the conspiracy hunts for Reds and "pinkos" in headline grabbing. Detectives fought over the right to escort basketball players past photographers at the jailhouse door. Before the basketball investigations were over, the scandal had implicated thirty-two players from seven colleges, who had allegedly manipulated the point spread of eighty-six games in twenty-three cities in seventeen states.

Colleges rushed to withdraw from doubleheaders in New York and elsewhere. Some colleges prohibited their teams from traveling to Madison Square Garden, even for the National Invitational Tournament. The sporting scribes wrote poignant articles about the sad lack of college spirit in Garden basketball. The *Daily Worker* seized the opportunity to run a lengthy analysis of the economics of big-arena basketball. The Communist paper found the manipulations of promoters a classic example of capitalist exploitation. Other critics blamed the point spread for the evil. The Converse shoe company severed its connection with Dick Dunkel, and newspapers stopped printing the spread.

The scandal presented an occasion for exploring the relationship of college athletes to academic work. As always happens in these investigations, it was discovered that academic training was often minimal. Long Island University had long had notoriously low academic standards. CCNY refused to schedule LIU on the grounds that the Long Island institution was a basketball factory rather than a college. City College had high academic standards, but as one CCNY player explained to Charles Rosen: "Forging transcripts was a widely accepted practice at City."

One reason mentioned for collegians' acceptance of bribes was that a professional basketball career was not all that attractive. The professional games didn't draw fans the way the college games did, and the salaries of the pros were modest. The collegians were already in the commercial big time, so they took the money while they could. Half a dozen fixed games in college earned more than the New York Knicks' $6,000 top salary for a season. But professional basketball was on the rise. The pro game had undergone its own revolution, becoming a more commercial production than when it was run by neighborhood ethnic groups. The professional teams were in a position to capitalize on the college debacle, and win over some of the fans having withdrawal pangs over the dwindling number of college doubleheaders.

CHAPTER

10

An Intimate Game
Becomes Big Business

Professional basketball underwent an almost complete transformation between 1941 and 1954. America's entry into World War II marked the beginning of a series of alterations in playing styles, economic organization, and the social context of professional ball. The adoption of the 24-second clock by the National Basketball Association in 1954 climaxed the radical changes which made possible the high-priced, fast-flowing, high-scoring game we know today.

Pro basketball began as the very physical, pushing, grabbing, and defensively oriented "cage game." It was still a rough sport when the NBA began operation in the 1950 season. Says Bruce Hale, a pro star of the late 1940s and early 1950s: "If I went out on the courts today and played like I did in my younger days I would foul out in five minutes."

When the big changes began the professionals were found almost exclusively in the industrial Midwest and in the Northeast. The midwestern teams were strong on hometown spirit. Some outfits were collections of graduates from colleges in and around the town; others were factory teams turned pro. A typical midwestern professional basketball town was Akron, Ohio, where bowling teams and basketball were part of the

extensive recreation programs at the Goodyear and Firestone
rubber plants. The midwestern game had expanded from half
a dozen organized teams in the mid-1930s to about fifty in
1941. They rarely had a set schedule, played only on week-
ends, and usually consisted of players who were moonlighting
from other jobs, such as the former Purdue All-American star
Johnny Wooden (of later UCLA coaching fame), who played
for a number of pro quintets while coaching high school in
South Bend. The recreation directors at Goodyear and Firestone tried to add stature to pro basketball in the area when
they led the organizing of the National Basketball League in
the fall of 1937. The National League had regularly scheduled
games, but on the eve of the war it was still a very short
schedule. The league tried to recruit players from around the
country, but pay was too low for the effort to be much of a
success.

In 1940, the NBL Chicago Bruins offered Santa Clara University All-American Ralph Gianinni $200 a month and a job
on the side at the racetrack of Bruins' official Charlie Bidwell.
"I turned them down," Gianinni explained. "It didn't seem
worth the trouble to move from California to Chicago. Besides, by remaining an amateur I was able to play for the San
Francisco Olympic Club. Hank Luisetti was on our team. The
Olympic Club was a great place; it had a nice steam room and
other facilties." Gianinni notes that while the pay for white
professional basketballers was low, it was even lower for black
professionals. "The Harlem Globetrotters were the world
champions the year I graduated from college, and the Trotters
played for peanuts."

In the East a revived American Basketball League was the
major focus for professional basketball activity. It, too, was a
weekend league, with low-paid players who were often moonlighting. Its strongest team was Eddie Gottlieb's South Philadelphia Hebrew All-Stars. They regularly drew close to capacity at their Saturday-night basketball game and dance at the
Broadwood Hotel ballroom. Throughout the eastern seaboard
the game was marketed with a dance, as it had been for half a

century. The players represented ethnic groups and neighborhoods rather than a whole city. They were part of neighborhood social life. People knew where to find them; in the case of the SPHAS a popular gathering place was the back room of a South Philly variety store, where the team whiled away the hours playing pinochle.

Considering the proven profitability of college basketball, and the sizable crowds when barnstorming pros like the Globetrotters or Harlem Renaissance came to town, one might have expected a slick, high-priced version of basketball professionalism before the World War. But the effort in this direction, a move to better financing that would lead to the NBA, came just after the war. The promotional push was sparked by the creation of the Basketball Association of America, which in its initial campaign of 1946–1947 launched the New York Knickerbockers, Boston Celtics, and Philadelphia Warriors (now the Golden State Warriors).

Eddie Gottlieb perceived the trend of the future and became the coach of the Warriors. He had been with the SPHAS for thirty years, first as a player and later as coach and owner. Gottlieb retained a loose tie with the SPHAS, and with his Jewish Youth League, which had long fed the team talent. The SPHAS went on playing the Broadwood for a number of years "because the Saturday night games were an institution in Philadelphia; they were the thing for the young people who didn't have a date," as the team ticket taker explained. The SPHAS were, however, a Jewish "institution," and sports for narrow segments of society were becoming passé. The postwar emphasis in sports was on a mass-media show. There was a similar trend in theater, a field Gottlieb knew well, having run a Catskills resort that produced many a noted Jewish comic, including Joey Bishop. It seemed time to move Philadelphia basketball beyond the Broadwood, just as the comics and actors of Borscht Belt establishments were reaching out to a broader audience.

*   *   *

Toward the end of World War II the sports pages of the nation were alive with projections of a postwar sports boom. One writer conjectured that every hustler with four bucks in his pocket was organizing a football league. There were enough prospects for spots on National Football League rosters for rival promoters to launch a rival big league, the All-America Conference. In baseball, *Sporting News* reported in the spring of '46 that enormous numbers of players were trying for spots on major-league baseball rosters. Those who failed to make the grade were sent to the Minors. There were soon twice as many minor-league baseball teams as there had been before the outbreak of the war. In basketball there was the new BAA, the upgraded NBL, half a dozen new minor leagues, new barnstorming quintets, and numerous announcements of teams and leagues that failed to materialize. In total, the number of salaried professionals in baseball, football, and basketball went from approximately 4,000 before the war to roughly 13,000 during the late 1940s.

The sports boom was sparked in part by public desire for diversions that could release the tensions built up by the trauma of the World War. Part of the trauma was the uprooting of old ties and social institutions—the uprooting of service personnel, their families who went to live near the military base, and the others who traveled to take work in defense plants. The loosening of ties to the neighborhood and old hometown provided professional sports promoters with a more receptive market for teams representing a broader constituency than before. The new Warriors of the Basketball Association of America, for instance, represented all Philadelphians. As for the South Philadelphia Hebrews, three of their 1946 players joined the new Warriors of 1947, a move paralleling the exodus of Jewish people from the old South Philadelphia neighborhoods.

The war made far more Americans physically fit and athletically well tuned, and consequently more interested in sport. When the war ended and New Yorkers rushed to grab tract homes in Levittown, they didn't set up a Little League and watch the kids play. At a heated community meeting over the use of Levittown's first softball field, the ex-GIs had their way. Youngsters were banned from the field during the weekend so that the adults could play ball. The kids were allowed on the field during the week, on the days when the water sprinkler wasn't going.

Women as well as men were charged with sporting interest by the war experience. It was the era of "Rosie the Riveter," the woman in the defense plant. The government set up sports programs in the plants to make the defense workers physically fit. Basketball appears to have been the most popular defense plant game, and women as well as men had their teams and leagues. In addition, barnstorming women's basketball teams like the Nashville Vultees and Rochester Filerets received substantial press buildup and drew sizable crowds.

The independent women of the war period broke tradition and in large numbers attended sporting events unaccompanied by male escorts. Despite the absence of the men gone overseas, basketball attendance at various levels had a steady rise during the war years. It was up each season in the college doubleheader circuit, at the annual AAU tournament in Denver, and at many of the statewide high school basketball tournaments. When the war ended, the GIs returned to find that many women shared with them a keen interest in sport. Photos of postwar crowds at Madison Square Garden reveal that women were as likely as men to jump up and down, shake their fists, and in other ways be thoroughly uninhibited and involved sports fans—an involvement that faded in the sexist 1950s.

During the war, sports were an integral part of rest-and-recreation programs for troops. R & R was just one military use for basketball. The game was widely utilized as a boot-camp training device. Over a million basketballs were provided and servicemen had over a hundred thousand teams, noted Col. Theodore P. Banks, who added: "Basketball made tremendous contributions in training personnel for combat duty and developing physical, mental and emotional stability for combat service. . . . Men who never played the game either undertook its study or enjoyed the role of spectators." Col. Banks could just as well have spoken of physical and mental development for postwar professional basketballers and their fans.

The military considered basketball especially useful in that the game could be played almost anywhere—on the decks of aircraft carriers or a few yards behind the front lines. The coach of the marines team that won the fifty-game season in the Guadalcanal League explained that on that rain-soaked island basketball was mostly a passing game, since "you can't dribble a ball in and out of gullies and through mud." There were better playing conditions for the troops in England awaiting the Normandy invasion. Over 20,000 of them participated in a two-month elimination tournament ending with games in Prince Albert Hall in London.

Quality basketball received broad exposure during the war, since the quality athletes were spread around, rather than being monopolized in the usual places. The vast majority of drafted and enlisted pros and college stars ended up playing on service teams. Others played for defense plants, where they had been assigned in lieu of military service. A sizable number of drafted collegians found themselves back in college, assigned to study sophisticated military technology. They were rarely sent to the old alma mater, however, but went instead to the schools with special military programs. As a sportswriter in Kansas described it: "The mainstay of the old home team is suddenly dumped into the cheering section of some bloody rival . . . and Mr. Big, All-American for years back, finds himself expected to do or die for the basketball gang at Podunk Tech." Thanks to the assignment of former All-American Howie Dallmar to the University of Pennsylvania, this traditional "Podunk Tech" of Ivy League basketball finally won an Ivy League crown, in 1945.

The war years were a nightmare for sports traditionalists. The Yankees temporarily stopped hogging American League pennants, and the St. Louis Browns actually won one, with a team loaded with 4-Fs. Military teams played in college football Bowl games. Teenagers performed on college basketball teams; and some college conferences ceased operation due to travel restrictions and a belief that quality was not up to the usual standards. A San Francisco *Chronicle* basketball writer sorely missed the Pacific Coast Conference, so he created his own "Super Seven Casaba League," consisting of local military and college teams. The writer declared that the players now had "a point to their labors, with big-league organization and recognition. . . . The Super Seven will have a champion, a scoring leader, and all the frills of the type usually reserved for leagues iike the Pacific Coast Conference."

The way sport was run uncovered hidden talent that might otherwise have never become part of the large pool of outstanding postwar athletes. The NCAA and AAU found it next to impossible to control the flow of athletes from one level of competition to another, and with great regret many of the prohibitions against amateurs playing pros were waived. "Sandlot Pitcher Duels Bob Feller in Shut-Out," ran the *Stars and Stripes* headline to one of the many stories in the army newspaper about unknowns getting their chance to prove themselves in service sport competition. Pros and amateurs played together on service teams, which in turn played colleges, industrial outfits, and professional teams. Fuel shortages led to travel restrictions that generally kept teams close to home playing against whoever was available. In 1943, for instance, Mitchell Field on Long Island had a bunch of pros on its basketball team. Mitchell Field had beaten a number of local colleges; then the team went into the den of a Jewish community house in Brooklyn. The community team had a ringer of its own in future New York Knicks center Hank Rosenstein. Mitchell Field was upset; and shortly thereafter Rosenstein joined the navy and had a couple of seasons with star-studded navy teams before coming to the Knicks.

Most military bases had a "varsity" or "post" team in the popular sports; and virtually every base had one of these teams for basketball. Typically, it was created through open tryouts; and from 1943 on the tryouts generally included both enlisted men and officers, a rare case of democracy in the military.

Playing performance in postwar pro basketball was much improved thanks to the uncovering of talent on service teams. Scouts for the postwar pro outfits discovered not only playground hot-shots but also the talent from little-known colleges. The BAA scoring leader "Jumpin' " Joe Fulks, for instance, came from the village of Kuttawa, Kentucky, and because he attended nearby Murray State College, where the competition was weak, his proficiency with an odd-looking behind-the-ear running jumper went unrecognized in basketball circles. Fulks joined the marines and was initially shunted off to a small base in Mississippi. After a few high-scoring games he was brought to play with the marines' all-star aggregation in San Diego; and after combat duty on Iwo Jima and Guam he joined the powerful fleet-marines team in the Pacific. The old pro Petey Rosenberg took notice of Fulks throwing them in for the fleet marines during a tournament in the Philippines. When Eddie Gottlieb was rounding up players for the Warriors, Rosenberg wrote to him urging him to sign up Fulks. Thanks to the shooting ability of Fulks, the Warriors won the BAA playoffs in the league's initial season of '47.

The Washington Capitols won the regular-season BAA honors in '47, with Red Auerbach as coach. Not yet thirty years old, Auerbach had been given his first coaching break by the navy. He was stationed at Norfolk Naval Station during the war, and somewhat by accident he found himself running a local navy team with half a dozen All-Americans and some All-Conference players thrown in. Hank Luisetti was expected to have this coaching job, but he came down with spinal meningitis. Auerbach was the officer of proper rank in the right place at the right time. When he later organized the Capitols he signed three players from his own navy team, and seven others who had played service ball in and around the Norfolk area.

The Rochester Royals won the NBL in 1947, with a starting five that had a combined total of fifteen seasons of service ball among them. The Warriors' starting five that season included one 4-F and four players with thirteen seasons of service ball. This kind of background was rarely acknowledged by the press of the late 1940s. The newspapermen, the writers of game program sheets, and others studiously avoided any mention of the wartime service game.

In its day service sport had become rather scandalous. Men were dying in the trenches while athletes were getting one season after another in "varsity" sports. According to Col. Banks there was still plenty of off-season front-line duty for college basketball lettermen in the service, and according to his figures the percentage of their time spent in combat was actually higher than the percentage for army and navy personnel in general. Nonetheless, service sports looked like the much-rumored favoritism that kept some baseball and football pros out of combat. Continuing pro sports in the midst of the war effort made many troops at the front hopping mad. "If a man can run, jump, and throw, he can jump a Normandy hedgerow with a full pack," a GI in France told a *Stars and Stripes* reporter.

Merely re-creating pro sports in the military didn't seem a particularly noble alternative. Between 1942 and 1946 there were some three dozen service basketball teams with entire rosters composed of top-caliber players. In 1943 and 1944 the Great Lakes Naval Training Station "varsity" had sixteen well-known court players, amateurs and pros. Experience in high-class service quintets readied the players for a receptive response when the war ended, and personable recruiters like Red Auerbach asked them to turn pro, officially.

The creation of star-studded service teams was rather inevitable, considering the avid sports fans among the military brass. A former midshipman states: "You had to become sports-crazy at Annapolis. It was part of our conditioning. We had to start each day running to the window and shouting to the world, 'Beat Army!'" The rivalry of Annapolis and West Point fed the professionalization of service sports. Bruce Hale, a postwar pro star, explained how the service game went big-time in Miami. "When I arrived at the Air Force Officers Training School there wasn't much going in basketball. The base officials weren't much interested. I organized a team that happened to have a few pros and some good young players. We beat everybody in sight. Then things got complicated. The navy considered Miami their town, and we had the best team. Some big admirals said, 'Let's stop this.' So they shipped in reinforcements, a bunch of All-Americans. We beat them too."

There were a few specifically selected all-star service teams that provided the players a taste of professional-sports working conditions, lengthy schedules, and extensive travel. These special teams were justified on the grounds that they boosted enlistments and servicemen's morale. Proceeds of their games went to worthy causes like the War Relief Fund. For worthy causes and morale boosting the powerful Wright Field "Air Techs" got travel clearance in 1945 and went 17,000 miles taking on the best basketball teams in the country. It was a traveling USO show. In Los Angeles the Air Tech opposition was a team from the Twentieth-Century Fox studios that had Carmen Miranda as water girl and Mickey Rooney as ball boy. The air force men also had assistants for this game: water girl Lucille Ball and ball boy Donald O'Connor. After the game Ms. Ball tried to get into the Air Techs' locker room, exclaiming: "This is my team, I want to see my boys."

Unique, chaotic, and a bit corrupt, the sports scene of the war years may not be what one would want in normal times. The war period was a revolutionary interlude in sports. It broke down rigid structures and provided opportunities for more people to become participants and sports fans. It was a revolution without a sense of direction, however. Structure and direction were provided in the more conservative postwar years. Much of it came from promoters eager to channel sports enthusiasm into commercial sports shows. For baseball and football, the kind of show they would become was foreordained. They had strong working models of businesslike sports organization. Basketball lacked a strong commercial model. Its future was wide open.

On June 6, 1946, the owners and representatives of eleven major arenas met at the Hotel Commodore across from Grand Central Station in New York. Their purpose was to create the Basketball Association of America and launch the New York Knicks, Boston Celtics, Philadelphia Warriors, Chicago Stags, St. Louis Bombers, Washington Capitols, Cleveland Rebels, and other franchises in Providence, Pittsburgh, Detroit, and Toronto. The BAA founders controlled the best indoor facilities of the East and Midwest. They had united to fit pro basketball into their arena schedule of college basketball doubleheaders, ice hockey games, ice shows, boxing matches, track meets, circuses, and so on.

The Basketball Association was a daring venture. Its founders were entering a business in which they had no experience, excepting one owner who had had a passing brush with pro basketball. What they knew of pro team sports management they knew from hockey—ten of the eleven were involved with ice-hockey teams.

In addition to being inexperienced in the business, they were going into battle against virtually all of established professional basketball. There was a conspiratorial air about the meeting at the Hotel Commodore, reminiscent of the locked-doors meeting at the Grand Central Hotel seventy years earlier at which the baseball moguls had created the National League. In 1876 the creators of baseball's big league showed their exclusiveness by declaring that only big cities could have a franchise. In 1946 the BAA founders displayed their stripes in a clause restricting franchises exclusively to arena owners. The established professional basketball teams of 1946 were owned by merchants, manufacturers, sportswriters, coaches, and assorted clubs and groups. Many teams represented towns that didn't have an arena; home games had to be played in high school gyms, armories, or ballrooms.

The new Basketball Association was a multiple threat to the existence of older professional teams. First, the new league had arena seating capacity and major metropolitan markets providing financial potential far beyond the reach of most of the older clubs. Then, too, the arena owners had well-established ties with local newspapers through their other activities and could therefore count on press coverage on a scale that had long eluded pro basketball promoters. The *New York Times*, for example, had for years given local pro teams no more than an occasional few lines in filler items at the bottom of the sports page. But the New York Knickerbockers received in-depth pre-game promotion and post-game reports from their very first BAA game on.

The Basketball Association was bringing rigid structure to professional basketball by introducing its exclusive scheduling. The BAA would play no outside club, with very rare exceptions. Throughout the prior half-century of the professional game it had been customary for teams in leagues to play up to half or more of their games against outsiders. Traditionally, pro basketball was like college basketball, a competitive mix of prestige teams and Mudvillian outfits. The owners of BAA clubs believed the similarity to the college game was a detriment to profitable production of the sport at the professional level. The BAA was putting professionals in such popular college doubleheader spots as Madison Square Garden and Boston Garden. The Association needed a distinctively classy show to compete with the college attractions. It was bad enough that fans found the collegians so exciting. On top of this there was the raging debate of 1947 and 1948 over the question "Could Top College Cagers Defeat Best Pros?" (this was the headline to one of many *Sporting News* discussions of the issue).

When the BAA entered the picture, basketball already had one so-called big-league organization, the National Basketball

League. From its beginning in the season of 1938 the NBL had operated in the traditional manner of the pro game, giving independents and minor-league quintets anywhere from two dozen to fifty or more games a season. There were annual invitational tournaments in professional, as in college and AAU basketball; and the National League was featured in the best of these, the Chicago World Professional Basketball Tournament. The World Tournament included the best of the NBL, the champions of minor leagues, and the leading independents. In March 1946 the World Tournament had drawn 115,000 spectators over a six-day span of afternoon and evening games. The BAA received invitations but never played in the World Tournament, which was discontinued after 1948.

The loosely organized clubs on the lower rungs of the sport needed tournaments and other games with top teams. Occasional stiff competition helped pay expenses and also made it respectable to be a member of these teams—to be one of those high school coaches like Johnny Wooden, who dabbled in pro ball on the weekend and was quite good at his part-time job on the side. The importance of open competition to non-league teams can be seen in the case of black American quintets. There was an unwritten law excluding blacks from all but the most inconsequential professional basketball leagues. The NBL made a few exceptions; six blacks played on the 1943 Chicago NBL team sponsored by the United Auto Workers union; one black played in the League in 1944; three in 1947; and in 1949 the entire Harlem Renaissance team played in the NBL as its Dayton franchise. But the color bar didn't officially come down until 1951, in the second season of the modern National Basketball Association. Before the racist ban was lifted the black teams had to get the teams in the white leagues to play them in outside games. The better black teams—the Globetrotters, Renaissance, and Washington Bears—had little trouble arranging these dates, although for less money than could have been earned in league play. The World Tournament in Chicago was open to black teams, and they showed

their ability, making the final foursome ten times in the tournament's ten years. The Globetrotters won it in 1939, the
Rens in 1940, and the Bears in 1943.

The response of traditional pro basketball to the BAA was
the formation of the fifty-two-team National Association of
Professional Basketball in October 1946. Its stated purpose
was to provide unified rules and regulations governing the
professional game. Unofficially, it was an attempt of the National League to rally support for the forthcoming struggle
with the BAA for basketball supremacy. To bolster its image
the National League coaxed the noted Purdue University
coach Ward "Piggy" Lambert into serving as League commissioner for the '47 season. Lambert also headed the broad federation. His high standing in basketball contrasted sharply
with the utter lack of basketball background for BAA commissioner Maurice Podoloff. He was president of a minor
circuit in professional ice hockey.

With the BAA standing for modernity and the NBL leading
the traditionalists, the 1947 season began with a battle over
the future of the professional game. It was the Association of
big-city franchises (with Providence thrown in) against the
League of small cities (with Chicago and Detroit thrown in).
Other NBL franchises in 1947 were located in Oshkosh and
Sheboygan, Wisconsin; the Tri-Cities (Moline and Rock Island, Illinois; and Davenport, Iowa); Rochester, Syracuse, Ft.
Wayne, Toledo, Indianapolis, Youngstown, and tiny Anderson, Indiana.

The interleague war officially lasted three seasons, ending
with a merger in the summer of 1949 that created the present
National Basketball Association. It was a struggle in which
differences between the two organizations ranged from the
behavior of fans to team financing.

BAA fans came to see a game. NBL fans came to a happen-
ing. In an effort to make pro basketball seriously big-league,
BAA teams avoided such frills as fans' free-throw contests at
halftime, roses for ladies' night, and similar gimmicks popular
in the NBL. Syracuse of the NBL had a radio announcer, Red

Parton, who traveled through the crowd at halftime with a hand mike interviewing lady fans and presenting orchids to those answering stock questions. Home games for the Tri-Cities team were spiced with the singing of Irish ballads by the team's star guard Billy Hassett.

The NBL had fanatics for spectators. Established rivalries between the League's older teams contributed to the fans' intensity, as did the relatively intimate atmosphere of the facilities for most NBL games. The BAA's cavernous arenas averaged over 12,000 seats, while the NBL averaged 6,500 seats, with a number of teams having home courts of only half this seating capacity. The Syracuse Coliseum was one of the noisier arenas. It had wooden chairs which fans banged up and down to rattle the opposition. Syracuse player-coach Al Cervi had a way of protesting referees' decisions by turning to the fans and waving his arms, a signal for chair banging. When the opponents went on a hot streak and noise failed to achieve its objective, the Coliseum ushers gave a hand, opening the doors to the winter air in an effort to cool the opposition. Finally, there were the Syracuse desperadoes who positioned themselves where they could shake the supports stabilizing the opponents' backboard. When the New York Knicks came to play in Syracuse after the merger creating the NBA, the sophisticated Knicks radio announcer Marty Glickman was livid with outrage at what he considered a circus atmosphere in the Syracuse Coliseum.

NBL star Bruce Hale remembers this Coliseum as but one wild place among many in the League. "Each place had its own idiosyncrasies," he notes. The 2,500-capacity high school auditorium that served the Oshkosh team had a stage at one end, close up to the court. Hale explains: "When we came to Oshkosh we always had to play against that stage in the second half. They let about a hundred kids sit on the edge. When we were trying a free throw they would all wave handkerchiefs and the like. It was quite distracting." Ft. Wayne played in the 3,800-capacity North Side High School gym, a throwback to the days of the enclosed cage game. "It was called the snake pit," Hale recalls. "It was surrounded by a six-foot wall. There was only room for the players and the bench below. The spectators were up above, yelling down on you." When Denver came into the NBL in 1949 it presented the menace of a court on a platform, which extended only a few feet beyond the playing floor. Past that point there was a three-foot drop.

The contrast in ownership of teams in the BAA and NBL reflected basic differences over what one expected to get out of investment in professional sports. The Basketball Association arena owners were expressly in the business of selling tickets —juggling schedules to bring a variety of attractions to a nameless mass audience. The BAA leadership included Ned Irish of the Knicks. He had become the quite-wealthy vice-president of the Madison Square Garden Corporation. The Boston Celtics were run by Walter Brown, president of the Boston Garden. The Chicago Stags were run by Arthur Morse, representing the Norris family that controlled Chicago Stadium.

Investment in NBL teams was made for many reasons besides filling the limited number of available seats. Sheboygan was owned by a collection of local businessmen, "city fathers who wanted to get their name in the paper," according to team general manager and coach Doxie Moore. Oshkosh was a similar community venture, as were NBL franchises in Tri-Cities and Syracuse. Companies owned by community stockholders in the latter two cities had been organized by two concessionaires from Buffalo who printed the scorecards for the teams around the League. One of the many promotional gimmicks in Syracuse was an annual "stockholders' night." The Ft. Wayne Pistons were owned by Fred Zollner, who, according to a colleague, was in the game because he "wanted the advertising for his piston company." The Indianapolis franchise was the creation of a basketball-loving grocer, Fred Kautsky. During the Depression he had made many friends by providing free food, and when he came to organize, his financial loans were easily arranged. The Toledo Jeeps were originally connected with the workers' recreation program at the jeep factory. The team was taken over and brought into the NBL by the proprietor of Buddy's Box Lunch, who sold hot lunches to factory workers in the Toledo area. The Chicago Gears represented a gear company; the Anderson Packers, a meat-packer; and Waterloo, Iowa, was brought into the League in '49 by the head of the lard department at the local Rath packing plant. The Denver franchise of '49 was a player-owned cooperative. One player served as team accountant; another was designated team auto mechanic; and forward Morris Udall (presently congressman from Arizona) became the team lawyer after passing his bar exam in midseason. Rochester was run by the hustling Harrison brothers, one of whom was the coach. Short on cash, they allegedly added to their income by scalping their own tickets.

The first battle in the basketball war of the late '40s was fought over the signing of the stars coming out of college. The NBL won handily, signing for the '47 season nearly twice the number of graduating All-Americans as did the BAA. And the small-town league won the All-American bidding battle again in '48 by a significant margin. The NBL also had the advantage of contracts with most of the outstanding older pros —its own older stars plus a number coaxed away from the American Basketball League, including one of the SPHAS. As BAA historian Leonard Koppett put it: "The National League had the players, the BAA had the cities and the arenas."

The NBL had an advantage in recruiting players in being the recognized "big league." And as Bruce Hale notes, players favored the NBL because "there was some doubt that the new league could fill all those seats. Playing to a near-empty house wasn't a pleasant prospect." The prime reason for NBL recruitment success, however, had to be its higher salaries. Top talent in the National League received $10,000 to $12,000, whereas the BAA had an initially announced $4,500 as the individual pay limit. It was quickly broken in numerous cases, but going into the BAA's third season the New York Knicks still have a $6,000 maximum.

Ned Irish, Walter Brown, and other BAA officials may have been new to pro basketball, but they knew something of efficient professional sports management. They ran hockey teams; five of them had franchises in the National Hockey League. When BAA club owners came to paying salaries they thought like hockey executives. "They paid their hockey players poorly and figured basketball players deserved the same treatment," quipped Sheboygan's Doxie Moore.

For its public image the NBL had to put extra effort into signing the best in the game. The League was stigmatized by franchises in what could be called hick towns. Its prestige franchise in Chicago had for a home court the amphitheater next to the odorous stockyards, while the local BAA Stags had Chicago Stadium, which was better located and had nearly twice as many seats. In addition, the NBL represented traditional pro basketball. In the opinion of the uninitiated, traditional pro basketball was a sport without class of the kind that attracted spectators of the sort found at roller derby or pro wrestling. Indeed, the NBL had its share of lowbrow hype. Doxie Moore recounts: "When I was coach at Sheboygan we had a hot rivalry with Oshkosh. To keep the interest high I had this act I pulled after games with Lon Darling (who ran the Oshkosh club). We'd get into this shouting match about who was going to do what to whom the next time around. The fans loved it."

A lack of class was evident in the arrangement by which the NBL's Chicago Gears signed George Mikan for the '47 season. Mikan was the number-one college pick, and would later be voted "the basketball player of the half century." Owner Maurice White of the Gears signed Mikan for a publicly announced $6,000 salary, plus a $6,000 bonus. Unannounced, however, was the nature of the bonus. Mikan had to earn it by scoring points: $5 for every basket, $3 for every free throw converted. This experiment in piecework failed. A couple of weeks into the '47 season Mikan told teammate Bruce Hale: "I don't think I can take this much longer. Every time I miss a shot I find myself saying, 'I just lost $5'; and when I miss at the line I feel I just blew $3." In the sixteenth game of the season Chicago played in Oshkosh, against a team whose coach had vowed to stop Mikan. The local team included some very physical players. One of them was a moonlighting football pro. The Oshkosh defense elbowed, pushed, and battered Mikan at will, bruising him considerably and holding him to a mere 2 points for the game. A week later Oshkosh manhandled Mikan again at a game in Chicago. He was sent to the foul line quite often, but missed many of his $3 shots. Immediately after the game Mikan announced he was retiring from pro basketball and vowed not to return until he had received in full his $6,000 bonus. Shortly before playoff time he received his bonus and returned.

National League officials enjoyed appearing to be big spenders. They called press conferences to boast of the high salaries of their players or to announce a special player's bonus, like a new convertible. Fred Kautsky liked to give catered steak dinners for his Indianapolis team. NBL front office people were making the most of basketball, which was usually their only involvement with pro sport. On the other hand, the BAA arena owners were merely trying to fill dates in their heavy promotional schedule of pro and amateur sports. While NBL leaders seemed adventurous, the BAA club owners appeared to have a patient, even casual, approach toward their basketball experiment. Ned Irish, for instance, made no special effort to fit the Knicks into the heavily booked Garden. During the Knicks' first season they had to play all but six of their regular-season home games in an armory, and they had only half their home games in the Garden the following season. Irish had gone into the Knicks venture with some doubts as to pro basketball's profitability. The college game seemed to be the brand of basketball that attracted the general sports fan.

The '47 season ended with twenty of the twenty-three teams in the two leagues losing money. The BAA admitted to collective losses of half a million dollars, and the NBL publicity director acknowledged that his league "wasn't too far behind" in overall losses. The money-winning teams were the NBL's Rochester Royals, who made a profit of about $40,000; the NBL's Kautskys, who made slightly less; and the Warriors of the BAA, who made a small amount. Their modest success was attributed to "the smart promotion of General Manager Ed Gottlieb." He generated a number of good home crowds by having the popular SPHAS play warm-up games. In both leagues the hopes of discovering new fans for professional basketball were dimmed. The few big crowds were almost all special promotions, as when the SPHAS, Rens, or Globetrotters were in a prelim game. The typical crowd was in the 2,500 range. This was a sellout crowd in Oshkosh and Sheboygan, but an embarrassment in the big arenas of other cities, particularly in the BAA. The Boston Celtics, for example, didn't once top the 10,000 figure in the Boston Garden, which then held 14,000 spectators. Boston was well into the 1949 season before the Celtics topped the 10,000 plateau.

Miserable attendance convinced four BAA club owners to throw in the towel after one season, leaving the league without franchises in Cleveland, Detroit, Pittsburgh, and Toronto. In the NBL, Detroit and Youngstown folded. Then there was the case of the Chicago Gears. George Mikan's retirement for much of the season had cost the team dearly at the box office, but then, the Gears had only averaged about 5,000 spectators a game in their 11,000-seat amphitheater even when they had "Big George." Gears owner Maurice White saw the attendance problem as one of the National League's image. While he could do little about its small-town stigma, he believed something could be done to give the League a more national and less midwestern appearance. He proposed to the NBL a massive expansion into the South and the Plains states, and he sent Gears starting guard Kenny Hale on a scouting expedition for likely locales for new franchises. White's scheme didn't sit well with other NBL owners. They told him that if he wanted to expand he could do it on his own. He did.

On November 2, 1947, the Professional Basketball League of America went into operation—a sixteen-team league with

Maurice White as the principal stockholder of every franchise, and with all players paid from the League's office in Chicago. It was called "the George Mikan league," since White had included his Gears team, with Mikan, who was expected to be the big box office draw. White had made millions during World War II supplying the gears that turned the guns on navy ships. Now he threw his profits into a far-flung venture that introduced league basketball into a number of future NBA locations: Atlanta, New Orleans, Houston, Kansas City, Omaha, the Minneapolis–St. Paul area, and Waterloo, Iowa, which was in the NBA for its initial 1949–1950 season. The PBL cost Maurice White hundreds of thousands of dollars and lasted only one month. "I gave up two years of college eligibility to turn pro, and now I'm out in the cold," lamented a player from the defunct Kansas City franchise. Forty players had jumped BAA contracts to sign in White's league. The BAA refused to allow them back. The NBL was more merciful with the disbanded Gears and the dozen other NBL players who had gone with the fallen league. They went back into the National League; and Mikan found himself on the new NBL team in Minneapolis, the Lakers.

"A dull and nameless champion" was the label tacked on the 1948 BAA winners. The champs turned out to be the BAA's new entry, the Baltimore Bullets, the previous year's champions in the American Basketball League of the old ballgame-and-dance circuit. As if having a lowly ABL team as champ weren't humiliation enough, the Warriors granted a rare exhibition game to the Eastern League's Wilkes-Barre Coal Barons and lost. BAA attendance was worse than in 1947. In Joe Fulks and Max Zaslofsky the BAA had a couple of players who were beginning to draw good crowds and excite the fans, but there were few others in the Association who came close to the drawing potential of a wide assortment of 1948 NBL stars, including Mikan and Jim Pollard of the Lakers, Bob Davies and Arnie Risen of Rochester, and Harry Boykoff of Toledo.

Even more than before, the BAA needed the NBL players;

and in turn, the loss of Chicago and Detroit franchises made the NBL more covetous of the Basketball Association's big-city exposure. To get the National League better exposure, a rather humbling deal was made with the BAA Chicago Stags. The Stags were in bad need of bolstering their own attendance, and toward this end they arranged for pre-game "National League window dressing," as *Sporting News* called it. For playing warm-ups for the Stags in Chicago Stadium the NBL teams earned about $500 a game; this was what remained in a deal granting them the first $1,500 from the gate, out of which they had to pay for the pre-game advertising and some game-related expenses of the Stags. On a number of occasions the Chicago press noted that the NBL prelim was the contest with the most fan interest and the superior players. Nonetheless, the NBL was in a subservient role.

National League teams received added exposure by frequent competition against minor-league teams and independents. Sheboygan, for example, had played fifty non-league games in '47. "We played anybody who gave a $300 guarantee," said Doxie Moore. That was the traditional way of pro basketball. The BAA stood in opposition to this tradition. At a secret peace meeting between BAA commissioner Podoloff and newly appointed NBL commissioner Doxie Moore, the BAA chief told Moore that a condition of peace was NBL abstinence from "exhibitions" against outside clubs. Moore refused, and later told the Chicago *Tribune*: "We have the best players and we are going to continue the policies which have made us strong. We will continue our policy of playing exhibitions, which are necessary for financial stability."

Not everyone in the NBL agreed with Moore's policies. The League was spending money on a scale far above that of traditional basketball. On this new economic plane the exhibitions were not quite so rewarding, especially considering travel time and expenses in going to out-of-the-way towns like Bismarck, North Dakota, where the local Phantoms came close to upsetting the Lakers of Mikan and company. Getting into Chicago Stadium as a preliminary attraction wasn't particularly lucrative either. It would be preferable to play in the feature game of the night; one way to do this would be to join the BAA.

The '48 season wound toward a close with staggering financial losses the general state of affairs in both leagues. BAA commissioner Podoloff offered the NBL a merger plan late in February: his league would drop Providence and let in Minneapolis, Indianapolis, and Ft. Wayne. Minneapolis club owner Max Winter had been thinking about a switch of leagues. Even with the great Mikan the Lakers were averaging about 5,000 of their possible 10,000 fans per home game; and Winter suspected the Lakers might get better fan support if games involved the Knicks, Warriors, and other teams from the big eastern cities. At Indianapolis, Fred Kautsky had a frustratingly high payroll to meet, and his young assistant openly suggested bolting to the BAA. Ft. Wayne owner Fred Zollner got the same message from the team coach. But the NBL was quick to refuse the uneven merger idea; and after a rush of phone calls it was announced that all owners had agreed to stay in the NBL and improve matters through careful expansion into more lucrative towns.

The weeks that followed the merger proposal were a case study in city slickers charming the hicks. In the interest of peace the BAA suggested a common draft of graduating collegiate players, and the idea was tentatively accepted. Arrangements were then made for the respective post-season league meetings to be held the same day in May at the same Chicago hotel. What transpired that day was described in the Chicago *Tribune* as "a parade" from the NBL office on the third floor down to the BAA office on the second floor, for what a BAA spokesperson called "exploratory talks." Max Winter later told the press he was going to be the first to go down and dicker with the BAA, but "when I got up to leave the room eight guys jumped up and blocked the door." While the diehards tried to coax Winter into keeping his team (and Mikan) in the NBL, Ft. Wayne and Indianapolis representatives slipped downstairs. Winter followed. Then the Rochester people decided they needed an exploratory talk and trudged downstairs, followed later by Toledo and Oshkosh. When the day ended, Minneapolis, Ft. Wayne, Rochester, and Indianapolis were all but officially in the BAA; and the NBL had no immediate response, because its press secretary was part of the Ft. Wayne contingent which was no longer in the League.

The National League refused to die. New franchises were secured in Denver, Detroit, and Hammond, Indiana; and the Toledo franchise was moved to Waterloo, which had a new 6,800-seat auditorium. Commissioner Doxie Moore was especially proud of the Hammond franchise; it offered something new in professional basketball—televised games. A nearby Chicago station agreed to carry them. The TV arrangement failed to materialize, however. When eastern officials of the station's network learned of the deal, they ordered their Chicago affiliate to back out. A year later telecasts of the new NBA were instituted from a New York office.

There was little reason to believe the National League would survive long enough to force the eventual merger that created the National Basketball Association. The NBL had lost many of its stars to the BAA, and this time around the BAA won the bidding war for graduating college All-Americans. The old league signed the future star Dolph Schayes to Syracuse, but there were few others of note. To survive, the old league had to experiment, as in the attempt at telecasts. In another experiment a player-owned-and-organized team in Denver was allowed in the League. Then, early in the '49 season the NBL's new franchise in Detroit folded. Commissioner Moore decided it was time to break the color bar in big-league basketball. He talked Bobby Douglas of the Harlem Rens into bringing the black team into the NBL. An arena in Dayton was secured to provide the Rens a midwestern home court; but the team played a couple of its NBL games in its usual haunt, Harlem's Renaissance Casino. The Harlem newspaper the New York *Age* suggested that NBL games so close to Madison Square Garden might make Ned Irish more interested in a merger.

Merger was far from the minds of the BAA leaders when

the '49 season began. They had George Mikan, the first tall center who moved with speed and agility. He had to be seen to be believed. Indeed, Mikan drew great crowds the first time around the home courts of BAA clubs. But by late February *Sporting News* was reporting a mixed picture of BAA attendance: up in five cities, about the same as the previous year in four, and down sharply in three. The typical attendance for a game was still embarrassingly low. When Joe Fulks scored a single-game record of 63 points against Indianapolis, only 1,500 spectators were on hand in the Philadelphia arena. Meanwhile, the NBL clubs featured more raffles, ladies' nights, and other gimmicks than ever before. *Sporting News* ran feature articles on how the promotions were generating attendance increases for Syracuse and the Tri-Cities. A number of NBL franchises, however, were in deep financial trouble.

Throughout the three-year war between the leagues the pros had played in the shadow of the collegians. Professional teams measured one another's worth in their numbers of young All-Americans from the colleges, rather than in quality old pros. No college team was more star-studded than the Kentucky Wildcats, the 1948 and 1949 NCAA champions. Their entire starting five made the 1948 U.S. Olympic basketball team. The climax of the postwar bidding battle for collegians came in the spring of 1949. Alex Groza, Ralph Beard, Cliff Barker, Wah Wah Jones, and Joe Holland were graduating from Kentucky.

The National League signed all of them. It was a victory of small-town spirit over the corporate mentality of the BAA. The Basketball Association clubs with high picks in the annual college players' draft were ready to pay good salaries for the Wildcats. However, the Kentuckians liked playing as a unit and didn't relish the prospect of being drafted and ending up on separate teams. The National League informed them they could be signed as a group; in addition, they would be given a sizable cash bonus, and on top of this they would be given their very own NBL franchise. It was a deal whereby the Kentucky stars took the bonus and used it to buy the controlling stock in a new Indianapolis franchise, making it a player-owned club. The player-owned Denver franchise of the NBL had been financially unstable, since the owner players started with little capital. The Indianapolis Olympians, as they were called, had the initial capital to sell a substantial amount of stock in the team while retaining control.

Shortly after the creation of the Olympians, negotiations began on the merger creating the National Basketball Association. For the 1950 season it was a seventeen-team league, with three divisions. Included were six franchises from the original BAA of 1947, and six franchises from the 1947 NBL. The basketball war wasn't about to end in a draw, however. From the beginning Ned Irish had stood fast on the principle of a league for big cities only. Irish used his influence, at this new juncture in the struggle, to arrange an NBA schedule that would isolate the clubs from the 1949 NBL that had come in with the merger. He didn't want them to get the prestige bonus of playing in Madison Square Garden. The new clubs from the NBL were put in the Western Division, except Syracuse—which, logic dictated, had to be in the Eastern Division. But logic didn't dictate the schedule for the 1950 NBA. The seven teams from the previous year's NBL each received only two games each against the ten teams from the previous year's BAA. The ten teams played each other at least six times. The schedule had Syracuse playing only two games against each of the teams in its own division, and seven against each club in the Western Division. To add insult to injury, Syracuse didn't get a game in the Garden, and of the clubs in the Western Division only Indianapolis received a Garden date. The "home games" the Knicks had with the old NBL clubs were either played in the armory or on a "neutral court."

The NBL clubs that had agreed to the merger were irate. Syracuse fans were so mad that when the Knicks came to town in the playoffs the desperadoes who occasionally shook the opponents' backboard got totally carried away. They dispensed with subterfuge, being unsatisfied with just shaking the backboard on shots from the field. The Knicks' Vince Boryla strolled to the foul line to find the backboard gyrating in anticipation of his shot. The Knicks had to scream at the ref before action was taken to clear the crazies from the backboard supports. Syracuse had five meetings with the Knickerbockers that season, counting the playoffs, and Syracuse won four of the five. The team was called the Nationals, in honor of the old National League. The Nats upheld the honor well in 1950, running up a 15–3 won–lost record against the charter BAA clubs, the Knicks, Celtics, Warriors, Washington Caps, Chicago Stags, and St. Louis Bombers.

The NBA was pruned back to eleven teams for the 1951 season. Chicago and St. Louis had dropped out because of poor attendance. Anderson, Sheboygan, Waterloo, and Denver either were voted out or quit in a huff, depending upon the source believed. What is known is that they were handed another insulting schedule for the coming season.

The retrenchment continued. Washington dropped out midway through the '51 season. Indianapolis called it quits after 1953, and the Baltimore Bullets folded early in the '55 season. Back in 1946 a group of arena owners had had a scenario for basketball's professional future in which they would play a major role. Only two of the group now survived, Ned Irish of the Knicks and Walter Brown of the Celtics. The Warriors were still alive, but Eddie Gottlieb was now their owner. The pride of the NBA was for a time the old NBL. Until Philadelphia beat Ft. Wayne in the finals of the 1956 playoffs, the NBA champions had been former NBL clubs— Minneapolis four times, Rochester and Syracuse one championship each. Three times in six years there was an all-NBL final. The old NBL kept five franchises in the NBA, and they are still alive, although no longer playing in the cities where they started. Syracuse remained in the NBA through 1963, the franchise then being transferred to Philadelphia. Over their fourteen-year span in the league the Nationals won six out of every ten games with their hot rivals from New York city. Rochester and Ft. Wayne lasted in the NBA through 1957.

The role of Syracuse, Rochester, and Ft. Wayne in the

NBA shows that success in pro sport is not necessarily correlated with winning games. The number of available seats for home games and the size of the team's marketing area are important factors. The teams with poor resources in these areas may pay high players' salaries, acquire good coaches, employ creative promotional techniques, and win plenty of games, and they may still end up out of the competition. Syracuse, Rochester, and Ft. Wayne all won more games than they lost in the NBA. The Nationals were second in their division in their final season, and the Pistons made the playoff finals in their next-to-last season.

In the late 1950s NBA attendance began to rise, boosted by the inception of the 24-second clock, which added to the action and the scoring. Then, too, national telecasts over the NBC network began in 1955, adding stature to the league. The faster the turnstiles clicked, the more disadvantageous the position of the teams with smaller arenas and marketing areas. There was no sharing of gate receipts; the home team took it all. When all teams had typically drawn from 3,000 to 4,000 a game, the differences in seating capacity were not crucial. Going all the way to the finals in the playoffs could turn a franchise from red to black ink as much as could a big arena for regular-season games. The extra games in the playoffs could equalize matters. But when overall attendance rose, arena size became all-important. By the mid-1950s Syracuse, Rochester, and Ft. Wayne had enlarged their home seating capacity, but were still toward the bottom of the league in this regard. Moreover, Syracuse was just a small town in drawing potential when compared with Philadelphia—where the team went in 1964, becoming the 76ers, the replacement for the Warriors, who had gone west. Rochester and Ft. Wayne were similarly small towns in comparison with Cincinnati and Detroit, the teams' new homes.

A quarter-century after he had led the small-town faction in the basketball struggle, Doxie Moore summed up what he had learned from the experience. "If all you are interested in is attendance you don't really need the best team. You can advertise a few stars, or appeal to the gambling crowd. There was a lot of betting on pro ball in my day, just as there was on the colleges. What it all boils down to is this: I learned you can play the game either of two ways, to win, or to make money. My teams won. I'm no longer in the business."

The exodus of small-city franchises from the NBA was rather inevitable in an era when professional sports in "the old hometown" were becoming anachronistic, even in the national game of baseball. During the 1950s hundreds of minor-league baseball teams folded. The reduction of the number of minor leagues in basketball from six in 1949 to one in 1953 was part of the same trend, whereby the entrepreneur with little capital was being squeezed out of the picture in the more popular games. In the process, a traditional avenue of mobility for enterprising individuals from groups climbing the social ladder was being closed.

The trend came at an unfortunate time for black Americans. It was their long-overdue turn to move into the American cultural mainstream. In film, theater, and the music world, as in sports, old restrictions were being swept aside, offering black performers a shot at fame and fortune. But there was all too little opportunity at the promotional level. In basketball, there arose no black Eddie Gottlieb, although there were qualified applicants for his role of former player turned organizer and club owner.

Among those who deserved to make a mark in the financial end of sports there was the 1947 UCLA basketball All-American Don Barksdale. He was later to show in the music world a promotional flair he might have brought to basketball. Barksdale had sort of a Jackie Robinson role in the court game. He was at first blocked from playing in the pro leagues by the unwritten law excluding blacks. Remaining an amateur, he starred on the 1948 U.S. Olympic team. It played a number of promotional games for the Olympics, and in these games Barksdale found himself pioneering in bringing integrated basketball into the segregationist states of Oklahoma and Kentucky.

The NBA was integrated in the '51 season, and in '52 Barksdale got his chance. "I became a thirty-year-old rookie," he says with a slight intonation of bitterness. He was a starter in the NBA through 1955, his last year. "I had a number of business interests in Oakland and San Francisco, and while I was tempted to keep playing I had to think of the future. I decided it was time to attend to business." Barksdale was a radio disc jockey, had produced the first black program on San Francisco television, and was beginning to enter the nightclub and music promotion sphere. By the early 1960s he had a string of nightclubs, and had become widely known in black music circles as a discoverer of promising young talent. Crooner Lou Rawls was one of the young performers Barksdale launched toward stardom. In recent years Barksdale has been a scout for the Golden State Warriors of the NBA, but his entrepreneurial abilities have been largely wasted, so far as sports are concerned.

In his book *Heaven Is a Playground*, Rick Telander presents a more contemporary case of underused black promotional talent. Telander describes the social scene at a predominantly black Brooklyn playground. In Rodney Parker, hotshots of the playground have a confidant and coach. A ticket scalper by trade, Parker expends endless hours, and puts up with much frustration, in his effort to help talented youngsters develop their game, keep up their school grades, and get scholarships to college.

Parker is virtually unemployed, and yet toils long hours for the playgrounders for no noticeable financial reward. All he gets is some small recognition in basketball circles as a capable talent scout. Telander finds Rodney Parker's motivation unexplainable. If Parker had been born fifty years earlier he would probably have run his own professional team, and perhaps become a basketball notable, as the Harlemite Bobby

Douglas did after organizing his Renaissance Five in 1922. Although Rodney Parker doesn't appear to be going anywhere, he doesn't give up. He is too imbued with the irrepressible attraction of the small-time hustler to sports. The hustler once had the power to make a neighborhood or some Mudville famous. It is rare these days.

The Women's Basketball League: Mudville Revisited

At one point it was the Irish, at another the Italians, and more recently the blacks. In any given period over the past hundred and twenty-odd years one can find a special energy being given to sports by segments of society striving to achieve a place in the American mainstream. The archetype is the bustling new urban center of the late-nineteenth-century Industrial Revolution, the town that expected to be the next New York but ended up just another Mudville. Recognition for a town, or the social assimilation of a group, rarely matches up to expectations. But while the expectations are high, significant contributions are made to sports.

The sporting world needs a periodic transfusion of new blood. The fervor in older groups dies, usually as modest gains are made and expectations become less idealistic. As the edge is taken off the daily struggle to exist, the hard road to sporting fame appears less inviting. The era of Jewish prominence in basketball passes; the stereotype of the football lineman with the long Polish name fades; the Irish-American prize-fighter becomes a rarity.

Today the media, the power-hungry coaches, and the public relations experts have taken such thorough control of the popular games that millions of Americans who might add new vigor to these games have decided instead to jog, ride surfboards, race bicycles, or go hang-gliding. The new activities are refreshingly without the bureaucratic hierarchy of the major sports, which are becoming ever more "Romanized" and turned into spectacles featuring a specially trained social caste, the athletes. It is a caste selected according to body measurements rather than fraternal or geographical bonds. Apprentices in sports are often taken from their neighborhood and sent to the junior high schools and high schools that have the coaches who specialize in turning out collegiate stars and future pros. The athlete is turned into a tool of the sports/entertainment industry. Not all the members of the new caste are superhuman, stereoid-fed, pep-pill-popping gladiators, but the promoters of TV network sports shows seem to prefer this kind of performer.

The Romanization of a sport is its reduction to a theatrical presentation for a nameless mob. The process is being hastened by the dissolution of strong social bonds in America. There is the vapid social life of the suburban bedroom community, and the empty streets and parks of the mugger-terrorized inner city. For millions of Americans it is easier to watch television than socialize.

In the 1970s millions of women decided they were through with tedium and social isolation. They created clubs, support groups, and a vital women's press, and developed high expectations of a better life. They became the latest in the procession of groups desiring to test their mettle in the competition of sports. They challenged the sports establishment, and with more than the passive protest of the young man who professes a preference for throwing a Frisbee over tossing a football. The women forced legislative and court action in behalf of their sports. Given time, though, women's sport will probably be transformed into a Romanized show. Women athletes will probably end up being isolated out on the female branch of the athletes' caste. For the present, however, women are giving to their sports the added spark that comes when the performers fight for the greater dignity of the whole group, rather than just their own egos and bank accounts.

In a sports world glutted with gladiators, women are advancing the appreciation of athletic performance because it is the very best the participating athletes can do, even if their best is not superhuman. This is the attitude found in road racing, where women have a major role; where there are different winners for different age groups; and where the announcer at the marathon loudly proclaims of each finisher over the public-address system: "Here comes another winner!"

The rise of women's sports and the portent of their future direction can be noted in the growth of the professional Women's Basketball League during its first two seasons of 1978–79 and 1979–80. The League has been in the forefront of the effort to provide a spectator following for women's sports. The Women's League's appeal has been decidedly human rather than superhuman. "The WBL plays below the rim. That's the way your typical fan plays basketball. Most people are incapable of dunking the ball," says WBL San Francisco Pioneers coach Frank LaPorte. The typical sports fan, however, has been conditioned to expect professional sports to be almost freakishly superb. Coach LaPorte and others claim that once a fan has seen a WBL game the return rate is excellent, but getting fans to that initial game has not been easy. In the League's first two seasons crowds of 2,000 were above normal size.

The problem is in selling it for what it is, which is not the NBA. San Francisco Pioneers spark plug Pat Mayo explains: "We readily acknowledge we don't have the strength of the men; we don't jump as high; and our hands are not as big. We use a slightly smaller ball than the men, for easier handling, but you won't see us waving the ball around in one hand. We are not trying to copy their style. There are some good shooters in our league, and you'll see crisp passing. Our games are worth watching."

Hustle is the most noted feature of play in the Women's Basketball League. The fans who show up have come to expect such sights as a loose ball being fought over by half a dozen players, all of whom have dived through the air and crashed to the hardwood in an effort to give their team the basketball. Heroes of the WBL have nicknames like "the Queen of the floor burns." After Julius Erving of the NBA saw a game of the women pros he exclaimed: "When they're not running, they're jumping. When they're not jumping, they're diving. When they're not diving, they're shooting. When they're not shooting, they're passing. These girls can really operate." A San Francisco sportswriter says of the WBL: "The action on the court makes the NBA seem almost laid-back in comparison."

The women often had to learn their hustle early in their career, compensating in playground games for lack of height with extra energy. Pat Mayo says hustle has always been her style. "When I see a ball going out of bounds I'm going to go for it." Coach LaPorte sees something more than personal style in the performance of his team: "They have something to prove; they're putting it on the line." In the words of WBL New York Stars coach Dean Memminger: "They're fighting for a cause"; and not wishing to be left out, Memminger adds: "I'm a liberationist."

Among the feminists of the 1970s there were those who saw little place for women's professional sports, which seemed like a female copy of the macho win-at-all-cost sports system of the jocks and media hucksters. These feminists felt it a virtue of women that they were generally reluctant to become the spectator fanatics who purchased a sports team's season tickets. It was argued that rather than copy the men, a preferable approach to sports for women would be the creation of informal mass participation on a grand scale. The reluctance of women to watch pro sports has confronted the Women's Basketball League. To the surprise of its promoters the large majority of the League's spectators were initially men, although the numbers began to equalize in the League's second season.

Practical considerations have made success of professional women's sports highly desirable for all but the most utopian feminists. Building a sport costs money, and the controllers of the American sports dollar have been reluctant to give women their share, for either informal or commercial enterprises. It has become necessary for women to prove by displays of sporting ability that they deserve their share; to prove that the adherents to traditional female images are wrong when they consider ambition, aggression, and competitiveness in a woman abnormal.

The issue was forced by Title IX of the 1972 Federal Education Amendments, which made women's sports a politicized civil rights issue. Title IX forbade sex-discriminatory programs, including athletics, by all educational institutions that receive federal money. Horrified athletic directors of the nation's colleges claimed that anything approaching the equalization of men's and women's athletic budgets would be unfair, because women's sports didn't pay their own way, didn't draw spectators. (Actually, the only sports in college paying their way were a few football teams and some basketball teams, with other rare exceptions.) College women were not asking for footballs, but they did ask for equipment and cash for the court game that they had been playing almost since the day Dr. Naismith invented it. As college athletic departments grudgingly began to comply with Title IX, the number of colleges fielding women's teams rose from 242 in 1974 to over 1,500 in 1980.

Gains for college basketball were obtained amid hostility and resentment by male administrators, a situation tailored to making militants out of the collegians later to play in the WBL. Women frequently had to resort to legal action to obtain funds. A collection of ugly situations was described in the January 1979 issue of *Women's Sports*. One incident was the firing of Colorado State University women's athletic head Mary Alice Hill, who had complained of a paltry $5,000 budget allotted to her teams. Although the students voted Hill the outstanding instructor in the department, the administration said she had to be removed because of such infractions as failing to park her car in the proper place, not dressing properly for class, and not posting her office hours. Hill sued and won a $65,000 judgment (which was later reduced upon a court appeal).

The expansion of college basketball made an attempt to form a professional women's league only a matter of time. WBL founder and president Bill Byrne explains: "The idea came to me in 1975 when a lot of attention was first given to Title IX. It didn't take a genius to see that big action was coming to women's sports. And that because of the nature of the game, basketball would be the biggest beneficiary of Title IX." Byrne's league, however, wasn't organized until 1978. In the mid-1970s respected leaders in women's basketball had put the damper on the professional idea, arguing that there were neither enough quality players nor women's fans. Cathy Rush, the highly successful coach of Immaculata College, stated in '77: "It will be a time for a pro league when you see as many little girls in playground pick-up games as little boys. . . . But there's not enough talent to stock a pro league yet." Nonetheless, the fervor of the women's movement in the mid-seventies made the creation of a professional women's league a tempting proposition.

Early in 1976 Jason Frankfort, a New York stockbroker turned restaurateur, decided it was time to cash in on the cause with pro basketball. He began laying plans for his Women's Basketball Association, with himself as self-proclaimed chairman of the board. Frankfort didn't appear to know very much about basketball, but he did know his way around the Madison Avenue crowd. For WBA public relations he obtained the services of the longtime feminist Jacqueline Ceballos, cofounder of the Association of Women Business Owners; and he selected as WBA commissioner Lois Geraci Ernst, the director of Advertising to Women, Inc. Ernst was known as the "poet of Madison Avenue," having dreamed up the Clairol slogan "You're not getting older, you're getting better," and the Coty perfume ad "If you want him to be more of a man, try being more of a woman."

In January 1977 Frankfort held a gala press conference announcing the Women's Basketball Association. At the time he had yet to sell a single franchise. He did have three players signed; and one of them, Karen Logan, was good for advertising purposes. She had had television exposure on CBS's *Challenge of the Sexes*, and on another occasion had beat Jerry West in a televised game of HORSE. The press conference was held in plush accommodations, with a well-stocked bar. Reporters were met at the door by cocktail waitresses in five-inch heels, satin boxing shorts, and T-shirts with the WBA logo. Commissioner Ernst introduced Frankfort as "chairman of the broads"; a good time was had by all; and the WBA never played a game. Karen Logan later received a $250 bill for her stay at the swank Plaza Hotel, a bill she thought Frankfort was paying. In December of '77 *Women's Sports* gave a scathing WBA obit titled "Women's Professional Basketball—Anatomy of a Failure." Amid this discouraging publicity the second attempt at a pro league was beginning, Bill Byrne's WBL.

Cathy Rush had said quality players would be hard to find. If they were out there, Byrne had probably the best opportunity of anybody in the country to find them. He ran the National Scouting Association, which provided scouting reports on collegians to assorted professional leagues. The National Football League and National Basketball Association have made highly laudatory comments on the quality of Byrne's scouting evaluations, and have cut back on their own scouting staffs to rely on Byrne's reports. What he had done for others, Byrne figured he could do in his own behalf in finding players for the Women's Basketball League.

One had to have a gambler's instinct to venture into women's pro basketball, and as the owner of a number of racehorses, Bill Byrne had this quality. He also had substantial experience in sports promotion. He had worked in the ill-fated

World Football League of the early 1970s; and the experience turned him off to the fast hustle for quick millions. While the WBL publicity evokes images of a high-powered women's version of the NBA, the League is really a low-powered operation. It began with a salary ceiling for players designed to keep costs low enough for teams to break even financially with a mere 2,500 spectators per game. The League started in the class of another Bill Byrne creation, the American Slow-Pitch Professional Softball League. This organization has been quite a successful addition to the fast-growing, easy-to-play, low-pressure version of softball.

The Women's Basketball League entered its initial '79 season with eight teams and a modest thirty-four-game schedule. The teams represented New York, Chicago, Dayton, Houston, Milwaukee, Iowa, New Jersey, and Minnesota. All franchises were male-owned. The club officers were generally men. The initial absence of women in team management was as much a reflection of the coldly businesslike situation in contemporary commercial sports as it was a commentary on the relationships of the sexes. The distance of the male owners in the WBL from women was no greater than the distance of many an absentee baseball and football club owner from the townsfolk of the owner's team. The ownership situation in the WBL has been similar to that in the NBA, in which the players are mostly blacks but the club owners are all whites. Thanks to the years of protesting by black sociologist Harry Edwards, the front office of many an NBA club now has blacks in important positions. In time, if it survives, the WBL will no doubt have more women in management roles. In its first seasons, it drew front office personnel from the male-dominated profession of the sports-public-relations expert—the ex-jock, and the former sports editor of the college newspaper, whose resumé includes jobs with assorted sports organizations.

In addition to the absence of women in management the WBL had only one woman coach in its first two seasons (a second was signed for the League's third season). One might have expected women coaches from the colleges to join, but some of them had doubts about the League's solvency, and others were intent on staying put in order to discourage the trend toward an ever-higher percentage of men in the ranks of college coaches for women's teams.

For coaches the League has recruited ex-NBA players who were looking for a coaching opportunity, ex-NBA coaches, and others enticed in with fringe benefits. Frank LaPorte, formerly a highly successful men's coach at St. Marys College near San Francisco, explains how he came into the WBL with the San Francisco Pioneers the League's second year. "I joined this league because I was offered the general manager's as well as the coach's position. In college I was only the coach; here, I am coach, and sort of the athletic director, too." La-Porte adds, "Coaching in this league is easy. It's refreshing. The players are so eager to learn. You tell them to do something, and they do it. And the way they hustle, the first time I saw them I couldn't believe it."

Whatever the WBL's founding owners lacked in emotional identification with the women's movement was more than made up for by the players. To participate in the League in its first seasons, players had to have a certain dedication to the cause. They certainly were not in it for the money. The League began with a top salary of about $15,000, with many players receiving as little as $5,000; and the Minnesota Fillies tried to get players to sign for $3,000, less than a mother with two kids could get on welfare in many states.

Low salary offers led some big-name ex-collegians to refuse to join the WBL. The former Delta State standout Lucy Harris was outraged at the WBL pay scale. She remained at her job in the Delta State admissions office and declared: "I know the women won't play for nothing."

The grand plan of the WBL seemed to be the establishment of an unillustrious league now that would be ready to go big time when the rapidly improving players then in college graduated. A comment by an official of the New Jersey Gems relating to the failure to sign the Montclair State College star Carol Blazejowski was eye-opening. Blazejowski, known as "the Blaze," had averaged 38 points per game her senior year. She felt the League should have put aside its pay ceiling in her case, and if necessary pooled resources to bring her into the fold. After she refused an offer that was barely in the five-figure range, the Gems official said: "She's making a mistake, in two years we may not even want her." Blazejowski angrily told *Women's Sports*: "These guys actually think that in two years three or four or five players will be coming out of college and be better than I am. . . . That's just impossible."

The National Scouting Association provided leads to talent that hadn't received the publicity of the Blaze or Lucy Harris. Good players were not all put off by low salaries. There was, after all, the cause to consider. Byrne waxed eloquent on the need for a professional women's league when talking to prospective players. In signing the New Jersey Gems star Wanda Szerementa, Byrne made a pitch about players taking a little now, so that players in later years could make $100,000 a season. Szerementa responded: "I hear you. Someday I'm going to sit in a rocking chair and say I helped pioneer that league." "We want this league to succeed so bad that we are willing to play for almost nothing to help it get off the ground," one player told the press; and said another, "Even if the League folds, I'll be able to say that I was there."

Before the Women's Basketball League there was hardly anyplace for a player to go after college. Says Pat Mayo: "It used to be that you might become a coach or p.e. instructor in high school or the like. But that was it. You didn't really have an opportunity to continue competing." Janice Thomas, one of the WBL's best jump shooters, got out of college a few years ago and took a job as a department store plainclothes guard. "I'm just glad the pros came along in my time," she says. "This is just what I've been waiting for for three years," exclaimed Gail Marquis, who had gone to France to continue playing after college. Karen Logan, who had previously signed with Frankfort's league, had before that played a number of seasons with a female version of the Globetrotters, a women's basketball comedy team called the Redheads. All the players had to dye their hair red. She welcomed the arrival of the WBL, signed early, and convinced the League officials to use the special ball she had devised, which was lighter and seven-eighths of an inch smaller than the regular sphere. The question of the WBL's salary range was put to her at the end of the League's initial campaign, and she responded: "Some made enough money last year, and I believe it will be a lot better this year. In five years, it will be a good career for women."

The initial WBL season raised some doubts about there being a second year. Overall attendance averaged about 1,500 a game. Newspaper coverage was quite poor. Home games typically received only little squibs; away games were rarely reported; and the papers only occasionally printed the League standings. The Chicago Hustle managed to get its games on a regular television channel, where the team outdrew the local hockey pros in viewers. But the other clubs either had no TV package or had only the limited exposure of cable television. Dayton and Minnesota franchises folded at year's end. The six survivors lost between $150,000 and $350,000 apiece.

In the off season the League was made to look second-rate when the graduating UCLA All-American Ann Meyers chose to sign with the Indianapolis Pacers of the NBA. After failing to win a spot on the men's team Meyers lowered herself to sign with the Gems of the WBL. Her flirtation with the NBA angered some players in the Women's League. "It was ridiculous," said New York Stars' center Althea Gwyn. "She was saying we weren't good enough." Gwyn predicted Meyers would be the target of more than the usual number of elbow jabs until she proved herself in the WBL. "After all, she put down women, and that's what we are," said Gwyn, the League's foremost thrower of elbows, hips, and forearms.

Despite its troubles, the WBL had survived one season; and its prospects for the future were made brighter by the accelerating interest in women's basketball at the lower levels. Between 1977 and 1979 the number of high school girls playing basketball had doubled to 550,000; and a number of women's teams in college had upped their average attendance to over 4,000 a game.

The WBL doubled its franchise price for the 1980 season to $100,000. Buyers were found to add teams to the league in San Francisco, Los Angeles, Dallas, New Orleans, St. Louis, Philadelphia, and Washington. Of the new clubs the San Francisco Pioneers turned out to be something special; and only secondarily because they were an expansion team that made the League playoffs. The Pioneers finished third in the League in attendance, and were averaging close to 3,000 a game at the season's end. The Pioneers had tapped the women in the community for fan support—support some had expected for the League from its beginning.

"We talked to every women's group in the area," said the Pioneers' owner, Marshall Geller. On opening night Dianne Feinstein took the spotlight and "as the first woman mayor in the history of San Francisco," she threw out the first ball. Women were not particularly numerous that evening, but by midseason they were comprising nearly half the spectators for Pioneers' home games at the Civic Auditorium. Group night for women's organizations caught on, and the percentage of women continued to rise, as did overall attendance. There were so many groups scheduled for a February game against New Orleans that the club provided childcare.

The sizable San Francisco lesbian community took to the Pioneers in a big way. Among the groups having nights at Pioneers' games there were the Lesbians Against Police Violence, and Maud's and Amelia's Bar. A San Francisco *Chronicle* reporter noted that the lesbian groups took great joy in cheering for themselves when their organizations were announced over the public address system. Gay or straight, the women fans of the Pioneers rooted for their team with an abandon that would make the fanatics of the old NBA Syracuse Nats envious. The fans made a special favorite out of the team leader in floor burns, Pat Mayo. A WBL All-Star specializing in tight defense, Mayo went on hustling for the team in the off season, working the phones and the typewriter in the club office. Before her recent marriage, she was Pat Cola-surdo, teammate of Blazejowski at Montclair State.

Where the cause leaves off and good sports showmanship begins is hard to tell in the WBL. The League's leading scorer, "Machine Gun" Molly Bolin of the Iowa Cornets, took it upon herself to give the League a hero to be worshipped. She made her own posters of herself and carried a supply around the League. Bolin believes she has a special role. "I'm aware that a lot of people are watching me because I was the first one signed and because I score a lot and all; to them I represent some kind of image of the League. . . . That's what we need, people to pick up on one area of the League."

One of her posters, showing her reclining in shorts and a tank top, seems to suggest the Iowa farm girl of the traveling salesman's dreams rather than Molly Bolin, the married woman with a four-year-old son. Asked about her posters, she explained: "I thought a little about the possible sexism in-volved, but 99 percent of the comments have been good. . . . I certainly won't say I'd do anything—but within the limits of good taste, I certainly want to do everything I can to promote the League." She sold out her first run of the posters in the 1980 season.

The publicity-starved Women's Basketball League has an open-door locker room press policy—an enticement to re-porters, who, the hope is, will conduct lengthy interviews that will find their way into the sports pages. League president Byrne has urged all owners and front office personnel to be-come as active as the Pioneers in scouring the community groups for support. "I must admit," said Byrne early in 1980, "our first year we had some owners who thought they could just put down the money and sit back and smoke their expen-sive cigars. We are now getting front office people who will work. We need it. We need to win the younger generation, the schoolgirls. We need to go to the schools; offer them discount tickets; let them in for a buck; but get them to the games."

The second season was another financial loser for the WBL.

Philadelphia and Washington had almost nobody watching their games and folded before the season was half over. Los Angeles folded later. Its press coverage was almost nonexistent. National press coverage consisted mostly of rumors that the WBL was about to go the way of the World Football League and professional team tennis. But another season was survived. The franchise price went to $500,000. Promoters in Omaha and Tampa paid their way in for the 1980–81 campaign.

Then disaster struck. First there was the Olympic boycott. The League had looked forward to increased interest in the women's game because of television coverage of the U.S. Women's Olympic team, but there was neither a U.S. entry nor U.S. telecasts of the Olympics. Two months after the non-Olympics four WBL franchises folded. The loss of Milwaukee and Houston was perhaps tolerable, but the collapse of the New York Stars and Iowa Cornets cost the league its two best teams. Backers of the new Tampa franchise had second thoughts and shortly before the new season opened the team was transferred to Boston.

The worst blow of all had to be the formation of a rival league, the Ladies Professional Basketball Association, hastily put together for operation in the 1980–81 season. The new league promised to honor the playing contracts held by surviving WBL teams, but the top performers on the defunct WBL franchises were considered free agents. Molly Bolin of the Cornets was coaxed into the new league by the opportunity to become both the team coach and a player for the LPBA Anaheim, California, franchise. Other LPBA franchises were located in Tucson, Phoenix, Albuquerque, and Oakland.

Hugo Roundtree, owner of the Oakland Oaklanders of the LPBA sounded much like Bill Byrne as he told the press of his eagerness to tap women's groups for support; and he pointed to a profit sharing arrangement for the players, which Roundtree felt was a good way to add a measure of women's control in his league of all-male club owners. However, the LPBA succeeded only in creating confusion in the women's game.

A month into the 1981 season the LPBA folded, while the WBL teetered on the edge of collapse. Although women's professional basketball is probably here to stay, the banner for the sport may well turn out to be some other entity than the WBL. Assuming the sport survives one has to wonder how long the current playing style and high emotional level will remain. Women's basketball is presently part of a cause, and reflects positively on women, as the old South Philadelphia Hebrew All-Stars reflected upon the Jewish community. But will the professional women basketballers still be diving for loose balls when the cause is forgotten and the women's game is just another part of the sports entertainment industry? Coach Memminger of the ill-fated New York Stars noted in 1980 that WBL players didn't resort to the backbiting and ego tripping he had known when he played in the NBA. He said of the women: "They don't squabble now, but give them time, they will."

Meanwhile, if you desire a sports show that's competent and lively, but not slick, check out the nearest showing of women's professional basketball, where the spirit of the old baseball nine from Mudville is alive and well.

Notes

This study is an outgrowth of a sports history series presented over radio station KPFA in Berkeley during 1975 and 1976. Listener-sponsored KPFA is noted for programs about radical politics, and for an effort to illuminate the "social significance" of music, art, and other aspects of culture. KPFA rarely discussed sports, and my initial program drew a letter of protest from a listener who felt baseball was too trivial a subject for an intellectuals' radio station. But there were favorable responses. The Berkeley avant-garde were not all snobs. Closet sports freaks reading *Sports Illustrated* inside a large volume of Shakespeare could be found on the campus of the Athens of the West. It seemed to me that a little evidence of "social significance" for sports might help the repressed fans own up to their hidden pleasures, at a time when various other so-called deviants were coming out of the closet.

Highly critical analysis of sports was something of a fad during the 1970s. While many arguments of the critics are supported in this book, the principal intent here has been to present models of sport reflecting a positive or at least a functional application of community spirit. For this, the historical approach has advantages. In the period before highly commercialized and monopolistic sport, the teams genuinely represented towns, neighborhoods, ethnic groups, and the like. Then too, before the decline of the American city, before the growth of the culturally vacuous bedroom suburb, and before the escape to the television set there was more readily analyzed social interaction in the American community. There was more opportunity to relate sports to daily life.

The source material for this study was quite varied. The more important sources will be listed in two sections: first, for the chapters on nineteenth-century sports; and second, for the sections on basketball.

NINETEENTH-CENTURY SPORTS

The sporting magazines surveyed deserve first mention: *The New York Clipper: Sporting and Theatrical Review*, 1858–62, 1867–98 (has excellent coverage of all sports until the early 1890s, when the sporting sections were reduced in size). *Spirit of the Times*, 1844–48, 1854–60, 1867–71, 1878–88, 1894 (pre–Civil War issues have good coverage of baseball and pro track; later issues contain superior coverage of amateur athletic club track and field). *Sporting Life*, 1883–1900 (valuable for baseball and pro track). *Sporting News* 1886–1900 (the "bible of baseball" was also in its first years a good source of reporting on pro track). *National Police Gazette*, 1877–95 (contains unique coverage of pro track, prizefighting, and lesser pro sports such as rowing, swimming, weightlifting, and wrestling). *Leslie's Illustrated Weekly*, 1875–1900 (contains a substantial pictorial record of late-nineteenth-century sports). *Outing*, 1885–91 (contains numerous articles on social life in the athletic clubs).

An overview of the sporting scene was obtained principally from: Harold Seymour, *Baseball: The Early Years* (1960); David Q. Voigt, *American Baseball—From Gentleman's Sport to the Commissioner System* (1966); Foster Rhea Dulles, *A History of Recreation* (1965); and John Durant and Otto Bettmann, *Pictorial History of American Sports* (1952).

Montague Shearman's *Athletics and Football* (1887) showed the British development of the system for organizing, conducting, and judging track and field. Frederick Janssen's *History of Amateur Athletics* (1885) contains historical sketches of prominent athletic clubs, such as the NYAC. Useful anecdotal material was found in: Preston D. Orem, *Baseball 1845–1881: From the Newspaper Accounts* (1961); Albert G. Spalding, *America's National Game* (1911); Jordan A. Deutsch et al., *The Scrapbook History of Baseball* (1975); Edward Grant Barrow, *My Fifty Years in Baseball* (1951); Alfred H. Spink, *The National Game* (1910); Harry Ellard, *Baseball in Cincinnati* (1907); Federal Writers' Project, *Baseball in Old Chicago* (1939); Morris A. Bealle, *The Washington Senators* (1947); and John Thorn, *A Century of Baseball Lore* (1974). An interesting discussion of Ernest Thayer and his poems about Mudville is presented in Tristram Potter Coffin's *The Illustrated Book of Baseball Folklore* (1975). Francis Richter's *History and Records of Baseball* (1914) contains a chapter on players' trade unions up to that time. Of help in understanding the sporting scene were: Alan Wykes, *The Complete Illustrated Guide to Gambling* (1964); Robert F. Kelley, *American Rowing: Its Background and Traditions* (1932); and Robert A. Smith, *A Social History of the Bicycle* (1972).

The daily newspapers not only provided sporting news, but through their accounts of election returns gave evidence of the substantial role of sporting people in politics. Newspapers consulted were: *New York Times*, 1856–1914; New York *Herald*, 1865–1900; New York *World*, 1880–1900; New York *Tribune*, 1885–91; Philadelphia *Public Ledger*, 1862–1905; Philadelphia *Inquirer*, 1888–96; Philadelphia *Taggert's Times*, 1890; Boston *Transcript*, 1866–87; Boston *Globe*, 1885–1902; Hartford *Courant*, 1868–79; Wilkes-Barre *Record*, 1883–87; Washington *National Intelligencer*, 1866–69; Cincinnati *Enquirer*, 1867–79; Chicago *Tribune*, 1865–1901; Atlanta *Constitution*, 1891; St. Louis *Globe-Democrat*, 1884–86; Cleveland *Leader*, 1871–72; Detroit *Free Press*, 1887–90.

The New York Public Library's Albert G. Spalding Collection contains essential information on the economics of baseball. Of special value to this study were: National League Constitution and Playing Rules, 1876, 1879; International Association Constitution and Playing Rules, 1877, 1878; International Association Yearbook, 1878; Eastern League Constitution and Playing Rules, 1885; the Henry Chadwick newspaper scrapbooks, 18 volumes; Chadwick *Base Ball Manual*, 1871; DeWitt *Base Ball Guide*, 1871–73; Spalding *Base Ball Guide*, 1878–1900; Wright and Ditson *Base Ball Guide*, 1884–86; Reach *Official Base Ball Guide*, 1883–1900; Spalding *Minor League Base Ball Guide*, 1889. A sizable collection of guidebooks for the 1880s and 1890s is also available at the Helms' Athletic Foundation library in Los Angeles.

Record keeping for nineteenth-century track and field was far less extensive than for baseball. The *New York Tribune Book of Open Air Sports* (1887) contained the earliest available comprehensive list of professional and amateur running, jumping, and walking records. Professional and amateur lists were also found in the *Clipper Annual*, 1888, 1892–94, 1896, 1898, and in the *Police Gazette Sports Annual*, 1896.

Pertinent scholarly articles on sports included: Steven A. Reiss, "Baseball Magnates and Urban Politics in the Progressive Era, 1895–1920," *Journal of Sports History*, spring 1974; J. Willis and R. Wettan, "Social Stratification in New York City Athletic Clubs 1865–1915," *ibid.*, spring 1976; Willis and Wettan, "L. E. Myers, World's Greatest Runner," *ibid.*, fall 1975; Edward Lamb and Mary Dawn Earley, "Weston the Walker," unpublished; Duane A. Smith, "The Leadville Blues of 1882," *Journal of Sports History*, spring 1977; Joseph S. Stern, Jr., "The Team That Couldn't Be Beat: The Red Stockings of 1869," *Cincinnati Historical Society Bulletin*, spring 1969; John R. Betts, "The Technological Revolution and the Rise of Sport," *Mississippi Valley Historical Review*, September 1953; L. A. Wilder, "Baseball and the Law," *Case and Comment*, August 1912; Steven A. Reiss, "Professional Sunday Baseball: A Study in Social Reform 1892–1934," *The Maryland Historian*, fall 1973.

The relating of sports to daily life was largely an exercise in checking the names of club members and officials given in the sporting papers against historical sources of an economic, social, and political nature. City directories proved extremely useful for identifying late-nineteenth-century sporting people. The directories—annual telephone book–sized compendiums —contained residents' addresses and occupations, membership lists for civic organizations, and other data. In cities where local newspapers were unavailable for a check of election returns, the directory lists of political officeholders sufficed. Directories for over a hundred cities with professional baseball teams were checked, most of the directory issues being located in the University of Pennsylvania's large collection on microfilm. The annual state government manuals provided biographical sketches of sporting people holding state political offices. Additional business connections for sporting people were found in a scan of such sources as *Street Railway Journal, Poor's Railroad Manual*, and *Bonfort's Wine and Liquor Circular* (variously titled from year to year). From various sources biographical data on 1,263 nineteenth-century baseball officials and club members was collected, and it is now on file at the Baseball Hall of Fame in Cooperstown, New York.

Between 1880 and 1930 city historical societies and university history departments produced an abundance of specific city histories, such as Morton Montgomery's *History of Reading, Pennsylvania 1748–1898*. The organizers of the more popular sports rarely had sufficient class standing to be featured in these volumes, but the histories did provide the context in which the sporting people operated. The following studies were also useful in understanding the period: Arthur M. Schlesinger, Sr., *The Rise of the City 1878–1898* (1933); Thomas Cochran and William Miller, *The Age of Enterprise* (1942); Daniel J. Boorstin, *The Democratic Experience* (1973).

The activities of the politician-sportsmen were illuminated by: Alexander B. Callow, *The Tweed Ring* (1966); Samuel P. Orth, *The Boss and the Machine* (1919); M. R. Werner, *Tammany Hall* (1928); Alfred Connable and Edward Silberfard,

Tigers of Tammany (1967); Lincoln Steffens, *Shame of the Cities* (1957 ed.). Also of value were: Gary Kyriazi, *The Great American Amusement Park: A Pictorial History* (1976); P. T. Barnum, *Barnum's Own Story* (1961 ed.); Oliver Ramsay Pilat, *Sodom by the Sea: An Affectionate History of Coney Island*; Hugh Bradley, *Such Was Saratoga* (1940), a history of the Saratoga Springs resort; two department-store histories: Leon Harris, *Merchant Princes* (1979), and Robert Hendrickson, *The Grand Emporiums* (1978); Stanley Wade, *Brewed in America: A History of Beer and Ale in the U.S.* (1962); two studies of temperance movements and prohibitionists: John Kobler, *Ardent Spirits* (1976), and J. C. Furnas, *The Life and Times of the Late Demon Rum* (1965). Robert and Helen Lynd's *Middletown* (1956 ed.) and Jane Jacobs' *The Death and Life of Great American Cities* (1961) provided a sociological understanding of city life.

BASKETBALL

James Naismith's *Basketball: Its Origins and Development* (1941) is the best volume for understanding the early years of the game. It is more than the memoirs of basketball's inventor. Included are chapters on the growth of the game in community-house, industrial, and college settings. The growth of women's basketball is also traced. Other books which helped fill out the picture of basketball's beginnings and first years were: C. Howard Hopkins, *History of the YMCA in North America* (1951); Alexander M. Weyand, *The Cavalcade of Basketball* (1960); Neil D. Isaacs, *All the Moves: A History of College Basketball* (1975); William G. Mokray, *Encylopedia of Basketball* (1962), containing valuable statistical information on the early college and professional game; and Jordan A. Deutsch et al., *The Sports Encyclopedia: Pro Basketball* (1975), containing an informative text on the economics of early pro basketball.

Basketball guides were useful not only for statistical data

but also for descriptive articles about teams and their organization, and for articles on teams of past years. The guides consulted were: *Spalding Basketball Guide*, 1899–1941 (originally *The Spalding AAU Basketball Guide*); *Reach Basketball Guide*, 1906–11, 1914–18, 1923–27; *Spalding College Basketball Guide*, 1907; *AAU Basketball Guide*, 1937–41; *NCAA Basketball Guide*, 1937–54; *Barnes Basketball Guide*, 1940–50; *Converse Basketball Yearbook*, 1940–78. The Converse annuals contain some enlightening reminiscences of basketball players of the early twentieth century. Spalding guides of the 1930s show the development of community basketball leagues and tournaments. The Reach guides are especially valuable for professional basketball coverage.

Sources for social and political matters relevant to basketball at the turn of the century were: Allen F. Davis, *Spearheads for Reform: The Social Settlements and the Progressive Movement* (1967); Lillian D. Wald, *The House on Henry Street* (1915); Oscar Handlin, *The Uprooted* (1951); William Thomas and Florian Znaniecki, *The Polish Peasant in Europe and America*, Vol. 5 (1920); *Playground* magazine, 1907–20. The trends in ethnic communities of recent decades were surveyed in Milton M. Gordon's *Assimilation in American Life* (1964 ed.) and Philip Rosen's *The Neglected Dimension* (1980).

For basketball's growth during the 1930s and 1940s the most frequently used source was *Athletic Journal*, for which monthly issues of 1931–56 were surveyed. While principally a high school coaches' journal, it carried in-depth analyses of economic and playing changes at the many levels of basketball. The aforementioned guidebooks were useful, along with the *Converse Yearbooks* of the late 1940s and early 1950s, in presenting an arena-by-arena analysis of college doubleheader fan support and profitability.

The daily newspapers with especially good basketball coverage from the late 1930s through the 1940s may be noted from a survey of papers in 57 cities. The survey was part of a project of collecting community and service team rosters for the files of the Basketball Hall of Fame in Springfield, Massachusetts. Noteworthy coverage of neighborhood and industrial basketball was presented in: the Brooklyn *Eagle*, Philadelphia *Inquirer*, Atlanta *Constitution*, New Orleans *Times-Picayune*, Washington *Post*, Chicago *Tribune*, and San Francisco *Chronicle*. The Denver *Post* contained outstanding coverage of top-level AAU basketball. Until the formation of the BAA for the 1946–47 season, professional basketball was given insultingly little coverage in the major daily papers, one exception being the Chicago *Herald-American*. The black American weeklies proved to be the superior newspaper source for professional basketball up until the BAA. In covering the games of the Harlem Rens, the New York *Age* reported on many a contest with a white pro team that rarely got a mention in the white dailies; the same was true for Harlem Globetrotter coverage in the Chicago *Defender* and Pittsburgh *Courier*.

Books of special value to the chapters on 1930s and 1940s basketball include: the aforementioned works of Weyand, Isaacs, and Mokray; Charles Rosen, *Scandals of '51: How the Gamblers Almost Killed College Basketball* (1978); Jack H. Bender, *Basketball Log* (1958); Ocania Chalk, *Black College Sport* (1976); Zander Hollander, *Madison Square Garden* (1973); Herbert U. Ribalow, *The Jew in American Sports* (1948); Leonard Koppett, *Twenty-four Seconds to Shoot* (1976). The elements of charm and pathos which have for generations marked playground basketball are captured in: Pete Axthelm, *The City Game* (1971); Rick Telander, *Heaven Is a Playground* (1976); David Wolf, *Foul* (1972); Daniel Rudman, *Take It to the Hoop* (1980).

A deeply felt thank-you is in order for Frank LaPorte, Pat Mayo, and Karl Heisler of the San Francisco Pioneers; Bill Byrne of the WBL; Bruce Hale, Doxie Moore, and Ralph Giannini for use of their scrapbooks, game programs, and other memorabilia, and for the insightful explanations of their basketball experience. Helpful firsthand reminiscences of basketball were also provided by Don Barksdale, Angelo Musi, George Barsi, Mike Iannolla, Max Spector, Herb Moritz, Ralph

Miller, Philip Rosen, and Ben Neff. Helpful criticisms and suggestions were made by Professor Paul Worthman of UCLA; David Voigt of Albright; and Harry Edwards and Lawrence Schechtman of the University of California at Berkeley.

Finally, mention must be made of the evidence supporting the contention that pro football originated, in part, as an anti-labor ploy. In researching life in the cities where sports originated, checks were made of trade-union activity. For 1880–94 the Bureau of Labor listed strikes and lockouts by city, across the nation; and for 1914–22 the annual report of the secretary of labor contained lists of the labor disputes mediated by the National Labor Conciliation Board—disputes involving many a pro football sponsor's establishment.

Index